720

for 11.10

Journey to Beatrice

Journey to Beatrice

Charles S. Singleton

(Originally published as Dante Studies 2)

The Johns Hopkins University Press
Baltimore and London

Reprint edition, 1977
The Johns Hopkins University Press, Baltimore, Maryland 21218
The Johns Hopkins Press Ltd., London
Originally published by Harvard University Press, 1958

Library of Congress Catalog Number 77-5266
ISBN 0-8018-2005-7

Preface

This second volume of Dante Studies is aimed at bringing into view the main outline of allegory in the *Comedy*, and is written on the persuasion that, for some time now, we have been reading the great work in what amounts to an amputated version. It is not that the text of the poem, as we have it, suffers from any serious lacunae. We would seem to have the work in its entirety as to text. The lacunae are rather in us, the readers, and reside in that deficient knowledge and lack of awareness which we continue to bring to our reading of the poem.

Let this indictment be confirmed by the fact that not one of the dozens of commentaries of the *Comedy* published in the last half century is concerned to follow the outline of the allegory in more than a sporadic manner, wherein the reader's attention is called to the merest *disjecta membra* of that continuous dimension of the poem. Small wonder that in our time we have deemed the allegory to be such a negligible part of the poetry.

There has been method in the madness of such a view, the signal instance in our own day being Benedetto Croce's reading of Dante. Yet no one seems to have noted that Croce's rejection of the allegory and the "allotria," as he called it, is but a late example of what is clearly a very old trend — as old as the Renaissance, in fact, which means about as old as may be, in this case, since that age followed so closely upon Dante's. Nor should this fact hold any special mystery for us, when we realize that the allegory of the *Comedy* is itself an imitation of Biblical allegory, as the Middle Ages conceived that matter; and it is common knowledge that the Renaissance soon disclosed a strong desire to discount and reject that way of reading Scripture. There came a time when God's way of writing allegory could no longer be taken seriously. Is it then anything surprising that Dante's allegory, an imitation of God's, should suffer the same rejection?

Dante's allegory is explicit in the theology of his day. We have only to learn to recognize it there when we meet it. And when we become able to do this, then at once we find ourselves confronted with an embarrassment of riches. Instead of one good text to cite in evidence of a given point or pattern, there are at least twenty. And indeed perhaps all twenty texts should be published rather than the one we must choose with such difficulty from among them, so that we may finally be persuaded that the poet constructed his allegory on points of doctrine firmly established and widely current in his time, that Dante built with materials which were, so to speak, public property. But that abundant documentation must wait for another time and place. Here it was possible to cite but the one text in most instances, not the twenty, and, with the one, hope to suggest the others.

Parts of the following chapters have appeared in the *Annual Report of the Dante Society*. I am grateful to the Society for permission to reprint these, retouched now to make them part of a comprehensive view of Dante's allegory.

CONTENTS

PART ONE · JOURNEY TO BEATRICE

Chapter I

The Allegorical Journey

In first *Studies*,[1] in a general way, two elements of the poem's structure were distinguished: allegory and symbolism. Such a distinction may be carried further, and its usefulness better evidenced, by an examination in far greater detail of each of these dimensions of Dante's *Comedy*. In the present volume, and first in order, must come a closer study of the allegory. Primacy may surely be claimed for this aspect of the great work. We have only to consider, for one thing, what a different poem this would be were it not first of all a narrative, the account of a journey. Take but that part of it away and the whole structure must collapse. Upon the outline of a journey all is threaded — even that other dimension, the symbolism of things seen. For it is of the essence of symbolism that things should point beyond themselves, be signs as well as things. But if "things" were seen to *point beyond* through the one hundred cantos of this poem and yet there were no going beyond to obey and enact their signs, their pointings would simply dangle without visible effect. The signs would be to no realized purpose. No unquiet heart yearning toward the goal which they so insistently and eloquently proclaim would be there to respond to them. The journey of the poem is the journey of the unquiet heart [2] and its presence in the structure constitutes the very heartbeat of the whole.

The signs visible in things are there for those who are still on the road of this life and move toward its proper goal — which is ever a goal beyond. These are road signs for the living. And Dante's most exceptional journey beyond, through the realms of the afterlife, is always the journey of a man who is still on the "road of our life" here. Only so can this be the double journey which it is: a journey *there*, through Hell and Purgatory and Paradise, and a journey *here*, an event in this "our life."

Just how this may be so in the poem has already been noted.[3] The literal event of Dante's journey beyond this life calls to mind the event of a kind of journey here. Thus, even as things do, so also does the literal journey point beyond itself. But there is a difference. The things which are seen in the journey beyond point upward with their signs to the One who judges, who punishes or rewards; whereas Dante's going, the journey as such, points back to the road of this our life and journey here.

The direction of this dual journey, once it gets under way, is the direction in which all signs point. It is a twofold *itinerarium* to God. Clearly the literal journey attains to such a goal. So also does the reflected journey which follows the literal as its very shadow and mirrored image. And between the two there is always the unmistakable distinction as to time and place. But it is the time and place of the journey in allegory that call for some special scrutiny. For we say that this is a journey here, in this life. The road of it is here, yet where is that? And we say that it takes place now, but how now? These are questions which do not arise with respect to the literal journey. Never did a poem locate more exactly or stage more concretely the vast scene of its unfolding action, nor was ever a poem more careful to tell its own time. This, literally, is the year A. D. 1300, this is Easter week, nor is the exact hour of day or night kept from us as we move along the way.

As for the time and place of the reflected journey, we come to see that a precise determination is not possible. For it, the familiar name in Dante's time was *itinerarium mentis ad Deum.*[4] But if this journey is "of the mind," whose mind shall we conceive this to be? There is but one possible answer: "whoever." Again we take stock of the double situation. In the literal journey the protagonist is definite, we may say who he is. He is Dante, Florentine by birth if not by custom. But the corresponding image, the shadow figure in allegory, has no determined identity. He is simply a "whoever": whoever, that is, may choose and be chosen, through God's grace, to move along the way of the mind which leads to Him in this life. The wayfarer, in allegory, is some Christian, any Christian. He is *homo viator*; but, strictly speaking, he is not Everyman. Rather is he "Whicheverman," whoever, that is, may be chosen for this journey to God while yet in this life where, willy-nilly, we all are wayfarers.

Such a going here will be a going of the mind and heart, for only so may we move toward God while we continue to dwell among the living. That such a journey here and now is an open possibility remains the basic postulate and, for Dante, the established doctrine on which he can construct the allegory of his *Comedy*.

If the protagonist of the mirrored journey is a "whoever," then the time of his journey will be a corresponding "whenever." Many have entered upon this *itinerarium mentis* in the past, many shall yet do so until the end of time. We must conceive that it takes place even now, in many Christian hearts. The time of the allegorical journey is thus indifferently past, present, or future, which means that its time is "whenever" time. And if we think again of the literal journey in this respect, we again note the basic difference between the literal and the allegorical. Protagonist and place of action could not be more exactly determined in the one, or less so in the other; and as for the time, we shall not think that the literal journey has taken place more than once or perhaps will ever take place again, whereas the *itinerarium mentis* is an event which repeats itself in the Christian heart as time unfolds, over and over again.

To be sure, in passing through Purgatory Dante makes mention more than once of his expectation that he will pass along this way again.⁵ But clearly any return journey on his part must necessarily be quite unlike the one which the poem represents to us. When he comes back to this place, no Virgil will guide him, nor will any Beatrice come to meet him at the top of the mountain. The return through Purgatory, if it happens, will be in the dimension of "the state of souls after death," ⁶ and will not be allegorical.

These points respecting the precise nature of Dante's allegory in the *Comedy* are evident enough and a good deal has been said of them in foregoing studies: ⁷ of the sense in which the journey to God is not one journey but two, as well as the further significant fact that the poem's main allegory, in this aspect, is an imitation of Scriptural allegory in one of its senses. Those senses are four. There is first the literal, which is historical. The words of the Psalm speak of the Exodus and denote an event in history. That event, in turn, may be seen to have meaning in three other senses, one of which is the "moral" sense. This, in the familiar jingle,⁸ is the sense which declares "quid agas," what the Christian should do. The departure of the children of Israel from Egypt thus, in this particular sense, signifies "the conversion of the soul from the grief and misery of sin to the state of grace," as Dante himself wrote in the Epistle to Can Grande.⁹

Now the poem's main allegory is a much closer imitation of this moral sense of Scriptural allegory than may at first be apparent. Not only is the literal event in the *Comedy* something of an Exodus in itself, but the event in the poem which is signified by the literal is exactly denoted in Dante's definition of the moral sense of Scripture. The *itinerarium mentis*, which is the other sense to be found in the literal journey through the after life, could have no better designation than that of a "conversion of the soul from the grief and misery of sin to the state of grace." This indeed, in its most general statement, is the subject of the main allegory of the *Comedy*, and is the event which these studies are now to scrutinize in its broader outlines.

"Conversion," we are to see, is a key notion for the whole allegorical journey, marking it off into three stages or phases.¹⁰

But, in passing, we may also remark that Dante's imitation of the moral allegory of Scripture bears an exact correspondence to its model, in time, place, and protagonist. For if the injunction which goes with that moral sense in Scripture is "quid agas," "what you must do," then this must be a sense addressed to the living, it must point to an action possible in this life. In short, it is moral, a meaning for all to see who may happen to find themselves in a dark and bitter wood of sin, who by God's grace may be privileged to turn, in a dawning light, toward a summit where justice and grace and reunion with God may be attained, and who from that first summit may be further privileged to rise to the higher peak of perfected grace and of final beatitude, *while still in this life.* And even as the moral sense of conversion signified in the Exodus is quite undetermined as to time and person, so also is this moral sense of the *Comedy.* Model and copy are both in terms of "whenever" and "whoever," in their allegory. And as for the place of the action, that is, of this conversion, its place is the soul: *mens.*

For all its undetermined character in these respects, however, the conversion of the soul from sin to grace was not, in Dante's time, without a precise doctrinal determination regarding its manner or shape as *event.* Whenever conversion took place, it would normally follow a recognizable pattern, through steps and stages to its completion. It becomes the purpose of the following chapters to retrace that pattern as established in the theology of Dante's day. What we have to realize here is something which applies generally to Dante's poem in all respects: *the poet did not invent the doctrine.* The shape of his poem is determined by the truth which it must bear and disclose in its structure, and that truth is not original with the poet. Dante sees as poet and realizes as poet what is already conceptually elaborated and established in Christian doctrine.

By his time, centuries of Christian meditation had determined what the essential outline of a journey to God in the soul, and in this life, would be. The poet does not formulate that conception, he holds to it, rather, as to something so well planted in the background of his reader's mind as to make it quite predictable that he, as poet, can call it up there; so that out of the unfolding literal journey through the life after death there may gradually arise the shape of this familiar journey in the soul. Dante's allegory is thus always in the manner of *evocation*: he calls the familiar to mind. A sense of recognition comes to the reader time and again, until a whole other pattern of meaning has taken shape. It is meant to be no small part of the pleasure of the poetry.

For us, of course, the difficulty lies just here. The once familiar shape of *itinerarium mentis ad Deum* is now become not so familiar. Certainly no poet could work with it in our day as Dante so confidently did in his. For now the pattern has first to be reinstated in the mind of the reader and made recognizable as a public and established thing, a truth shared generally by Christians. Then only can it be evoked in the manner of allegory.

No doubt some readers of the poem will say that our efforts at reinstatement are hardly worth what they cost. They will tell us that for all we may do, we shall not transform ourselves into "readers of Dante's time." And the truth of this must be granted. Indeed, there will always be a considerable difference between having, as by natural inheritance, a certain familiarity with a body of doctrine, and having this by a deliberate effort made to recover it and reinstate it in our minds. Yet, granting the discouraging difference, what else can we do? The truths which the poet built into his poem seemed to him to be enduring truths. That this has not proved to be the case is no fault of poet or poem. It is better not to speak of fault at all, in any way. We must simply observe that this has come about: the unquiet heart of the Christian pilgrim has grown quiet, and the very notion of a journey of the mind and heart to God *in this life* now requires such an effort of the historical imagination as would have been a veritable scandal to the mediaeval mind.

Some readers there may be, however, who, in order to become adequate readers of this poem, stand ready to make the effort of reestablishing in the background of the mind what the mediaeval mind took for granted: the broad and certain outline of a possibility, open to man now, in this life, which is a great drama of salvation. This possibility is that of an *itinerarium mentis ad Deum*

as a real event, taking place in the life of some individual: a conversion from the grief and misery of sin to the state of grace as an
actual happening in the soul — and, for this mediaeval poet, one
which can come alive in the mirror of allegory.

*   *   *

Itinerarium mentis: "mind" will hardly translate the term.
"Soul" does better, or "mind and heart," for the heart is surely
involved. St. Augustine, indeed, would have insisted that the heart
comes first in this matter, that such a journey is above all a journey
of love.[11] And, following Augustine, a long and vigorous tradition
held to such an emphasis, down to Dante's own time. St. Thomas
Aquinas, though inclined to place the accent on *mind* rather than
on heart,[12] still gives due recognition to Augustine's stress on the
affective part as the primary element whenever he writes of that
love which is charity, and of the role of charity in the life of any
wayfaring Christian entering upon the journey to God:

> The charity of the wayfarer can increase. For we are called way-
> farers by reason of our being on the way to God, who is the last
> end of our happiness: In this way we advance the more the nearer
> we get to God, who is approached "not by steps of the body but
> by affections of the soul" (Augustine, *Tract. in Joan.* xxxii) and this
> approach is the result of charity, since it unites man's mind to God.
> Consequently it is essential to the charity of the wayfarer that it
> can increase, for if it could not, all further advance along the way
> would cease.[13]

Yet Thomas insists that the soul achieves union with God not
through love alone, which is an operation of the will, but through
intellect as well. The two faculties function inseparably and simultaneously with respect to their proper end, which is God:
"anima conjungatur Deo per intellectum et affectum," [14] the soul
is united to God through intellect and love. Nor was Thomas
alone in holding to this view. It is necessarily shared by all who
think on such matters and in such terms, since the simple acknowledged truth is that the rational or intellective soul, the
immortal part of the human creature, is made up entirely of these
two faculties, intellect and will. The intellect "sees" or knows,

the will loves. The object of intellect is truth, the object of the will is the good. The two faculties cooperate in their movements, it being the function of intellect to discern and present its object to the will, whereupon the will moves to attain the object discerned under the aspect of good. This, indeed, is the reason why Thomas and others insist on the primacy of intellect in the movements of the rational soul. The will can only move toward an object presented to it by the intellect. Without the seeing faculty of intellect, love in the soul is truly blind.[15]

Readers of the *Paradiso* especially know how often the poet has focused attention on this order in the operation of the two faculties.[16] Repeatedly, in verses such as the following, Dante asserts the primacy of intellect in regard to the last happiness, the Beatific Vision. Thus, high in *Paradiso* Dante is told by Beatrice of the angels, what also applies to the saints, that beatitude consists primarily of the act of *vision* (that is, of intellect) and not of the act of love which follows upon vision:

> "E dei saper che tutti hanno diletto
>   quanto la sua veduta si profonda
>   nel vero in che si queta ogni intelletto.
> Quinci si può veder come si fonda
>   l'esser beato ne l'atto che vede,
>   non in quel ch'ama, che poscia seconda."
>   *Paradiso* XXVIII, 106–111.

> "And you must know that all have delight in so far as their vision penetrates into the Truth in which every intellect finds rest. Hence it may be seen that blessedness is founded on the act of vision, not on that of love which follows after."

Beatrice's words on the primacy of intellect agree with the doctrine of St. Thomas, and students of theology are prompted accordingly to speak of the "intellectualism" of Thomas because of just such stress.[17] Both the theologian and the poet are well aware of the truth that it is the will which moves finally to possess the object discerned, completing the total act. Indeed, when it is a question of moral action, then the will may well be the first concern. Justice or inner rectitude in the soul is first of all a matter of the condition and orientation of the will, and the virtues which are such a necessary part of that rectitude pertain above all to the will.[18] Yet the goal of any moral journey must be an apprehended good, and it is the intellect which apprehends, not the will.

In short, the two faculties of the rational soul are coordinated in their respective operations. Each has a function complementary to the other and together they make up one total act. Indeed, they are thus so closely conjoined in their movements that we speak of them as two rather than one only because we find that we must think of them so, as faculties separate and distinct one from the other — or so St. Thomas instructs us:

> The mind is moved to God both through intellect and through love, and these two movements of the mind can *be* at the same time, although they cannot be *thought* at the same time; for one is the rule of the other, and it is by an act of the intellect that the will's object is presented to the will; for the object of the will is an imagined or conceived good, as the Philosopher says.[19]

Clearly, to understand any journey of the mind to God we shall have to remain alert to movements in soul as they pertain to both of these faculties.

In such a journey as Dante has represented in allegory, a first goal and attainment under Virgil's guidance is announced in terms of the will and its condition, for when Virgil has led Dante as far as he may, he dismisses him in these words:

> "Libero, dritto e sano è tuo arbitrio
> e fallo fora non fare a suo senno."
> > *Purgatorio* XXVII, 140–141.

> "Free, straight and sound is your will and it would be wrong not to do as it discerns."

Here both faculties are being kept in view. The *arbitrio* must be the will, but the *senno* of the will, the discerning part, must be the reason or intellect.

If the goal to which Virgil leads, in this journey in soul, is essentially a condition of rectitude in the will, then that higher goal to which Beatrice leads in her turn is one in which intellect is primary, even as we have heard her say of the angels who are ever present at such a goal: "si fonda l'esser beato ne l'atto che vede." Hence, in even a fleeting glimpse of these matters, we take note of the necessity of realizing which faculties are involved, *what moves* in movement toward God. The very goals of the journey, whether intermediate or final, must be given and are given in terms of will and intellect. They are the coordinated and cooperating functions of the rational soul in all of its movements.

There are three guides in this journey to God, as Dante has represented it: Virgil, Beatrice, Bernard. In the case of the last named, special considerations enter in, since if Bernard is in any sense a "guide," his role as such is quite different, actually, from Virgil's and Beatrice's. But with due allowance made for differences, we do come to see that this trio of "guides" represents the fulfillment of a pattern, a journey conceived as movement by three "lights"; and light, of course, pertains to intellect. But we come to see that we must also think here in terms of a complementary pattern of three phases of movement pertaining to the will, best seen and understood as three "conversions."

It will be our first concern, therefore, to distinguish two master patterns or paradigms in this matter of a journey to God in the soul, and they are two for the reason noted, namely, that the faculties involved are two, intellect and will. Only by seeing such broad patterns may we then recognize those which are subordinate to them as parts of the whole, and see how these shapes of doctrine are made manifest in the concrete substance of a poem.

The present volume of studies is mainly concerned with that area of the journey which extends to a first goal, at the end of the *Purgatorio*, a goal which proves to be Beatrice herself. When that point is reached, when Beatrice takes over as guide, only two of the three lights and two of the three conversions in these master patterns have come into play. Yet any attempt to understand this journey up to its first goal in isolation from the entire pattern of three lights and three conversions extending all the way to the end which is God, is doomed to be abortive and fall short of true understanding.

Notes

1. *Dante Studies 1, Commedia: Elements of Structure*, the preceding volume of this series, hereafter cited as *Dante Studies 1*.

2. The phrase will always recall St. Augustine, in the opening of the *Confessions*: ". . . quia fecisti nos ad te et inquietum est cor nostrum donec requiescat in te."

3. See *Dante Studies 1*, ch. i.

4. Or *itinerarium mentis in Deum*. See, for one, the treatise by Saint Bonaventura bearing this title. Another phrase, used by Thomas Aquinas in outlining his own great work, evidences the same notion: "de motu rationalis creaturae ad Deum" (*Summa Theologiae* I, q. 2).

5. *Purgatorio* II, 91; XIII, 133; and *passim*.

6. The phrase is Dante's own, in the Letter to Can Grande: "status animarum post mortem" (*Opere di Dante*, ed. Società Dantesca, Florence, 1921, p. 438).

7. *Dante Studies 1*, especially ch. 1.

8. Littera gesta docet, quid credas allegoria,
   moralis quid agas, quo tendas anagogia.

9. *Epist. ad Can. Gran.*, 21.

10. Aquinas, *Summa Theol.* II–II, q. 19, a. 2, ad 2: "Bonum morale praecipue consistit in conversione ad Deum."

11. See G. Combès, *La charité d'après saint Augustin* (Paris, 1934).

12. See P. Rousselot, *L'intellectualisme de s. Thomas* (Paris, 1908).

13. *Summa Theol.* II–II, q. 24, a. 4, resp.: "Caritas viae potest augeri. Ex hoc enim dicimur esse viatores quod in Deum tendimus, qui est ultimus finis nostrae beatitudinis. In hac etiam via tanto magis procedimus quanto Deo magis propinquamus, cui non appropinquatur passibus corporis, sed affectibus mentis. Hanc autem propinquitatem facit caritas, quia per ipsam mens Deo unitur. Et ideo de ratione caritatis viae est ut possit augeri; si enim non posset augeri, iam cessaret viae processus."

14. *Summa Theol.* I–II, q. 101, a. 2, resp.

15. On this point other relevant texts in Aquinas may be considered: *Summa Theol.* I, q. 43, a. 3, resp.: "Et quia cognoscendo et amando creatura rationalis sua operatione attingit ad ipsum Deum, secundum istum specialem modum Deus non solum dicitur esse in creatura rationali, sed etiam habitare in ea sicut in templo suo." *Summa c. G.* II, 87: "Finis enim animae humanae et ultima eius perfectio est quod per cognitionem et amorem transcendat totum ordinem creaturarum et pertingat ad primum principium quod Deus est." *In IV Sent.* d. xvii, q. 1, a. 3, sol. 3: "Movetur autem mens in Deum et per intellectum et per affectum." See also below, note 19. But such statements by Thomas, as indeed by contemporary theologians, are legion. On the

primacy of intellect Thomas even finds it possible to cite St. Augustine for support: "Praeterea, intellectus est fortior in cognoscendo quam affectus in diligendo; unde dicit Augustinus (*In Psalm.* CXVIII, serm. viii), 'Praecedit intellectus, sequitur tardus aut nullus affectus.' " For a fundamental statement of the point by Thomas, see *Summa c. G.* III, 25: "In omnibus agentibus et moventibus ordinatis oportet quod finis primi agentis et motoris sit ultimus finis omnium: sicut finis ducis exercitus est finis omnium sub eo militantium. Inter omnes autem hominis partes, intellectus invenitur superior motor: nam intellectus movet appetitum, proponendo ei suum obiectum; appetitus autem intellectivus, qui est voluntas, movet appetitus sensitivos."

16. *Paradiso* XV, 73–78; XXVI, 28 ff.; XXIX, 136 ff.; and *passim.*

17. See Rousselot, *L'intellectualisme de s. Thomas.*

18. Aquinas, *In IV Sent.* d. xvii, q. 1, sol. 1, ad 1: "Tota ista rectitudo [i. e., inner justice, as defined here] a voluntate originaliter est, quae est principium merendi et demerendi; sed etiam est in aliis partibus animae quasi rectificatis, sicut in subjecto."

19. *In IV Sent.* d. xvii, q. 1, a. 3, sol. 3: "Movetur autem mens in Deum et per intellectum et per affectum, et hi duo motus mentis simul esse possunt, quamvis non simul cogitari possint: quia unus est regula alterius, et per actum intellectus praesentatur suum objectum voluntati, quia objectus ejus est bonum imaginatum vel intellectum, ut Philosophus dicit."

For the close cooperation of the two faculties, see, for instance, *Summa Theol.* I, q. 59, a. 2, ad 3: "Quia bonum et verum convertuntur secundum rem, inde est quod et bonum ab intellectu intelligitur sub ratione veri, et verum a voluntate appetitur sub ratione boni. Sed tamen diversitas rationum ad diversificandum potentias sufficit."

Chapter II

The Three Lights

There is [1] a kind of vision for which the natural light of intellect suffices, such as the contemplation of invisible things according to the principles of reason; and the philosophers placed the highest happiness of man in this contemplation; [2] there is yet another kind of contemplation to which man is raised by the light of faith, as are the saints in this life [*in via*]; and [3] there is that contemplation of the blessed in Heaven [*in patria*] to which the intellect is uplifted by the light of glory, seeing God in His essence, as the object of beatitude — and this contemplation is not full and perfect except in Heaven; yet sometimes one is uplifted to this contemplation by rapture even while still in this mortal life, as was Paul when in rapture [II Cor. 12.2: "I know a man . . . whether in the body or outside the body, I know not, God knows, rapt even to the third heaven"].

Thomas Aquinas, In Isaiam Prophetam.[1]

Vision is a function of intellect, and vision is possible only through the medium of some kind of light. And since it seems, according to St. Thomas, that one may speak of distinct kinds of light, intellectual vision will differ in kind according to the light afforded.

All readers of the *Comedy* (at least those who read and give thought to the poem as a whole) are well aware that we must speak of three "guides" along Dante's way. The pattern of three in this regard is evident enough. The wayfarer completes a journey to God, moving first with Virgil, then with Beatrice, and finally with Bernard. In this an order is apparent, involving degree and hierarchy. The direction of the movement is ever upward, so that Beatrice as guide is higher than Virgil, and Bernard higher than Beatrice. And order is to be noted in another respect as well: the lower leads to the higher, Virgil to Beatrice at the summit of the mountain of Purgatory, Beatrice to Bernard at the last summit where God is seen in His essence.

Time and again in the poem, Virgil and Beatrice are seen as kinds of light.[2] Yet the poem presents them so always in the manner of poetry, obliquely or allusively, by suggestion and by metaphor. As guides, for instance, both are said to be "suns," [3] lighting the way of Dante's journey which, since it is one of intellect, must pass through some of the biggest questions of this our mortal life. There is also the matter, repeatedly stressed, of Virgil's limitations. Virgil will declare that he can "discern no further," that Dante will have to wait until Beatrice is guide in order to attain to further and higher light on a given question. And the questions, in these moments, are always of some matter touching on faith or revealed truth, and lie, for that reason, beyond Virgil's ken.[4]

It is by the cumulative effect of all such pointers and turns of phrase along the line of the entire journey that the allegorical pattern of the *itinerarium* is disclosed. Never will the poet enter into direct discourse on the matter, speaking his allegory outright. The pattern of it emerges through the figures of the three guides, through an occasional and reiterated reference to their nature and function. The guides are "lights" (Virgil or Beatrice) or one of them may preside over the area of a third and last light (Bernard).

Now any reader who understands that Dante as poet does not invent his patterns in allegory, but adopts them as notions already existing in the thought and doctrine of his day, may quite naturally

be led to search that thought and doctrine for such conceptions as
are thus sensed to inform the poem's structure. And if, in so doing,
he should come across a passage such as the above in St. Thomas,
he must surely meet it with some shock of recognition. This *is*
the pattern of Dante's allegory in so far as it is a journey of intellect; and his allegory clearly pertains to intellect, being movement of mind by or through or under (all are possible) three
kinds of light. In this formulation by Thomas, moreover, we even
note a special provision for an experience in rapture which, as
we shall see, matches the event at the end of the poem, where
Bernard is guide.

But the inquiring reader will not therefore conclude that Dante
must have taken such a scheme as this from St. Thomas. Or, if he
is at first tempted to think so, let him but carry his search a little
further and discover that Thomas can lay no special claim of
ownership in this matter at all. He as theologian is, like the poet,
dealing with shapes of doctrine already elaborated in a long tradition.

We may therefore take the distinct formulation of this trio
of lights by St. Thomas simply as representative: it is an expression characteristically clear and concise of a conception which
Dante in his turn dealt with as something "public," familiar to his
readers and evocable in the mode of allegory. But that conception
is no longer so familiar, and we shall become better readers of the
poem only through making a special effort to retrieve it. It can
therefore help, in this direction, if we examine yet other formulations by St. Thomas of this notion of three lights.

From one such, we learn something about the specific nature
of these lights that appears well worth our knowing: namely, that
each of the three may be said to be natural to some order of
existence. In noting this, we realize that the idea of this trio is not
merely one attaching to the "mystical" notion of a journey to
God in this life; on the contrary, this pattern of three lights and
modes of vision is, as it were, built into the very structure of
existence, marking off orders of being — though it remains, of
course, essentially a matter of ways of seeing God or knowing
God, and theology in such matters is, more often than not, con-

cerned with man and the way open to man. What we may learn, therefore, is that by one of these lights and in one of these modes, the highest, God knows Himself, and that such a light is natural to Him alone; that by the next lower or middle kind of light and vision, the angels know God in a manner natural to them; and that finally there is a third and lowest light and manner of seeing God, which is natural to man. There are, thus, two modes of vision and two kinds of light by which God is seen which are higher than man's natural mode of knowing Him; and surely here, in reading Thomas on this point, we may expect a sense of recognition on the part of any reader of the *Comedy*:

Therefore, to know God, man, as he is after the fall, needs a medium which is like a mirror, in which there arises a likeness of God Himself. For we must reach "the invisible things of Him . . . by the things that are made," according to Romans 1.20. Man in the state of innocence, however, did not need this medium, but he did need a medium which is somewhat like the species of the thing seen, because he saw God through a spiritual light which was given to the human mind by God, and which was a kind of expressed likeness of the uncreated light.

But he will not need this medium in heaven, because he will see the essence of God in itself and not through any intelligible or sensible likeness of it, since no created likeness can so perfectly represent God that one who sees through it can know the essence of God. Yet, he will need the light of glory, which will be a kind of medium under which God is seen, according to Psalms 35.10: "In Thy light we shall see light." The reason for this is that this sight is not natural to any creature, but only to God. As a result, no creature can reach it by his own natural power, but to acquire it one must be enlightened by a divinely given light.

The second sight, through a medium which is an intentional likeness, is natural to the angels, but above human nature. Accordingly, for it man needs the light of grace.[5]

We may note yet another statement by Thomas of essentially the same concept of three lights, and again he takes thought of man in the state of innocence. Which light did man have before the Fall, in Eden, and what remains with man after the Fall? The student of Dante's poem will be particularly alert to the relevance of such questions. The Journey, as Dante gives it, is a return to

Eden, and in Eden Beatrice comes. In fact, thought of Beatrice may bring us to pay closer attention to the several names which Thomas continues to assign to that middle light which Beatrice must somehow represent:

> The third sight is proper to human nature; hence, it alone remains in man after the fall. Therefore, it is clear that the sight by which man in the state of innocence saw God was midway between the sight which we now have and the sight of the blessed.
> Accordingly, it is clear that after the fall man needs a triple medium to see God: creatures themselves, from which he rises to knowledge of God; a likeness of God, which he gets from creatures; and a light from which he receives the perfection of being directed toward God. This light may be the light of nature, such as the light of the agent intellect, or the light of grace, such as that of faith and wisdom. In the state before the fall, however, he needed a double medium: one which is a likeness of God, and one which is a light elevating and directing his mind. The blessed, however, need only one medium, the light of glory which elevates the mind. And God sees Himself without any medium, for He Himself is the light by which He sees Himself.[6]

It is well to turn now from such general formulations [7] of this scheme of three lights to a particular consideration of each light in itself, testing the whole scheme for its possible presence in the poem and paying closer attention to the concrete manifestations of it there. In doing this, however, it is also well to remain in touch with the whole pattern of three taken together, for by the whole is the part finally understood.

It must be decided in what order we should consider these lights. In the poem, the order of the journey to God is upward, of course, the wayfarer moving from lowest to highest. Yet we have already noted of this poem what can doubtless be said of many another: that we have full understanding of it only from the end. Hence, even though our chief concern and proper subject in these studies is the journey as it extends to the first summit only, where Beatrice comes, we shall for the moment continue to look from the last end and to trace the journey back from there.

*   *   *

THE LIGHT OF GLORY

"There is that contemplation of the blessed in Heaven [*in patria*] to which the intellect is uplifted by the light of glory, seeing God in His essence, as the object of beatitude." God is Himself the light by which He sees Himself. But God may give this His light to certain of His creatures that "in His light they may see light," knowing Him in direct vision, in His essence. This sight is man's ultimate beatitude, the Beatific Vision in which all desires of the rational creature grow quiet, being fulfilled therein.[8]

To such high vision only the blessed in Heaven may attain; there alone is that light of glory given through which sight of this highest order is made possible: given to those human souls who are there in-gathered as a harvest out of time, and to the angels, first and higher creatures. No reader of the *Paradiso* will ever forget the spectacle as the poem represents it: the great Rose of the blessed, the bee-swarm of the angels, the Light pouring down from above and striking upon the convex surface of the *primum mobile* to form there a pool of reflected light which is itself the yellow center of the Rose.[9] To that place Dante is guided by Beatrice, but as he reaches it, Beatrice leaves him to take her seat in the amphitheater of the blessed and St. Bernard replaces her. It is Bernard, not Beatrice, who must preside over the end of the long journey.

The change of guides is the clear signal of a change of "lights," a passing from whatever we may conceive the name of Beatrice as "light" to be, to what we may recognize, from the now familiar scheme, to be the last light of three, the light of glory. There are verses here to mark this and to declare attainment of this last light:

> Lume è là su che visible face
>   lo creatore a quella creatura
>   che solo in lui vedere ha la sua pace.
>
>   *Paradiso* XXX, 100–102.

> There is a light up there which makes the Creator visible to the creature, who finds his peace only in seeing Him.

"Creature" here is in the singular, but one is of course aware of the plural intention. All "high creatures" are meant, angelic and human, who have "intellect and love," [10] all creatures therefore who dwell here, in Heaven and in God's presence. Gazing up into the descending Light, each attains to such measure of the Beatific Vision as grace and merit may determine, for "ogni dove in cielo è paradiso": there are as many mansions here as there are creatures.[11] But we must take note of a point of signal importance for our understanding of the end of this action, and it is one which the poet has carefully built into the final scene. The Light descending here is *lumen gloriae*, even as the verses just noted make evident. Yet, as *first* presented, the whole scene in Heaven is a vision of how the saints and angels partake of the light of glory where the former sit in the Rose and the latter fly about. Now in St. Thomas's Latin (in the passage translated above) there is a term which can prove most useful in this connection: *in patria*. Its usefulness lies in the fact that it is one of a pair, *in via* being the other and opposing term: *in patria*, *in via*, familiar phrases in mediaeval theology. The notion expressed by *in via* is the same as that which informs the familiar term *homo viator*, a conception central to the scheme of the allegorical journey as Dante represents it. To attain to *patria* is to make an end of our pilgrimage *in via*. It means to pass from the condition of *homo viator* to that of *homo comprehensor*; and what is comprehended or possessed, of course, is the vision of God in His essence.

Now the important point about the whole scene *in patria*, at the end of the poem, and one too often overlooked, is this: in a first moment Dante sees the saints and the angels as *comprehensores*, sees how it is that they all find their peace here in the descending light of glory; but, in this first moment of the scene at the end, Dante the wayfarer does not himself partake of that light directly.[12] This order in the staging of the final scene at the end is dictated by reasons artistic as well as theological. Yet the theological reason is the determining element (or shall we not say that with Dante the two are one?). In any event, the final scene reveals a concern to keep the ultimate experience of the light of glory separate and to respect the radical distinction between the experience of it *in patria* and *in via*. And having our eye expressly on the allegory of a journey in the poem, we may see the importance of this. Only if the poet can stage the attainment of the end of the journey in terms of an experience *in via*, can he keep his allegory. Here is a man reaching *patria* at the end of his long ascent, and here *in patria* he is to have the ultimate vision of God in His essence. But even so, this vision must be that of one who is *in via* — else this becomes a literal journey merely and would cease to be in the double focus of allegory.

The experience of the light of glory had by one still in this life is the terminal focus of the whole poem and its proper end. At that end there is a remarkable merging of the line of the literal journey *there* and the line of the journey of soul *here*. On the instant of that merging the poem ends. All the while the experience of those who are already *in patria* and the experience of one who is still *in via* are kept distinct.

Bernard replaces Beatrice. For one thing, of course, the poet wanted to behold Beatrice where she takes her seat in the Rose beside ancient Rachel, and to address to her there the magnificent paean with which he says goodbye.[13] And he desired also to linger with the whole spectacle of the Rose, inviting his reader to rejoice in the symmetry and balance, the beauty of order to be seen in the very seating arrangement of the blessed, and finally to focus upon the loftiest place, allotted to Mary, with whom that movement of grace had begun which had brought him finally to this high place. In a sense, the action of the whole poem now comes full circle, for it began with Mary.[14] And at this point one might further remark that if Dante's poem were only a vision of "the state of souls after death," it would have to end with this spectacle of the saints in glory. But precisely because the line of a journey is also there and must be brought to its completion, the poem does not end in the focus of "state of souls after death." It ends where a journey ends.

The end of the journey is shown as a struggle, a mighty effort to attain to this high experience, all the while that it fades away. Why? Because such is always the nature of any experience of God in His essence on the part of one still in this life, *in via*.[15] St. Paul had found it to be so, and so no doubt had St. Bernard himself experienced it, who, on the claim of the poem, had "en-

joyed this peace in contemplation." [16] It is this, indeed, that quali-
fies Bernard to guide here. He had been here before, while he was
yet *in via*, among the living, *homo viator*.

*   *   *

THE LIGHT OF GRACE

"There is yet another kind of contemplation to which man is
raised by the *light of faith*, as are the saints in this life." Such a
name for the second or middle light of three is but one among
several possible names. Others already noted in the statements
by St. Thomas are "light of wisdom" (*sapientia*) and "light of
grace." [17] Or, for this same middle light, there is yet another
name: "revelation." This we may see in still another formulation
by Thomas of the familiar pattern of three lights:

> Man's knowledge of divine things is threefold. The first is when
> man, by the natural light of reason, rises through creatures to the
> knowledge of God. The second is when the divine truth which sur-
> passes the human intelligence comes down to us by revelation, yet
> not as shown to him that he may see it, but as expressed in words
> so that he may hear it. The third is when the human mind will be
> raised to the perfect intuition of things revealed. . . .
>
> And since natural reason rises to the knowledge of God through
> creatures, while on the other hand the knowledge of God by faith
> comes down to us by divine revelation, and since the way of ascent
> is the same as that of descent, we must needs proceed by the same
> way in those things above reason which are an object of faith, as
> that which we followed hitherto in those matters concerning God
> which we investigated by reason. [18]

The passage in the *Contra Gentiles* is pivotal, serving to introduce the fourth and last book of that work and declaring a significant change in method. Up to this point, Thomas writes,
inquiry and argument in his *Summa* have proceeded according
to natural reason. In short, the method throughout the first three
books has been primarily that of "philosophy"; now, in the
fourth book, it is to be that of "theology," the science in which
first principles are given, not by reason, but through faith and revealed truth. [19]

Faith, revelation, theology. The terms are not synonyms, of course, but in this context they bear the closest connection, as is evident in Thomas's way of writing about them. They form a kind of cluster of names to be linked with the other two names, *wisdom* and *grace*. These, then, are all terms which out of various perspectives of allegory may be properly assigned to Beatrice in her role as the middle light. We have yet to understand this. At the moment it is important to observe that each of these names easily lends itself to the metaphor of light, and that we are here concerned with a journey to God as an operation of intellect, always seen as taking place by some kind of light.

If the reader on encountering the above statement has Beatrice in mind as the second light, he will be struck by the particular turn of phrase: "the divine truth which surpasses the human intelligence comes down to us by revelation." One thinks at once not only of Beatrice's actual descent to the summit of the mountain where Virgil's guidance must end and hers begin, but also of the way in which Paradise itself continues to "descend" to meet the wayfarer as he moves upward from sphere to sphere with Beatrice. In this sense we may note that the movement of the whole canticle, as long as she is guide, continues to repeat the initial descent of Beatrice. The poet, moreover, is at pains to stress this point. Souls of the blessed are met in all the spheres of the heavens, and Beatrice must explain that they of course do not dwell there but only descend to manifest themselves there to one *in via* for the same reason that Holy Scripture condescends to speak to us:

> "Qui si mostraron, non perchè sortita
>   sia questa spera lor, ma per far segno
>   della celestial c'ha men salita.
> Così parlar conviensi al vostro ingegno
>   però che solo da sensato apprende
>   ciò che fa poscia d'intelletto degno.
> Per questo la Scrittura condescende
>   a vostra facultate, e piedi e mano
>   attribuisce a Dio, ed altro intende."
>
> *Paradiso* IV, 37–45.

"Here they showed themselves not because this sphere is allotted to them, but to give a sign of the heavenly rank which is least exalted. It is necessary to speak thus to your faculty, since only through sense perception does it apprehend that which it then makes worthy of intellect. For this reason Scripture condescends to your capacity, and attributes feet and hands to God and means otherwise."

Such verses can prompt us to think of at least one notable difference in this respect between the view of Dante the poet and that of Thomas the theologian. We have seen the latter noting explicitly that the truth of revelation is not shown to man "that he may see it, but as expressed in words so that he may hear it." But no poet could afford to adopt such a position, and it is interesting to observe Dante declaring as much in these verses. A poet, who must see (that we in turn may see), must insist that man learns only from sense experience even at these transcendent heights. Thus the whole realm of *Paradiso* through which Beatrice guides must descend (condescend!) to speak to him (and to us) *sensibilmente*. It is the way of poetry. And Thomas had not a very high opinion of that way.[20] Yet this radical difference in their views may not bring us to deny to Beatrice the name of "Revelation" as she guides through the high realm of the heavenly spheres. This is the area of revealed truth, and one understands why a poet would leave unanswered the question of whether he was here in the flesh or not;[21] for, whatever the answer, Dante is determined to behold this realm as poet and as no theologian would ever attempt ot see it:[22] *sensibilmente*. Of course, certain gradations will be apparent in this respect, as the journey moves from the lowest sphere to the highest. Images in any way resembling those of the natural world will become fainter and fainter, fading and passing gradually to the geometrical or "unnatural." These would resolve themselves into pure light and music were it not that metaphor and simile, even in this highest and most rarefied region, continue to speak concretely to the eye.

However, for all the "sense" experience which is had in this high sphere where Beatrice guides, the poet has made it clear beyond any doubt that this journey with her is one "surpassing the human intelligence." To pass from Virgil's guidance to that of Beatrice means, when measured on the familiar pattern, to pass from journey by the first of the three lights to journey by the second. As for signals of the transition, these are several and they are most explicit. Thus, at the summit of the mountain, when Beatrice has replaced Virgil as guide, Dante the wayfarer puts a question designed to point up the line between two lights which has just been crossed:

> "Ma perchè tanto sovra mia veduta
>   vostra parola disiata vola
>   che più la perde quanto più s'aiuta?"
>
> > *Purgatorio* XXXIII, 82–84.

> "But why do your longed-for words fly so above
>   my sight that, the more it tries, it loses them?"

Whereupon Beatrice's answer can be that Dante has now come into quite another "school" than Virgil's "human" one:

> "Perchè conoschi" disse "quella scola
>   c'hai seguitata, e veggi sua dottrina
>   come può seguitar la mia parola;
>   e veggi vostra via dalla divina
>   distar cotanto. ... ."
>
> > *Purgatorio* XXXIII, 85–89.

> "In order that you may know," she said, "the school you have followed and may see how its doctrine can follow my words; and that you may see how far your human way is from the divine way. . . ."

While he was still guide, Virgil himself spoke of his "school" [23] and of its limits, more apparent now that Beatrice is guide; and the very fact that Virgil guided to a given point and no further, because he could "discern no further," stressed even more the fact of those limits. Yet the full implication and true nature of the transition from Virgil's school to Beatrice's could not be more emphatically affirmed than it is in the first canto of the *Paradiso*, in a verb invented by the poet to mark that "crossing over": *trasumanar*. As a verb, the coined term is striking enough; but it is the more so in being, in this context, a verb of motion. As it is used here, it can only mean "to pass beyond the human," and this is indeed what the journey is doing now. The particular point in the poem where the verb comes is important (it is used nowhere else by Dante). Here, in the first canto of the *Paradiso*, Dante has begun to move with Beatrice upward from the summit of the mountain, "pure and disposed to rise up to the stars":

> Trasumanar significar per verba
> non si poria; però l'essemplo basti
> a cui esperienza grazia serba.
>
> *Paradiso* I, 70–72.

To pass beyond the human cannot be expressed in words; therefore, let the example suffice him for whom grace reserves the experience.

Itinerarium now passes "beyond the human" and movement now (on both levels of meaning) will be by grace, by *lumen gratiae*, grace of a kind not given to Virgil. The whole context of this *terzina* becomes rich with the meaning which the curious verb brings in.

In the verses immediately preceding we were shown Dante and Beatrice in that pose which in itself declares much respecting Beatrice's guidance here, and which we must think proved so monotonous to Botticelli when he came to illustrate the *Paradiso*: Beatrice looking ahead and up toward the next sphere and the goal beyond, and Dante gazing upon her:

> Beatrice tutta nell'eterne rote
> fissa con li occhi stava; ed io in lei
> le luci fissi, di là su remote.
>
> *Paradiso* I, 64–66.

Beatrice remained with her eyes wholly fixed on the eternal wheels and on her I fixed mine, withdrawn from above.

Immediately before the *terzina* beginning with "Trasumanar" come verses comparing the experience so designated to a strange metamorphosis suffered by one Glaucus once, on a remote shore of Boeotia:

> Nel suo aspetto tal dentro mi fei
> qual si fe' Glauco nel gustar dell'erba
> che'l fè consorte in mar de li altri dei.
>
> *Paradiso* I, 67–69.

> Looking at her, I inwardly became such as Glaucus became
> upon tasting the grass which made him consort with the gods
> of the sea.

To understand the allusion it is necessary to recall Ovid's account of the curious event, how one day this Glaucus had gone to
fish from a grassy shore where no herds ever grazed, where not
even bees gathered honey; how there, when he laid his catch on
the grass, fish already half-dead appeared to regain life. Ovid has
Glaucus tell his own story:

> I stood for a long time amazed and in doubt, seeking the cause of
> this. Had some god done it or was it the grasses' juice? "And yet
> what herb could have such potency?" I said, and plucking some of
> the grass with my hands, I chewed what I had plucked. Scarce had
> I swallowed the strange juices when suddenly I felt my heart trem-
> bling within me and my whole being yearned with desire for an-
> other element. Unable long to stand against it, I cried aloud: "Fare-
> well, O Earth, to which I shall nevermore return!" and I plunged
> into the sea. The sea-divinities received me, deeming me worthy of
> a place with them, and called on Oceanus and Tethys to purge my
> mortal nature all away.[24]

Here, as so often, it is rewarding to follow to its source the
poet's reference, for only so does its full relevance become apparent. Dante, gazing upon Beatrice and ready to begin his upward flight with her, is as Glaucus was when he tasted of the
grass. He too, like Glaucus, suddenly desires another element
(only Ovid's verses, not Dante's, declare this) and suffers a sea-
change to a higher, god-like nature. "Farewell, O Earth!" Unlike
Glaucus, he will return; but like Glaucus, he leaves earth now for
another element or "sea," in which he is received by those whose
element this is. When Dante comes into the moon, souls appear to
greet him as so many faces reflected in water,[25] and others in the
next sphere come to meet him as fish come to what is thrown upon
their waters.[26] These, of courses, are human souls, and this "sea"
can be said to be theirs only in a quite special sense, being merely
the place where they are shown or revealed; but clearly when
Dante compares his experience to that of Glaucus, who became
"consort in the sea with the other gods," he has more than human

souls in mind. The "gods" must be the angels, first of all, even though these do not appear here.[27] We do well indeed to understand this in connection with a point which St. Thomas made concerning the second or middle light of three: namely, that it is a light natural to the angels. This "sea," then, is the natural element of those high creatures. And as Dante, like Glaucus, becomes "consort in this sea with the other gods," we shall understand these "other gods" to be those angelic creatures whose proper realm this lofty region is, and whose natural light is second in the scale of three. A light natural to angels must necessarily be transhuman, one remove above man. The angels' area is this middle one, their "sea" is here.[28]

If the comparison of Dante's experience to that of Glaucus is to prove valid in any strict sense, then it must be that transition from Virgil's school to Beatrice's necessarily implies something of a real metamorphosis, some radical change of nature in the one who undergoes the experience. Such further meaning does in fact find its confirmation in the very name (among the several noted) that does justice to Beatrice in her role as guide: "the light of grace." For grace, as the middle light, means sanctifying grace; and to come into such grace from a condition deprived of it must mean to undergo an elevation of man's very nature, as St. Thomas tells us in a passage of his *De Veritate* where he speaks again of the three lights reaching from man to God:

> Now in his nature man is proportioned to a certain end for which he has a natural appetite and for the obtaining of which he can work by his natural powers. That end is a contemplation of divine things such as is possible to man according to the capabilities of his nature; and in this contemplation philosophers have placed man's ultimate happiness.
> But there is an end for which man is prepared by God which surpasses the proportion of human nature, that is, eternal life, which consists in the vision of God by His essence. That vision is not proportionate to any creature whatsoever, being connatural only to God. It is therefore necessary that there be given to man not only something by which he can work toward that end or by which his appetite should be inclined to that end, but also something by which man's very nature should be raised to a dignity which would make such an end suited to him. For this, grace is given. But to incline

his will to this end charity is given; and for carrying out the works by which that end is acquired, the other virtues are given.[29]

Thus, man's nature may be raised above its own natural proportion and powers to a dignity that is *transhuman*. Beatrice is in fact the *lumen gratiae* by which this takes place, and the grace in question can be none other than that here defined by Thomas. We recognize the clear evidence of this, noting that charity and the other virtues, as required by Thomas, do indeed attend Beatrice when she comes. They are her handmaids. To be sure, such virtues concern primarily the will and not the intellect. But grace itself is a kind of light and as such must pertain directly to vision, to that operation of the intellect which precedes movement of the will in any *itinerarium mentis*.

It would be an easy matter to go through the *Paradiso* extracting and listing the many points at which Beatrice is presented as a kind of light; but it would then be necessary to restore each verse and *terzina* to its context, wherein her allegorical meaning is declared in characteristically oblique and allusive ways. One such passage may be noted here for the clear manner in which it speaks of grace as the light by which love is kindled, and then of the "ladder" or way of ascent by both light and love, that is, intellect and will. These particular verses addressed to Dante are spoken by no less an authority than the soul of Thomas Aquinas, in the heaven of the sun:

> e dentro all'un senti' cominciar: "Quando
>   lo raggio della grazia onde s'accende
>   verace amore e che poi cresce amando,
> multiplicato in te tanto resplende,
>   che ti conduce su per quella scala
>   u' sanza risalir nessun discende. . . ."
>
> Paradiso X, 82–87.

And within one I heard begin: "Since the ray of grace by which true love is kindled, and which then grows in loving, shines so multiplied in you that it is leading you up that stair which no one descends without reascending. . . ."

The "ray of grace" in this instance is not said to be Beatrice. Yet, in the action of the poem, the term may be seen to be her proper name as guide. She is *lumen gratiae*, and vision by such a light does indeed serve to kindle the kind of love which is "true" because its other name is charity. Movement up the ladder is thus by both light and love, intellect and will.

In the way of intellect, which is one of light and vision, it is Beatrice's eyes that become the adequate symbol or "medium," as all readers recall. Thus, the poet speaks specifically of her eyes as "lifting the wayfarer from the summit of the mountain," [30] and in the *itinerarium mentis* she is the one who "emparadises the mind." [31]

The point in the poem at which Beatrice's eyes do in fact become the symbol of seeing by a new kind of light (new, following upon Virgil's guidance) is clearly marked. Even before Dante is permitted to cross the stream at the summit that separates him from her, he sees Beatrice strike a new pose. She turns, now that the confession of his sins has been wrung from him, to gaze upon the gryphon, the "double beast" which unmistakably represents Christ in His dual nature, human and divine.[32] Beatrice remains in this pose until Dante has been brought through the dividing waters to stand before her and look into her eyes. What he now sees there is the revelation of one of the deepest mysteries of the Christian faith, a revelation which can be had through grace alone: the two natures of Christ, now in one aspect and now in the other.[33] Nothing could more clearly declare the several names which Beatrice at this moment, and henceforth, takes on as guide — "light of grace," "light of faith," and "light of revelation" — all of which find their basis in that "transhuman" mode which is explicitly designated in the poem, vision beyond Virgil's "school" and beyond man's natural powers.[34]

* * *

THE NATURAL LIGHT

"There is a kind of vision for which the natural light of intellect suffices, such as the contemplation of invisible things according to the principles of reason; and the philosophers placed the highest happiness of man in this contemplation." Does Virgil represent such a light in the journey to God? While Virgil guides, there would not seem to be any "contemplation of invisible things," in the sense in which St. Thomas means this here; yet Virgil does emerge in the action of the poem as the kind of light which the "philosophers" had, who did not have the second and higher light of faith and of sanctifying grace — a fact already apparent in Virgil's confessed limits as guide.

In the matter of "contemplation of invisible things" by the natural light of intellect, it must be acknowledged that Virgil does not appear to fit the pattern (except perhaps at one significant point).[35] There are some special reasons for this to be seen in particular patterns within the master pattern of three lights. The important point at the moment is that Virgil as guide can and does represent a first movement toward God by the natural light, even though "contemplation of invisible things" is not a significant or prominent part of that movement. Virgil, as we shall see, guides toward a condition of justice at the summit of the mountain, at which summit contemplation as such can begin for the wayfarer (as a dream in *Purgatorio* will make evident).[36] In this sense, Virgil has a role in a subordinate pattern of event ending with Beatrice at the summit and known in established doctrine as "justification of the ungodly" (*justificatio impii*), an inner event in the soul involving conversion and rectification of the will. But this is a matter to be examined when the journey is viewed especially as a movement of the will.[37] Then we shall be in a position to observe that, as the first guide, Virgil has a function in the way of the will as well as of the intellect. Here we are concerned primarily with intellect, "light" being always a matter pertaining to that faculty.

That Virgil figures in the action of the poem as a kind of guiding light has been noted, and is not, in any case, a matter for which any reader of the poem will require a long array of single verses and *terzine* to be cited in evidence. Once the fundamental fact itself is recognized, that we have to do with a pattern of three lights, and when two of the three have been distinguished for what they are, then Virgil's role as the guide who represents the third (in descending order) becomes a fact which no one may fail to recognize. It is enough to note that he, like Beatrice, is called a "sun," a "luce," a "lume," that he, like Beatrice, is said to constitute a "school." The further fact that Virgil leads to Beatrice and that the transition from him to her is a *trasumanar* quite clinches the point. If movement with Beatrice is trans-human, then movement with Virgil must be an *umanar*, within the proportion of our human nature.

Indeed we have to note, in the statements by St. Thomas, that several specified features and limits were prescribed for the lowest light. It is a light, first of all, natural to man. Such a light would remain with man even after Adam's sin and after the privation of sanctifying grace which resulted from that sin. Thus it is the light by which the "philosophers" saw whatever truths they did see, since they were deprived of the light of faith or of revelation or of sanctifying grace, and could move in the way of intellect only by the natural light of reason. That light was their only guide *in via*. Plato, therefore, and Aristotle, and all the other virtuous pagans "who did not sin" [38] had this light, natural to man, and no other light of intellect than this. Because this is so, these "philosophers" shall never enjoy that higher light which is Beatrice and which is the light given to the "saints" *in via*; nor of course shall they ever see by that yet higher light of glory which is man's last beatitude. What was denied them in this life is denied them in eternity. Every reader knows the pathos that attaches to the figure of Virgil because of this hard truth.

Virgil, then, when urged by Beatrice to rescue the wayfarer from his struggle before the beasts, moves from his place among the "philosophers" where they dwell in their hemisphere of light in Limbo [39] (this being the evident sign of the natural light which they had in this life) and takes on a function as guide which, allegorically, is that very light itself: *lumen naturale*. The whole extent of Virgil's guidance proves then to be considerable, if we count the cantos. It lasts in fact through nearly two-thirds of the whole journey, down through all of Inferno and up to the very summit of Purgatory. Certain minor complications arise here, to be sure, which we may only remark in passing. One is the evident fact that Virgil actually does not know his way up the mountain of Purgatory, but must ask time and again and be told — a curious predicament, to say the least, for one who is chosen to serve as guide through this second realm of the life beyond. On the other hand, such was not the case through Inferno, for the good reason that Virgil had been that way before, down even to the bottom of the pit.[40]

Nonetheless, and allowing for such minor problems as may present themselves in this regard, Virgil, as a light, can be none other than that light which is natural to man, which does not exceed the proportion of his nature, which remains with man even after loss of sanctifying grace.

Notes

1. *In Isaiam Prophetam*, ch. i: ". . . sciendum quod non quaelibet visio intellectualis est visio prophetalis: est enim quaedam visio ad quam sufficit lumen naturale intellectus, sicut est contemplatio invisibilium per principia rationis: et in hac contemplatione ponebant philosophi summam felicitatem hominis. Est iterum quaedam contemplatio ad quam elevatur homo per lumen fidei sufficiens, sicut sanctorum in via. Est etiam quaedam beatorum in patria ad quam elevatur intellectus per lumen gloriae, videns Deum per essentiam, inquantum est objectum beatitudinis; et hoc plene et perfecte non est nisi in patria, sed quandoque ad ipsam raptim elevatur aliquis etiam existens in hac mortali vita, sicut fuit in rapto Pauli."

The doctrine of "the three lights" has yet to be thoroughly studied in the theology of Dante's time. All evidence points to the fact that it was a much more familiar conception than Dante studies have recognized it to be. Further study is wanted. When it is undertaken, it must surely pay attention to the connection which the "three lights" have with what are referred to as "three goods" or "three perfections," meaning three "states." See, as examples, Aquinas, *In III Sent.* d. i, q. 1, a. 4, ad 1: "Est triplex perfectio, scilicet naturae, gratiae, et gloriae"; Albertus Magnus, *Summa Theol.* II, tr. xiv, q. 90 (ed. Borgnet, XXXIII, 173): "Tria bona sunt in quibus perficitur homo, scilicet bonum naturae, bonum gratiae et bonum gloriae"; Alexander of Hales, *Summa Theol.* I–II, Inq. IV, tr. iii, q. 3, tit. 1, ch. 1, in a "sed contra" (ed. Quaracchi, II, 729): "Status gratiae est status medius inter statum naturae et gloriae." Anyone undertaking such further study will find many helpful pointers in H. Bouillard, *Conversion et grâce chez s. Thomas d'Aquin* (Paris, 1944), and in René-Charles Dhont, *Le problème de la préparation à la grâce*, Etudes de science religieuse, V (Paris, 1946).

2. See E. A. Fay's *Concordance of the Divine Comedy* (Cambridge, Mass., 1888) s.v. "lume" and "luce" for the many instances.

3. For Virgil: *Inferno* XI, 91; for Beatrice, *Paradiso* III, 1; XXX, 75.

4. As one of several instances, *Purgatorio* XVIII, 46–48:

> Ed elli a me: "Quanto ragion qui vede
> dir ti poss'io; da indi in là t'aspetta
> pur a Beatrice, ch'è opra di fede."

5. *De Veritate* q. 18, a. 1, ad 1: "Homo igitur in statu post peccatum indiget ad cognoscendum Deum medio, quod est quasi speculum, in quo resultat ipsius Dei similitudo; oportet enim ut per ea quae facta sunt, in invisibilia eius veniamus, ut dicitur Rom. 1. Hoc autem medio non indigebat homo in statu innocentiae; indigebat autem medio quod est quasi species rei visae; quia per aliquod spirituale lumen menti hominis influxum divinitus, quod erat quasi similitudo expressa lucis increatae, Deum videbat. Sed hoc medio non indigebit in patria, quia ipsam Dei essentiam per seipsam videbit, non per aliquam eius similitudinem vel intelligibilem vel sensibilem cum nulla creata similitudo adeo possit perfecte Deum repraesentare, ut per eam videns ipsam Dei essentiam cognoscere aliquis possit. Indigebit autem lumine gloriae in patria, quod erit quasi medium sub quo videtur, secundum illud Ps. 35.10: 'In lumine tuo videbimus lumen,' eo quod ista visio nulli creaturae est naturalis, sed soli Deo; unde nulla creatura in eam ex sua natura potest pertingere; sed ad eam consequendam oportet quod illustretur lumine divinitus emisso. Secunda autem visio, quae est per medium, quod est species, est naturalis angelo: sed est supra naturam hominis. Unde ad eam indiget lumine gratiae."

6. *Ibid.*, continuing immediately: "Tertia vero est competens naturae hominis; et ideo ea sola sibi relinquitur post peccatum. Et ideo patet quod visio qua homo Deum in statu innocentiae vidit, media fuit inter visionem qua nunc videmus et visionem beatorum. — Patet igitur quod homo post peccatum triplici medio indiget ad videndum Deum; scilicet ipsa creatura, ex qua in divinam cognitionem ascendit; et similitudine ipsius Dei, quam ex creatura accipit; et lumine quo perficitur ad hoc ut in Deum dirigatur; sive sit lumen naturae, ut lumen intellectus agentis, sive gratiae, ut fidei et sapientiae. In statu vero ante peccatum indigebat duplici medio: scilicet medio quod est similitudo Dei; et quod est lumen elevans vel dirigens mentem. Beati autem uno tantum indigent medio, scilicet lumine elevante mentem. Ipse autem Deum seipsum videt absque omni medio, ipse enim est lumen quo seipsum videt."

7. For another such, stated in different terms, see *Summa Theol.* I, q. 93, a. 4, resp.: "Cum homo secundum intellectualem naturam ad imaginem Dei esse dicatur, secundum hoc est maxime ad imaginem Dei, secundum quod intellectualis natura Deum maxime imitari potest. Imitatur autem intellectualis natura maxime Deum quantum ad hoc quod Deus seipsum intelligit et amat. — Unde imago Dei tripliciter potest considerari in homine. Uno quidem modo, secundum quod homo habet aptitudinem naturalem ad intelligendum et amandum Deum; et haec aptitudo consistit in ipsa natura mentis, quae est communis omnibus hominibus. Alio modo, secundum quod homo actu vel habitu Deum cognoscit et amat, sed tamen imperfecte; et haec est imago per conformitatem gratiae. Tertio modo, secundum quod homo Deum actu

cognoscit et amat perfecte; et sic attenditur imago secundum similitudinem gloriae. Unde super illud Ps. 4.7: 'Signatum est super nos lumen vultus tui Domine,' Glossa distinguit triplicem imaginem: scilicet creationis et recreationis et similitudinis. Prima ergo imago invenitur in omnibus hominibus; secunda in iustis tantum; tertia vero solum in beatis."

8. On "rapture," see especially Aquinas, *Summa Theol.* II–II, q. 175. Also his *De Veritate*, q. 13, a. 1, "De Raptu."

9. *Paradiso* XXX.

10. *Paradiso* I, 106.

11. *Paradiso* III, 88–89.

12. The signal of the change for Dante the wayfarer from seeing by the *reflected* light of glory to seeing through it *directly* is given by St. Bernard at the end of Canto XXXII (140–144). The last canto of the poem comes into the single and simple focus on Dante experiencing directly the uplifting light of glory.

13. *Paradiso* XXXI, 61–93.

14. *Inferno* II, 94.

15. For the two ways of seeing *in patria*: Aquinas, *De Veritate* q. 13, a. 2, resp.: "Similiter et lumen gloriae dupliciter menti infunditur. *Uno modo* per modum formae connaturalis factae, et permanentis; et sic facit mentem simpliciter beatam; et hoc modo infunditur beatis in patria. — *Alio modo* contingit lumen gloriae mentem humanam, sicut quaedam *passio transiens*: et sic mens Pauli in raptu fuit lumine gloriae illustrata. Ipsum etiam nomen raptim et transeundo ostendit hoc esse factum."

16. *Paradiso* XXXI, 111.

17. See quotations above; also *De Veritate* q. 18, a. 1, ad 4: "In contemplatione Deus videtur per medium quod est lumen sapientiae, mentem elevans ad cernenda divina; non autem ut ipsa divina essentia immediate videatur; et sic per gratiam videtur a contemplante post statum peccati, quamvis perfectius in statu innocentiae." For the identification of the light of faith with the light of grace, see *Summa Theol.* I–II, q. 109, a. 1, resp.: "Altiora vero intelligibilia intellectus humanus cognoscere non potest nisi fortiori lumine perficiatur, sicut lumine fidei vel prophetiae; quod dicitur lumen gratiae, inquantum est naturae superadditum."

18. *Summa c. G.* IV, 1: "Est igitur triplex cognitio hominis de divinis. Quarum prima est secundum quod homo naturali lumine rationis per creaturas in Dei cognitionem ascendit. — Secunda est prout divina veritas, intellectum humanum excedens, per modum revelationis in nos descendit, non tamen quasi demonstrata ad videndum, sed quasi sermone prolata ad credendum. Tertia est secundum quod mens humana elevabitur ad ea quae sunt revelata perfecte intuenda. . . . Quia vero naturalis ratio per creaturas in Dei cognitionem ascendit, fidei vero cognitio a Deo in nos e converso divina revelatione descendit; est autem eadem via ascensus et descensus: oportet eadem via procedere in his quae supra rationem creduntur, qua in superioribus processum est circa ea quae ratione investigantur de Deo."

19. *Ibid.*: "Competunt autem verba praemissa nostro proposito. Nam in praecedentibus de divinis sermo est habitus secundum quod ad cognitionem divinorum naturalis ratio per creaturas pervenire potest: imperfecte tamen et secundum proprii possibilitatem ingenii. . . . Restat autem sermo haben-

dus de his quae nobis revelata sunt divinitus ut credenda, excedentia intellectum humanum."

20. See *Summa Theol.* I, q. 1, a. 9. Thomas' judgment on the poets in this respect repeats Aristotle's and, for that matter, Plato's. See note 22 below.

21. *Paradiso* I, 73–75; II, 37–42.

22. Aquinas, *Summa c. G.* III, 47: "Si autem alias substantias separatas in hac vita intelligere non possumus, propter connaturalitatem intellectus nostri ad phantasmata, multo minus in hac vita divinam essentiam videre possumus, quae transcendit omnes substantias separatas. Huius autem signum hinc etiam accipi potest, quia quanto magis mens nostra ad contemplanda spiritualia elevatur, tanto magis abstrahitur a sensibilibus."

23. *Purgatorio* XXI, 33.

24. *Metamorphoses* XIII, 940 ff. I have given the translation of F. J. Miller, Loeb Library (Cambridge, Mass., 1944), II, 295.

25. *Paradiso* III, 11 ff.

26. *Paradiso* V, 100.

27. For angels called "gods," see *Inferno* VII, 87. This is frequent enough. See Aquinas, *Summa Theol.* I, q. 63, a. 7, resp.: "Et videtur haec opinio consonare positioni Platonicorum quam Augustinus recitat in lib. De Civ. Dei VIII et X. Dicunt enim quod omnes dii erant boni, sed daemonum quidam boni, quidam mali; deos nominantes substantias intellectuales quae sunt a globo lunari superius. . . ."

28. Aquinas, *Summa Theol.* I, q. 62, a. 3, ad 3: "Quamvis gratia sit medium inter naturam et gloriam ordini naturae. . . ." And see the quotation above wherein this middle light is said to be *natural* to the angels. Also Aquinas, *De Veritate* q. 8, a. 8, ad 6: "Intellectus angeli quantum ad hoc est medius inter intellectum divinum et humanum"; *ibid.*, q. 18, a. 5, ad 5: "Sicut natura angelica est media inter naturam divinam et corporalem. . . ." It is to be noted that before sin Adam had this kind of vision, regained by Dante at this point. Aquinas, *De Veritate* q. 18, a. 1, ad 12: "Angelus in statu naturae conditae non vidit Deum per essentiam; sed hoc ei competebat solum per gratiam. Adam autem in statu innocentiae per gratiam habuit illum modum visionis quem habet angelus per naturam . . . et ideo dicitur sicut alter angelus." Finally, see Dante's recognition of this general point in the *Epist. ad Can. Gran.*, 28: "Intellectus humanus in hac vita, propter connaturalitatem et affinitatem quam habet ad substantiam intellectualem separatam, quando elevatur, in tantum elevatur, ut memoria post reditum deficiat propter transcendisse humanum modum."

29. *De Veritate* q. 27, a. 2, resp.

30. *Paradiso* XVII, 113–114.

31. *Paradiso* XXVIII, 3.

32. *Purgatorio* XXXI, 79–81.

33. *Ibid.*, 121–123.

34. Aquinas, *Summa Theol.* I–II, q. 109, a. 7, resp.: "Cum enim decor gratiae proveniat ex illustratione divini luminis, non potest talis decor in anima reparari, nisi Deo denuo illustrante; unde requiritur habituale donum, quod est gratiae lumen."

35. *Purgatorio* XIII, 13 ff., where Virgil prays to the *visible* sun for guidance.

36. See Chapter VII, below.
37. See next chapter, "The Three Conversions."
38. *Inferno* IV, 34.
39. *Inferno* IV, 67 ff.
40. *Inferno* IX, 22 ff.

Chapter III

The Three Conversions

> Every movement of the will toward God can be termed a conver-
> sion to God. And so there is a threefold turning to God. The first
> is by the perfect love of God; this belongs to the creature enjoying
> the possession of God; and for such conversion, consummate grace
> is required. The next turning to God is that which merits beatitude;
> and for this there is required habitual grace, which is the principle
> of merit. The third conversion is that whereby a man disposes him-
> self so that he may have grace; for this no habitual grace is required,
> but an operation of God, Who draws the soul towards Himself,
> according to Lam. 5.21: "Convert us, O Lord, to Thee, and we shall
> be converted." Hence it is clear that there is no need to go on to
> infinity.
>
> Thomas Aquinas.[1]

We are now concerned with movement of the will as distinguished from that of intellect, movement which is a turning
towards God on the part of the will. Such is the specific meaning
of "conversion" for St. Thomas and for the theology of Dante's
day.[2]

If "conversion" is understood in this sense, one perceives at once
its relevance to the notion of a "journey" to God. Indeed, in the

above statement we recognize a trio and sequence of movements toward God presenting the closest correlation to that scheme of three lights we have been concerned to examine in some detail. And remembering a first truth respecting *itinerarium mentis ad Deum*, namely that any movement toward Him will be not a matter of intellect alone or of will alone, but of the two in coordinated operation, we may with good reason seize upon this scheme of three conversions in the certain persuasion that here we find nothing less than the other half of the master pattern of Dante's allegory that we require.

With the present sequence, as with that of three lights, we might again proceed to examine in detail the manner in which the poet has carried out such a design in the events of his journey. But what has already been noted in this respect regarding the three lights is now so easily applied to these three "conversions" that extensive examination under separate rubrics appears superfluous, especially in the matter of the highest light and the last conversion, at the end.

In the above formulation of "conversions" St. Thomas begins at the summit of the scale, where the final movement toward God is through perfect love and consummate grace. For now it is a question of love of course, since love concerns the will. And the coordination, here at the summit, of a movement of love with movement of intellect, which is a matter of light, is evident enough. This highest conversion is made possible through consummate grace, which in the other scheme is simply the light of glory. Movement of intellect comes first, and its movement is by light; whereupon the will moves towards God to possess Him in love, and this is the end of the last conversion, this is final beatitude for all "high creatures," that is, for angels and for men. The last conversion, of which St. Thomas speaks, takes place in the poem, therefore, where Bernard comes in as guide, replacing Beatrice. "Light of glory," "consummate grace," "last conversion" are thus all facets of one event which we must conceive as having such distinct parts since two faculties are involved and not merely one: intellect which sees and will which turns and moves. We remember, of course, that for Dante the wayfarer, the whole final experience is one in rapture, as it was for Paul: a rapture in which the will is not confirmed forever in consummate grace, as happens with the blessed and with the angels in the presence of God. With respect both to intellect and will, the experience in rapture which may be had while man is still *in via* can have but the briefest duration, even as the poem represents it.

If such cursory remarks appear sufficient to distinguish the essential nature of the last turning of the will towards God (such is its simplicity), the two lower conversions are not, perhaps, so simple to undertsand. Special questions can arise in regard to them, and one question in particular which was extensively discussed in the theology of Dante's time. These two lower conversions, then, appear to call for a somewhat closer scrutiny.

* * *

CONVERSION WITH BEATRICE

The second or middle conversion takes place with Beatrice. In it, as in the highest conversion, one readily perceives the co-ordination of "light" in the pattern of intellect with "conversion" in that of the will. Furthermore, we have already remarked the particular manner in which Beatrice is seen to differ from Bernard in her allegorical role as guide. The same difference holds between Virgil and Bernard. For in the allegory of three lights, Virgil and Beatrice are themselves the two lower lights, whereas Bernard is not the last light at all (as, for reasons noted, he could not possibly be).

While we take note of this difference as we turn from the highest conversion with Bernard to the next lower conversion with Beatrice, we remark also the similarity between the two moments: for even as the light of glory is that same consummate grace by which the final conversion of the will is realized, so now is the light of sanctifying grace that same lesser grace by which the second conversion of the will takes places, a turning to God which merits beatitude. Only through habitual grace, as St. Thomas tells us above, can such merit be obtained; and habitual grace is but another name for sanctifying grace. Beatrice is such grace, and her advent is predominantly in terms of light for that reason. She is *lumen gratiae*, the light of grace descending to the wayfarer who attains to the summit of the mountain and is made ready to receive her. Beatrice is thus that grace by which a man is made "pleasing" to God, as the name in Latin most commonly used to denote it explicitly affirms: *gratia gratum faciens*.[3]

But the advent of Beatrice is not merely advent of light. By such grace as she (in allegory) is, man's whole nature is transformed, elevated above the limits of what is natural to man. A *trasumanar* takes place, not in the intellect alone but also in the will. A new orientation of the inner man prevails, *itinerarium mentis* "turns" and moves in a new way. Through sanctifying grace the soul is uplifted and turned toward God as to its special object of beatitude. By such grace alone do we become the "adopted sons of God."

That a new kind of light and new ordering of the will attend the advent of sanctifying grace, which is Beatrice's advent, is witnessed by the presence of the two virtues, faith and charity, in her retinue. For faith pertains to vision, and charity pertains to the will. Both are virtues which are special gifts of God, accompanying the gift of sanctifying grace by which He directs both will and intellect unto Himself. By faith it is given to us (while yet *in via*) to know God as our ultimate and true Beatitude. By charity we adhere to God through a love which reaches to Him as such Beatitude. Thus, of the seven virtues attending Beatrice as her handmaids, two there are, faith and charity, which must be seen to be chief among them all.

But since we are now concerned, above all, with "conversion," which is movement of will, we may look especially to the presence of charity in Beatrice's advent. We have only to know that red is the established color of that virtue [4] to remark that charity's color is indeed the dominant one in the whole scene of Beatrice's coming. Of course, charity is but one of the theological virtues (each having its own symbolic color), and in this awareness we should note the colors which mark off and divide the whole triumphal procession which brings Beatrice: white, green, and red — "faith, hope, and charity, these three." No one, moreover, will forget how the Apostle had ruled that of these three, the greatest is charity,[5] and with this the poet has shown his predictable agreement. The dominant color of Beatrice's attire is charity's color: she is "vestita di color di fiamma viva," meaning that the greatest of the virtues attending sanctifying grace must be charity, which is love. Moreover, if we turn to that other group of four maidens attending Beatrice, the four cardinal virtues, we note that all four are dressed in a single color in which the red of charity predominates.[6]

The virtues pertain to the will, as St. Thomas has told us, and when movement or conversion of the will is our first concern, the virtues call for special attention. By such virtues as those which here attend Beatrice, the will of a man *in via* is directed to God as the object of beatitude. Among them, charity is chief, for it is through charity that the will receives its due orientation to God as our last end. Charity is one kind of love, and love is the proper name for all movements of the will. Indeed, as the poem affirms, the soul "moves by no other foot" than that of love.[7]

Charity (as with the grace through which charity is given) means an elevation of man's power beyond what is natural to man and proportionate to his being. It is, in its origin and source, *transhuman*, being a love available to man only when given from beyond him and his human limitations: given by God. Only with charity is merit had with God. Charity is the very root of merit.[8]

What we are remarking, in short, is simply an established point of doctrine: that the second conversion is conversion through sanctifying grace and the infused virtues, charity predominating. Representing such grace, Beatrice comes at the summit of the mountain, and with her is that virtue without which all is a mere tinkling cymbal, without merit before God. Such is the second and central conversion in the pattern of three.

*   *   *

CONVERSION WITH VIRGIL

As for the third and lowest conversion in the threefold pattern, one notes the explicit stipulation by St. Thomas that for this "turning of the will" no habitual grace is required. "Habitual grace" is "sanctifying grace," which, in the allegory of the three guides, is Beatrice. We have therefore to conceive of a first turning to God (in ascending order) by way of "an operation of God Who draws the soul towards Himself." But this, as St. Thomas also states, is that conversion whereby "a man disposes himself so that he may have grace." Now clearly a question arises here: is this first conversion a matter of man disposing himself, or is it God who disposes? The ambiguity in Thomas's wording can seem puzzling and calls for some special attention. Already we sense that this lowest conversion is precisely the area of Virgil's guidance in the journey, and for this reason the question takes on a particular interest. We note one further point also in Thomas's formulation: the first or lowest conversion prepares for the second. Accordingly, we are told that in the first conversion a man disposes himself so that he may have grace, by which we know that Thomas means sanctifying grace, which comes at the point of the second conversion, and is the goal of the first.

The particular question whether, in this first conversion or movement toward God, man disposes himself to receive grace, or whether he is disposed thereto by God, may easily be seen as related to the great issue of Pelagianism. Not that the Pelagian controversy as such had continued very much alive into the time of St. Thomas and Dante: Augustine's victory almost a thousand years before had been too complete for that. One may speak of the "semi-pelagianism" of some of St. Thomas' earlier writings, for instance,[9] but we know that with Thomas there is no question of a denial of original sin or a denial that death came into the world through that sin. The issues are settled, and although the questions as questions appear in the *Summas*, the Response in each case is always predictable. Still, there were facets of that issue which lingered on as "semi-pelagian" questions and remained open at least to fresh formulation in the 12th and 13th centuries. This was due in large part to the Aristotelian revival which provided new avenues of approach. Such a question is the one posed above concerning the first conversion. The issue and central concern here becomes precisely the line of distinction, if any, to be drawn between nature and grace, in the matter of this preparation for the reception of sanctifying grace.

The influence of Aristotle's thought may be discerned time and again in the treatment which the question receives at the hands of Thomas and of his master Albertus Magnus, to choose that pair as representative. The tell-tale signs of this influence are the terms in which the question of the first conversion is constantly cast: *form* and *matter*. The usage is typical, of course, nor does it originate with Thomas or Albertus; it appears to begin with the theologian Philippe le Chancelier, who, in his *Summa* written around 1230, was the first to conceive of sanctifying grace as *form* in the Aristotelian sense. Not that some other theologian would not have had this thought had Philippe not hit upon the fruitful idea. Still it is one of the earlier signs of that general re-casting of Christian theology into Aristotelian molds of thought which was to prevail.[10]

The definition of habitual grace as form is a matter of some importance, for it opens the door to a conception of a whole process of conversion on an Aristotelian pattern. "Form," in Aristotle's sense, brings with it inevitably the notion of "matter," and between those two polar terms lies "process," which is their real relation one to the other. That process is generation (*generatio*), and we may safely say that no pattern of thought deriving from Aristotle (in this case, of course, from the *Physics*) found more favor in philosophy and theology from Philippe's time through Dante's than did this one.[11] It pervaded the thoughts of poets, as well, so that a famous poem by Guido Guinizelli is built around the Aristotelian notion of generation; [12] and one meets with it time after time in Dante's earlier works [13] as well as in the *Comedy*. Indeed, any idea of process whatever would almost certainly be conceived in Dante's day in the pattern of the Aristotelian *generatio*. It is not surprising, therefore, to discover that the main outline of the poet's allegory was in fact determined in large part by this conception.

Generatio is essentially a movement toward form. Such, literally, is the most general definition of the term; "generatio est motus ad formam." [14] What moves toward "form" is, of course, some "matter." The movement itself is essentially an alteration, a process of change in a given matter by which that matter is prepared or disposed to receive the form. The whole process of "becoming" moves from a beginning which is privation of form to an end where the form is received. And the movement has, as its first goal, a condition which is a "disposition to receive the form."

Thus, if sanctifying grace is "form," as Philippe decided and as many another theologian conceded it to be, then must there not be some process that would culminate in the reception of such a form? Would there not be some "matter" which at a beginning point is deprived of that form, but which, on the established pattern of Aristotle, would "move" toward that form, being made ready to receive it? "Matter" in this case would surely be the soul, or some faculty of the soul. Thus sanctifying grace would be the form of the soul, and there would be a movement of soul toward form, a process by which the soul is "disposed" to receive the form.

It is of interest to note that before the entire question of the reception of sanctifying grace in the soul was recast into this Aristotelian mold, there was no clear formulation at all of the problem of a preparation for grace. There had been other questions arising out of the Pelagian and "semi-pelagian" positions, of *initium fidei* and so forth, but the notion of a process which is a *praeparatio* or *dispositio* for grace took on a positive and clear outline only when the Aristotelian concept of a process of generation by which matter receives form came to prevail.[15]

This clearly becomes a point of very particular interest to our consideration of the substance and basic structural progression of Dante's poem, when we realize that the whole area of Virgil's guidance in the *Comedy* is that of *praeparatio ad gratiam*, and that had the Aristotelian notion of *generatio* not prevailed so generally in the thought of the poet's time, the event of the journey would not have been at all as it is.

If, then, sanctifying grace is "form," and if the process of conversion is construed on such a pattern of *generatio*, what exactly are we to understand the "matter" to be which is made ready to receive that form? The matter is, in the broadest sense, some human creature, of course, as Thomas tells us:

> It can be clearly shown from what has been said, that man is unable to merit God's assistance. For everything is in the position of mat-

ter in regard to what is above it. Now matter does not move itself to its perfection, but needs to be moved by another. Therefore, man does not move himself to the effect of obtaining the divine assistance, for this is above him: rather indeed is he moved for this purpose by God. Now the motion of the mover precedes the movement of the thing moved both logically and causally. Consequently, the divine assistance is not given to us because by our good deeds we previously move ourselves to obtain it, but rather do we advance by our good deeds, because of God's prevenient help.[16]

The question of merit here is the familiar one, but is not at the moment the matter of main concern. That is rather the notion of form and matter, and we note in this regard the important point: "everything is in the position of matter in regard to what is above it." Thus, since sanctifying grace is above ("transhuman," as we were noting) and is the form, it must be that the human creature is the matter.

The matter which receives the form (when the form is habitual grace) is, broadly speaking, the soul. Or again, matter may be conceived as man's nature simply, in that sanctifying grace is said to "inform" the very nature of a man, uplifting it to a condition above nature.[17] But in a more limited sense (in no way contradicting the broader view) the matter which receives the form in this case is thought to be the will. For this reason the whole question falls properly under the notion of conversion, which is movement of the will. It is thus the will which is made ready to receive the form. Hence there is a first phase of movement or change, a period of *dispositio*, wherein the will is made ready to receive. Then, at the end of the process, the form is received and the movement is complete.

Now this final moment of the reception of form, where movement ends, must, on the pattern of the three conversions, be precisely the moment when sanctifying grace is given; and this, as already noted, must mean that the event, in the pattern of *generatio*, extends to and includes the second conversion. Such is in fact the case, and in the next chapter we shall examine this pattern of event under the familiar name which it bears in theological doctrine: *justificatio impii*.

However, the first conversion as such, if we hold to St. Thomas's formulation, does not extend so far as to include the moment when sanctifying grace is given, for that moment is itself the second conversion. Instead, the first conversion may extend only as far as the process of preparation or disposition of the matter extends — which, to return to the outlines of event in the poem, is precisely as far as Virgil leads and no further. And if this is so, then we must say that the process of preparation for the reception of grace takes place under a natural light, for we have seen that Virgil must be such a light in his role as guide. To move with Virgil must mean to move within human limits and within the proportion of man's nature, as regards the light by which the movement takes place. But if this is true of light, i.e., of intellect in its movement, it must likewise be true of the movement of will, which is the specific matter in process of being made ready to receive the form. The first conversion in this sense will therefore be an event entirely within the confines of the human, of what is natural to man.

By way of these terms we come back to the problem that appeared inevitably to arise in the statement by Thomas respecting this first conversion. Does man dispose himself to receive sanctifying grace, or is it God who disposes him to this grace, drawing the soul to Himself through this first phase of the process? Evidently, the problem here comes only with respect to God's part in this action. For if movement through this first stage is conceived as a matter merely of "man disposing himself," no problem arises, since this is precisely a human area, this conversion lying within the confines of man's natural powers, as witnessed by the fact just noted that movement here is by natural light. The very fact of such limits would seem indeed to require that this be a process in which no other powers than man's own are involved. This would mean that man is on his own through the first phase of movement toward God.

But St. Thomas will not have it so. Man does dispose himself for grace, but we must not fail to see that God's hand is also there, drawing the creature to Him.[18] In the final analysis, we touch here on the crux of the question and the essential terms of its formulation. It comes down to this: is it possible for God to draw a man to Himself without such an operation on His part exceeding in any way the confines of the natural, or the limits of man's nature?

Can such an operation be so conducted by God that man may be said to dispose himself even though it is an operation of God? But how shall we not think of God's intervention in this case as "grace" of some kind, since His intervention is for no other purpose than that of drawing a man to Himself? And can we properly speak of an event as being entirely *natural* when it is brought about by such Divine intervention? Or if we hold to the notion that such intervention must be called grace and yet can not be habitual or sanctifying grace, in what sense can this be held? Is there a kind of grace that leads to sanctifying grace, and yet does so within natural confines?

One may be sure that when they allowed such questions to arise, the theologians knew the solution to them, and theirs were answers which, for Dante, carried the greatest weight of authority. The importance of these questions lies for us in the evident fact that, translated into the action of the poem, they all concern the figure of Virgil himself and his role as guide to Beatrice.

Many a treatise on the question of grace will be found to touch upon this point in just the terms noted, and to provide answers which interest us for the light they bring to the allegorical signifi- cance of Virgil as first guide in the journey. Light, for instance, can be had from such a statement as the following, forming part of the general discussion of grace in the *Summa Theologiae* of Thomas:

The preparation of the human will for good is twofold: — the first, whereby it is prepared to operate rightly and to enjoy God; and this preparation of the will cannot take place without the habitual gift of grace, which is the principle of meritorious works, as stated above (a. 5). There is a second way in which the human will may be taken to be prepared for the gift of habitual grace itself. Now in order that man prepare himself to receive this gift, it is not neces- sary to presuppose any further habitual gift in the soul, otherwise we should go on to infinity. But we must presuppose a gratuitous gift of God, Who moves the soul inwardly or inspires the good wish. For in these two ways do we need the Divine assistance, as stated above. . . . Dionysius says (Div. Nom. iv) that "God turns all to Himself." But He directs righteous men to Himself as to a special end, which they seek, and to which they wish to cling, ac- cording to Ps. 72.28: "It is good for me to adhere to my God."

And that they are "turned" to God can only spring from God's having "turned" them. Now to prepare oneself for grace is, as it were, to be turned to God; just as, whoever has his eyes turned away from the light of the sun, prepares himself to receive the sun's light, by turning his eyes towards the sun. Hence it is clear that man cannot prepare himself to receive the light of grace except by the gratuitous help of God moving him inwardly.[19]

Here we see the clear outline of a first period or preparation for grace, or (because Thomas is again proceeding typically from higher to lower) a first lower way in which the will is made ready for good. And this way is unmistakably the first or lowest conversion, as outlined in the preceding statement of the three. Now, in this first phase in which man prepares himself (again the particular conception), it is not necessary, St. Thomas tells us, to suppose that the gift of sanctifying grace is present in the operation — "otherwise we should go on to infinity." Nor is it hard to grasp the necessity of this on strictly logical grounds. But beyond that necessity we can hardly fail to sense that Thomas is determined to have a first period of *praeparatio* preceding the attainment of sanctifying grace, such a phase being directed to that attainment as to its terminus and goal. Logically, therefore, the goal cannot be conceived as present in the movement itself toward the goal, or we should continue to move back indefinitely. But the fact that there is a first preparatory phase is there for Thomas, supporting the logical necessity. And such a "fact," we are in a position to note, is there for him because of the Aristotelian model in the background: the notion of *generatio* which is a movement toward form.

This is the more evident, indeed, when we realize that Thomas was ready to grant that the attainment of sanctifying grace could be instantaneous, if God so willed. In terms of "preparation for grace," God may bring about a perfect preparation for grace which is instantaneous and simultaneous with the infusion of the grace; or God may grant that there be a first imperfect *praeparatio* or process, extended in time, through which the soul, or more specifically the will, is gradually made ready to receive and is brought to perfect preparedness. Thus, to the question "whether

any preparation or disposition for grace is required on man's part,"
Thomas replies as follows — making, it will be noted, an essential
distinction between habitual grace and the grace which is oper-
ative during the phase when the soul is being made ready to receive
it:

> Grace is taken in two ways: — First, as a habitual gift of God.
> Secondly, as a help from God, Who moves the soul to good. Now
> taking grace in the first sense, a certain preparation of grace is re-
> quired for it, since a form can only be in disposed matter. But if
> we speak of grace as it signifies a help from God to move us to
> good, no preparation is required on man's part, that, as it were, an-
> ticipates the Divine help, but rather, every preparation in man must
> be by the help of God moving the soul to good. And thus, even
> the good movement of the free-will, whereby anyone is prepared
> for receiving the gift of grace, is an act of the free-will moved by
> God. And thus man is said to prepare himself, according to Prov.
> 16.1: *It is the part of man to prepare the soul*; yet it is principally
> from God, Who moves the free-will. Hence it is said that man's
> will is prepared by God, and that man's steps are guided by God.[20]

Then, in two replies to objections in the same article, Thomas
uses the terms "imperfect preparation" and comes to the notion
that there can be a perfect preparation from God which is instantaneous, simultaneous with the infusion of habitual grace, as happened to Paul on the road to Damascus:

> A certain preparation of man for grace is simultaneous with the
> infusion of grace and this operation is meritorious, not indeed of
> grace, which is already possessed, but of glory which is not yet pos-
> sessed. But there is another imperfect preparation, which sometimes
> precedes the gift of sanctifying grace, and yet it is from God's mo-
> tion. But it does not suffice for merit, since man is not yet justified
> by grace, and merit can only arise from grace. . . .
> Since a man cannot prepare himself for grace unless God . . .
> move him to good, it is of no account whether anyone arrive at
> perfect preparation instantaneously, or step by step. For it is written
> (Ecclus. II. 23): *It is easy in the eyes of God of a sudden to make
> the poor man rich*. Now it sometimes happens that God moves a
> man to good, but not perfect good, and this preparation precedes
> grace. But He sometimes moves him suddenly and perfectly to good,
> and man receives grace suddenly. . . . And thus it happened to
> Paul, since, suddenly when he was in the midst of sin, his heart was

perfectly moved by God to hear, to learn, to come; and hence he received grace suddenly.[21]

We may remark in passing that, in the matter of the shape which Dante's *Comedy* was to take, it was indeed of some account "whether anyone arrive at perfect preparation instantaneously, or step by step." Take away the preparation which is step by step, and all of *Inferno* and almost all of *Purgatorio*, in so far as they are conceived as a journey, must vanish. And Virgil would have no function whatsoever in the poem.

But it is important not to lose sight of what we have remarked as the crux of the question: in this phase of preparation by degrees, God's intervention is called by Thomas a "gratuitous gift" of God, a "divine assistance." We learn that "grace may be spoken of in two ways." God's first operation then, in moving the soul towards sanctifying grace, must itself be called a kind of grace.

Clearly we are here very close indeed to the heart of the question. If God intervenes with His grace in the first phase or conversion, directing the movement towards its goal, how then may this be seen as an operation in which "man disposes himself"? To any student of theology it is at once apparent that we confront here the familiar problem of grace and free-will, as may be seen from a further statement by Thomas on the specific question of the preparation for sanctifying grace:

> Man's preparation for grace is from God, as Mover, and from the free-will as moved. Hence the preparation may be looked at in two ways: — First, as it is from free-will, and thus there is no necessity that it should obtain grace, since the gift of grace exceeds every preparation of human power. But it may be considered, secondly, as it is from God the Mover, and thus it has a necessity — not indeed of coercion, but of infallibility — as regards what it is ordained to by God, since God's intention cannot fail, according to the saying of Augustine . . . that "by God's good gifts whoever is liberated, is most certainly liberated." Hence if God intends, while moving, that the one whose heart He moves should attain to grace, he will infallibly attain to it.[22]

Attainment to sanctifying grace is the completion of a process of justification (to be considered in the next chapter), and the movement towards that end is a preparation to receive. As such it is the first of three conversions. Such movement takes place, in the action of the poem, under Virgil's guidance. It is therefore an event to be conceived as falling within natural limits. It is, we recall, an *umanar*. Yet we must grant, also, as we have seen, that the movement is directed by God.

For all such essential requirements we find ample provision in the established theological conception of this first conversion. God's providence extends throughout the universe, of course, operating within the boundaries of the natural everywhere. But the direction which He gives to the human creature in that providential order, whenever His direction is intended to draw such a creature to Himself, may properly be called by the special name of grace, of *gratia gratis data*, to distinguish it from sanctifying grace (*gratia gratum faciens*).[23] St. Thomas at times appears to prefer other names for this first guidance within natural limits: *auxilium Dei, misericordia Dei*. But, for Thomas especially, the essential truth about it is that it is providential, that as a first movement in soul it is willed by God and cannot therefore fail of its appointed end. "Hence if God intends . . . that the one whose heart He moves should attain to grace, he will infallibly attain to it." [24]

In considering these points of doctrine, one cannot help feeling that we are indeed very close to Dante's poem with its first movement toward grace under Virgil's guidance.[25] The journey through *Inferno* is a "fatale andare," as it continues to be through the second realm of *Purgatorio*. This is a journey which may not fail of its appointed goal. This man's way (and in his we are to see ours always, as an open possibility) is given by a power which descends from on high. It is a ladder which God extends to the creature whom He chooses to call to Himself.[26]

The ladder is three-sectioned and is to be understood both in terms of *light* and of *movement of will*. Virgil guides through the first section which is within "nature" or natural bounds, and which is a preparation for the second higher section which is Beatrice's.[27] If God did not offer his help in such manner, extending it all the way down into the natural order, we should face no problem of a first phase of guidance through such an order at all. But through His mercy, God does so extend His *auxilium*; God Himself choosing to observe degree, giving His help first through the lowest order, to prepare the soul for the next higher.

The concept which we require of theology, in this respect, is not wanting. We have to do here with an order and process which is moral, of course; and a moral order is an order of finality, an order directed to an end or goal. Now St. Thomas gives us what is needed here as a concept, and with the clearest kind of label: *ordo naturalis ad gratiam*.[28] Here are all the elements as required. The first conversion is an *ordo*, that is, a providential ordering or directing of the creature by God. The order is natural, in that it is within confines which do not exceed human nature. But it is an order toward an end. It is *ad gratiam*, having as its goal a grace which is beyond the natural.

Thus the first conversion, though natural, is directed to what is above nature: sanctifying grace. It is even more essentially directed to such grace in that it is a preparation to receive it. St. Thomas is given to using another term for this aspect of the matter: *habilitas ad gratiam*.[29] For the "matter," in this case, is a nature able to receive the "form" when made ready to receive it. Such a "making ready to receive" is the first of the three conversions.

Notes

1. *Summa Theol.* I, q. 62, a. 2, ad 3: "Quilibet motus voluntatis in Deum potest dici conversio in ipsum. Et ideo triplex est conversio in Deum. Una quidem per dilectionem perfectam, quae est creaturae iam Deo fruentis. Et ad hanc conversionem requiritur gratia consummata. Alia conversio est quae est meritum beatitudinis. Et ad hanc requiritur habitualis gratia, quae est merendi principium. Tertia conversio est per quam aliquis praeparat se ad gratiam habendam. Et ad hanc non exigitur aliqua habitualis gratia, sed operatio Dei ad se animam convertentis, secundum illud *Thren.* ult.: 'Converte nos, Domine, ad te, et convertemur.' Unde patet quod non est procedere in infinitum."

2. For "conversion" as understood by the theologians of the 13th century and by St. Thomas in particular, see Henri Bouillard, *Conversion et grâce chez s. Thomas d'Aquin*, to which I am greatly indebted. See pp. 1–2: "Dans la langue théologique actuelle, conversion désigne souvent l'acte par lequel un pécheur se repent et commence une vie meilleure. Mais on réserve volontiers le mot à l'acte par lequel un incroyant vient à la foi. . . . Ce n'est pas ainsi qu'il faut l'entendre chez Saint Thomas. Conversion y a un sens plus large où se reconnaît encore l'inspiration néoplatonicienne de Saint Augustin: c'est le mouvement par lequel la créature raisonnable se tourne vers Dieu. Elle consiste à adhérer à Dieu par l'amour. . . . 'Converti ad Deum est amore ei adhaerere.' *II Sent.* d. v, q. 2, a. 1." Thus in *Purgatorio* XIX, 106, even a pope can speak of his "conversione . . . tarda."

See also by Bouillard, "La théologie de la grâce au xiii⁰ siècle," in *Recherches de science religieuse*, XXV (1948), 469 ff.

3. Aquinas, *Summa c. G.* III, 150: "Est autem et alia ratio propter quam praedictum Dei auxilium *gratiae* nomen accipit. Dicitur enim aliquis alicui esse *gratus*, quia est ei dilectus: unde et qui ab aliquo diligitur, dicitur *gratiam* eius habere," etc.; and III, 151.

4. Augustine, *Quaestionum in Heptateuchum*, PL 34.734: "Coccinum caritas, quod fervorem spiritus igneo colore testatur."

5. I Cor. 13.13.

6. *Purgatorio* XXIX, 131.

7. *Purgatorio* XVIII, 44.

8. Aquinas, *Summa Theol.* II–II, q. 182, a. 2, resp.: "Radix merendi est caritas."

9. On this point see especially Bouillard, *Conversion et grâce*, pp. 92 ff., 222 f.; he makes it quite clear that St. Thomas is not "semi-pélagien."

10. *Ibid.*, p. 37: "Philippe le Chancelier, dans la *Summa de bono*, rédigée aux environs de 1230, ouvrit une voie nouvelle, en appliquant les schèmes aristotéliciens de matière et de forme." See the whole account of this point here. Also p. 214: "Le problème de la préparation à la grâce, par exemple, ne se pose que dans une théologie où la grâce est conçue comme forme, au sens aristotélicien."

11. *Ibid.*, pp. 214 ff.

12. "Al cor gentil ripara sempre amore."

13. *Convivio* II, i, 10. "Ancora è impossibile però che in ciascuna cosa naturale ed artificiale, è impossibile procedere a la forma, sanza prima essere disposto lo subietto sopra che la forma dee stare: sì come impossibile la forma de l'oro è venire se la materia, cioè lo suo subietto, non è digesta ed apparecchiata. . . ." So also Thomas Aquinas, *Summa Theol.* I–II, q. 4, a. 4, resp.: "Unde sicut materia non potest consequi formam, nisi sit debito modo disposita ad ipsam . . . ," and time after time, whenever *process* is treated.

14. Aquinas, opusc. 27, *De Principiis Naturae ad Fratrem Silvestrum*: "Generatio est motus ad formam"; and *passim* in other works.

15. See note 10 above.

16. *Summa c. G.* III, 149.

17. See the quotation from St. Thomas above, p. 29.

18. See *In II Sent.* d. xxviii, q. 1, a. 4. On the point of the "free will moved by God," see *In IV Sent.* d. xvii, q. 1, a. 5, sol. 1, ad 3: "Voluntas

non trahitur in justificationem per modum coactionis; sed ut libere velit illud ad quod Deus eam movet." It is a "cooperation" essentially: *In IV Sent.* d. xvii, q. 1, a. 2, ad 1, "Cooperatio voluntatis, quae praeparatio dicitur." The point is reflected in *Purgatorio* VIII, 112–114:

> "Se la lucerna che ti mena in alto
> truovi nel tuo arbitrio tanta cera
> quant'è mestieri . . ."

19. *Summa Theol.* I–II, q. 109, a. 6, resp.

20. *Ibid.*, q. 112, a. 2, resp.

21. *Ibid.*, ad 1, ad 2.

22. *Ibid.*, q. 112, a. 3, resp.

23. *Ibid.*, q. 111, a. 5, resp.: "Gratia enim gratum faciens ordinat hominem immediate ad coniunctionem ultimi finis. Gratiae autem gratis datae ordinant hominem ad quaedam praeparatoria finis ultimi." See Bouillard, *Conversion et grâce*, p. 61 and *passim.*

24. On this whole point the discussion by Bouillard is fundamental.

25. Dante is "called" by Virgil, to use the technical theological term (*vocatio*). Or, we may say that a first *vocatio* takes place when Dante the wayfarer first turns toward the light, in Canto I, *Inferno.* On *vocatio* in this sense, see Aquinas, *In S. Pauli Epist.*, 707; or *Summa Theol.* I–II, q. 113, a. 1, ad 3: "Vocatio refertur ad auxilium Dei interius moventis et excitantis mentem ad deserendum peccatum." For the moment of Dante's turning toward the dawning sun, see *Summa Theol.* I–II, q. 109, a. 6, resp.: "Hoc autem est praeparare se ad gratiam, quasi ad Deum converti; sicut ille qui habet oculum aversum a lumine solis, per hoc se praeparat ad recipiendum lumen solis, quod oculos suos convertit versus solem. Unde patet quod homo non potest se praeparare ad lumen gratiae suscipiendum, nisi per auxilium gratuitum Dei interius moventis."

26. *Purgatorio* XXI, 21: "la sua scala," that is, God's.

27. Aquinas, *Summa Theol.* I, q. 2, a. 2, ad 1: "Fides praesupponit cognitionem naturalem sicut gratia naturam et ut perfectio perfectibile."

28. On this most important point, the very basis for Virgil's guidance to Beatrice, see Bouillard, *Conversion et grâce*, p. 191, where many texts are referred to. Typical of the many statements to be found is the following in Aquinas, *In IV Sent.* d. xvii, q. 1, a. 5, sol. 1: "Inest recipiente ordo naturalis ad recipiendum illum effectum . . . sicut patet de infusione animae rationalis. Et similiter est de justificatione impii . . . quia ordo naturalis inest animae ad justitiae rectitudinem consequendam." Bouillard notes (pp. 37, 64) that Philippe le Chancelier speaks already of a "dispositio habilitans ad gratiam suscipiendam."

29. See Bouillard, p. 35, for the important references, which are many. Others to be noted are Aquinas, *De Malo* q. 2, a. 12, resp.: "Impossibile est quod per peccatum tollatur totaliter bonum naturae, quod est aptitudo vel habilitas ad gratiam"; q. 2, a. 11, ad 12: "habilitas ad gratiam totaliter se tenet ex parte naturae."

Chapter IV

Justification

Justification can be defined as "movement towards justice." This may well seem over simple and too vague to have much meaning, but it is a definition which St. Thomas and contemporary theology found satisfactory: "justificatio est motus ad justitiam." [1] Such bare terms call, of course, for further definition. What are we to take "justice" to mean in such a formula? And what, moreover, shall we understand "movement" to be?

The answer to the latter question is readily found in theological doctrine following the triumph of Aristotle with the schoolmen of the thirteenth century. "Movement," in this instance, must mean "alteration" (*alteratio*) taking place in a given subject or "matter"; movement will mean change in the "matter" with respect to an end. [2] That is to say, obviously, that justification is to be conceived on the pattern of the Aristotelian conception of *generatio*, which, we now know, is "motus ad formam." This being so, one must think of such a process in terms of the two elements involved, matter and form. Movement to form is thus change on the part of the matter to the end that it may receive the form. By such a change a given matter is "made ready," is "disposed," to receive. The whole movement ends when form is received by the matter which has been prepared for it. One thus conceives a process which has extension in time and manifests two successive moments or phases. The first is the moment of *preparation*, the second the moment of *completion*, at the end, when form is attained.[3]

But if justification as movement be so conceived in this recognizable and simple outline of event, what meaning can the two terms "matter" and "form" have in such a conception? Surely the form in this case, i.e., that which is the end of the movement, will be justice itself. But justice in what sense? And as for the "matter" which will thus undergo change in preparation to receive justice, what will that be?

Such concepts, at first sight, are no doubt quite strange to us. We need some fuller statement which can clarify the meaning of these elements of a process. And for this we may once more turn to St. Thomas' view on this point as one representative of the doctrine which came to prevail following the Aristotelian revival. For one thing, we shall see, and with no surprise, to be sure, how closely Thomas is following Aristotle, not only in taking *generatio* to be the mold in which the whole notion of justification is cast, but in the very conception of justice which is thought to lie at the end, as the form. Or, perhaps, in order that this may be the clearer, we might first recall a definition which Aristotle himself, in the *Nicomachean Ethics*, gives of justice. It is the definition to which St. Thomas will be seen to refer:

> Metaphorically and in virtue of a certain resemblance there is a justice, not indeed between a man and himself, but between certain parts of him; yet not every kind of justice but that of master and servant or that of husband and wife. For these are the ratios in which the part of the soul that has a rational principle stands to the irrational part; and it is with a view to these parts that people also think a man can be unjust to himself, viz. because these parts are liable to suffer something contrary to their respective desires; there is therefore thought to be a mutual justice between them as between ruler and ruled.[4]

Justice, then, as Aristotle would understand it here, is justice within, justice as the inner rule of the rational part of the soul over the other parts. Justice is that same right order in the soul of which Plato wrote in the *Republic*. It is a matter of a man's inner disposition, of reason's rule over those faculties which are properly subject to reason — the passions, the sensitive appetite.

In turning, now, to St. Thomas' definition of justice in this sense, we shall hardly avoid being struck by one thing: Thomas extends Aristotle's definition in a notable way, carrying it quite beyond anything Aristotle or Plato intended. To be sure, for Thomas, justice remains a matter of order in the inner man, but for him that order is, first of all, one which is due subjection to God and to God's will. This, as St. Thomas means it, brings a Christian requirement into the matter of justice not dreamt of by the Philosopher. Of course, students of Aquinas will at once recognize here a common manner of thought with him. Aristotle, in this case, a given definition in Aristotle, is used as far as it can carry our understanding of the matter in question. Whereupon, if it is then evident to the Christian theologian, by the revealed truth of Christian doctrine, that the point to which Aristotle can bring us is not the whole truth, and if the revealed truth can carry us further, then we proceed further with that. Only St. Thomas, typically, will not make explicit mention of the point at which we pass beyond Aristotle, will make no specific acknowledgment of any limitation or shortcoming on the part of his Philosopher. Thomas seems simply to assume that his Christian reader will know and understand where that point is, without his calling attention to it. A clear instance is the definition, modelled on Aristotle, which Thomas gives of justice in the sense concerning us here:

> Justification taken passively implies a movement towards justice, as heating implies a movement towards heat. But since justice, by its nature, implies a certain rectitude of order, it may be taken in two ways: — First, inasmuch as it implies a right order in man's act, and thus justice is placed among the virtues. . . . Secondly, justice is so called inasmuch as it implies a certain rectitude of order in the interior disposition of a man, in so far as what is highest in man is subject to God, and the inferior powers of the soul are subject to the superior, i.e., to the reason; and this disposition the Philosopher calls *justice metaphorically speaking* (Ethic. v.11). Now this justice

may be in man in two ways: — First, by simple generation, which is from privation to form; and thus justification may belong even to such as are not in sin, when they receive this justice from God, as Adam is said to have received original justice. Secondly, this justice may be brought about in man by a movement from one contrary to the other, and thus justification implies a transmutation from the state of injustice to the aforesaid state of justice. And it is thus we are now speaking of the justification of the ungodly, according to the Apostle (Rom. iv.5): "But to him that worketh not, yet believeth in Him that justifieth the ungodly," etc. And because movement is named after its term *whereto* rather than from its term *whence*, the transmutation whereby anyone is changed by the remission of sins from the state of ungodliness to the state of justice, takes its name from its term whereto, and is called *justification of the ungodly*.[5]

When we shall have seen finally, and as clearly as may be, that the whole "movement" of Dante's *Comedy*, conceived in allegory as a journey, is itself a "movement toward justice," then we shall recognize the close relevance to the poem of such a conception of justice and justification as St. Thomas here offers us. If justice means right order in the soul and right order before God, then we shall see that such is indeed Dante's conception in the poem; such is, in fact, the "end" of his journey. It may be that we shall be helped to see this in clearer outline if we recall an image which is given in certain verses of the *Purgatorio*, when the journey reaches the first terrace, where pride is purged. There, as so often elsewhere, "we" are addressed, readers who are proud Christians in need of the sternest warning respecting this our gravest sin:

> O superbi cristian, miseri lassi,
>   che, della vista della mente infermi,
>   fidanza avete ne' retrosi passi,
> non v'accorgete voi che noi siam vermi
>   nati a formar l'angelica farfalla,
>   che vola alla giustizia sanza schermi?
> Di che l'animo vostro in alto galla,
>   poi siete quasi entomata in difetto,
>   sì come vermo in cui formazion falla?
>
>   *Purgatorio* X, 121–129.

O proud Christians, woeful wretches, who sick in the mind's vision, place trust in backward steps, do you not see that we are

worms born to form the angelic butterfly which flies to justice
without shields? How is it that your spirit soars so high, when
you are as imperfect insects, like the larva lacking its full formation?

What the verses and their metaphor declare of pride and its
effect is evident enough. Pride stops us short of full formation.
By pride we are arrested at a first and imperfect stage of growth.
We are as butterflies to be, but remaining in pride, at the larva
stage, we shall never become the winged creatures we were created to become. But it is the notion of justice and of movement to
justice as to a goal which interest us especially here. For if we do
attain to our full formation, then justice is the end to which we
fly, a justice "sanza schermi," which must mean a justice before
God. And it is through such an image as this that we may profitably look at the entire *itinerarium* to God as the *Comedy* presents
it, asking ourselves where it is along the way that the first phase
of this movement ends and the second begins: in short, within the
metaphor, where does Dante pass from larva stage to butterfly?
The answer is easy. This surely is when Dante passes from Virgil
to Beatrice; and it is clear, looking through the image, that if
Dante had not passed on to Beatrice, he would never have had his
"wings." With her he flies upward to justice, becoming "angelic,"
even as Glaucus became like a sea-god.

But there must be a goal of justice short of that final justice at
the end of the *Paradiso*, before God. Another justice is, in fact,
reached before that. It lies precisely at the point where the journey
attains to Beatrice, and is therefore at the summit of the mountain
of Purgatory. One may view this justice, to be sure, as the beginning of movement toward that other higher and perfect justice
before God. But it is this first justice as goal which most concerns
us in the present study, together with the whole process or movement through which that goal is reached. For when justification
is conceived as a movement toward justice, a movement which a
poet may represent as a journey, then the kind of justice which
lies at the top of the mountain is that justice which is the end
goal of justification. Indeed, the attentive reader of the poem must
have some sense of this from the outset, for the mountain which

he is given to see in the first canto is surely, in some sense, the very mountain of Purgatory which is later climbed; and, on that moral landscape of the first canto, the mountain seen must be none other than the "mountain of justice" of which Scripture speaks, meaning a mountain having justice at its summit, a mountain to be ascended. In that first prologue scene, the sun is shining upon that summit. Must this not be the "sun of justice" (*sol iustitiae*) also known to us from Scripture? And then later the reader will see, when he reaches the summit with Dante, that Beatrice comes there in the figure of a rising sun; and there too he is reminded, where she comes in triumph, that the Sun had no finer chariot than hers.[6]

But such meanings come clear only through perspectives yet to be examined. Enough at the moment if we note the limits of our present concern with the outline of this journey. At the summit of the mountain lies a kind of justice which is a goal for Dante, the wayfarer.

That we should think of justification as completed when the summit is reached is something which the very definition by St. Thomas can strongly suggest to us. One notes how in the context of justification, Thomas has remembered Adam and the justice that he, in his creation, received from God. This indeed is an element of the statement by Thomas which makes his whole formulation of special interest for present purposes. Eden, that very place wherein Adam received justice, is precisely what lies, in Dante's conception, at the top of this mountain. There, in Eden, Adam received justice by "simple generation," as Thomas puts it. For Adam was without sin. This being so, one might think that Adam's receiving justice (as a form is received) would not be viewed in the pattern of *generatio*. But Thomas does so view it, for Thomas can regard Adam as being, in a first moment, without the form which is justice, as being (without sin) ready or disposed to receive that form, and then, in a second moment, as receiving justice. And we know that two such successive moments suffice as the essential elements to make this a case of "generation," even if it is *simple* generation.

Adam lost this gift of justice when he lost Eden. And men, after

Adam, are no longer placed here, at this summit, at birth. Men are born in a fallen condition. No longer is justice given to a man by simple generation because no man, after Adam, is without sin, either Adam's or his own. But the question must be put: may not a man, some men, regain Eden and the justice that was originally given to man there? May not regeneration replace the simple generation which would have continued to be in Eden, had the first man not fallen in sin? May we not regain justice through a journey back to Eden?

Dante's journey in the poem is such a regeneration, and whatever the specific answers to the questions must prove to be in strict theology (and these we shall see), his journey to Beatrice at the summit is in fact a return to Eden and, in some sense, to justice.

Regeneration, however, is not a matter as simple as that original generation in which Adam received justice, when he was without sin. Regeneration is complex. It is a matter of a man rising out of his sinful nature and out of his own burden of actual sin, to attain to justice. Sin and the consequences of sin in the soul must first be put off, before justice (which is the form, in this instance) may be received in the soul. And, since *generatio* is defined as movement, this must mean of course that the matter which is made ready to receive the form is the soul, or, as we shall see, the will, more exactly, since justice specifically means right order in the will. Such, in any event, is the matter to be disposed; and, as St. Thomas has indicated, we must keep our eyes on two terms or points of reference in viewing the process. There is the term "whence" and there is the term "whereto." Clearly, in this instance, the "whence" is the condition of sin (which a poet can figure as a dark wood), and the "whereto" is a condition of justice (which a poet can place at the summit of a mountain). And between the two terms, the two contraries, lies process, which is alteration. Therefore a movement "away from" is at the same time an "approach to." The process might be named with respect to either term, but, even as Thomas says, we must consider the end in these matters and give a name to the movement according to its goal, the "whereto." Thus, since justice is that goal, this movement will properly be termed justification; and in this more complex kind of generation, it will be known specifically as the "justification of the ungodly" (*iustificatio impii*).

The journey to Eden and to Beatrice is such an event, and when we have understood it, we may mark off its phases. Movement with Virgil as guide is movement as preparation. This is the first phase, extending from the beginning in the dark wook of sin all the way to the summit of the mountain. In this first phase, a matter is disposed to receive the form, a soul is made ready for justice. And the aspect of movement "whence," as indicated by St. Thomas, is made plain enough in the climb up the mountain. The wayfarer is led through one terrace of Purgatory after another, and as he moves, a burden of sin and the consequence of sin is put off.[7] *Impedimenta* to the reception of the form, as St. Thomas would say, are removed;[8] and all the while there are varying statements in metaphor of what those obstacles are: they are "stains," "knots," "blemishes," left in the soul or the will through sinful acts.[9] And the seven letters "P" inscribed upon Dante's forehead are the visible sign of those *impedimenta*. These are marks which must be erased in the long hard climb. And so they are, one on each of the terraces of Purgatory. All have been removed (*remotio* is Thomas' term) when Dante comes finally to stand upon the top-most level, at the summit: at which point exactly, Virgil turns to him and speaks the words which announce that the goal "as far as Virgil can discern" has now been reached. And as he reads Virgil's words, the reader who has in mind the conception of justice and of justification which we were concerned to note in Aristotle and in St. Thomas will recognize that those words declare an attainment in terms which clearly mean "justice." This is justice *metaphorice dicta*, justice in the interior disposition of a man, justice which is right order in the will:

> Come la scala tutta sotto noi
>   fu corsa, e fummo in su 'l grado superno,
>   in me ficcò Virgilio li occhi suoi,
> e disse: "Il temporal foco e l'etterno
>   veduto hai, figlio, e se' venuto in parte
>   dov'io per me più oltre non discerno.

Tratto t'ho qui con ingegno e con arte.
  Lo tuo piacere omai prendi per duce,
  fuor se' de l'erte vie, fuor se' de l'arte.
Vedi lo sol che in fronte ti riluce;
  vedi l'erbetta, i fiori e li arbuscelli,
  che qui la terra sol da sè produce.
Mentre che vegnan lieti li occhi belli
  che lacrimando a te venir mi fenno,
  seder ti puoi e puoi andar tra elli.
Non aspettar mio dir più nè mio cenno:
  libero, dritto e sano è tuo arbitrio,
  e fallo fora non fare a suo senno;
per ch'io te sovra te corono e mitrio."

Purgatorio XXVII, 124–142.

When all the stair was put beneath us, and we stood on the topmost step, Virgil fixed his eyes on me and said: "You have seen the temporal and the eternal fire, my son, and you are come to a point beyond which I discern no further. I have brought you here with intelligence and skill. Take henceforth your pleasure for your guide. You are out of the steep and the narrow ways. See the sun that shines on your brow; see the tender grass, the flowers, and shrubs, which the earth here produces of itself alone. Until the fair eyes come rejoicing which with their tears sent me to you, you may sit and you may go among these things. Await no further word nor sign from me. Your will is free, straight and whole, and it would be wrong not to follow its discernment; wherefore I crown and miter you over yourself."

Now, with an eye on the Philosopher's definition of justice above, and again on St. Thomas' extension of that definition, it is important to take note of one thing here: this justice to which Virgil has led, and which he thus announces, is justice only as far as Aristotle goes in his definition. If Dante's will is now free and straight and whole again, and if it would now be wrong not to follow its "senno," this must mean that the rule of reason over the lower parts of the soul, of which Aristotle and Plato spoke, has now been attained. Indeed, Plato's great metaphor of the *Republic* emerges in Virgil's last words: "I crown and miter you over yourself." Right order in the soul brings to mind right order in the state. Reason and right will now rule in the soul; and in the state, by suggestion, there would now rule that one universal monarch through whom alone, as Dante believed, the world would come to justice in all its parts.[10]

This is justice as far as Virgil can discern. Virgil's limit here is thus precisely the limit of ancient pagan wisdom itself, the wisdom of the "philosophers." Beyond this limit is Beatrice, beyond is justice as St. Thomas' definition would have it extended beyond Aristotle, in Christian terms unknown to a Virgil or a Plato or to "the Philosopher." The poet's deliberate design is here most evident. Virgil may guide only as far as the natural light extends, that light which is the only light that was given to him in life, or to those who now dwell with him in Limbo.

Clearly this whole pattern of event is one which we may profitably refer back to those two master patterns of three lights and three conversions already examined. By the light of those we may see that this whole movement or journey to justice, to which we rightly assign the name *iustificatio impii*, must be thought to extend through the area of the first light and over into the area of the second, or, on the other pattern, to reach through the area of the first conversion and over into that of the second conversion. Such a measurement of justification on those two broad paradigms serves to show us exactly how the two phases of the process of justification are to be distinguished. Those two phases are, as we know, 1) preparation to receive a form and 2) reception of the form. Now, the whole area of Virgil's guidance is the area of preparation; and such an area, on the pattern of three lights and three conversions, is precisely that of the first light in the one scheme and the first conversion in the other. We come to see that all three notions, "preparation," "natural light," "first conversion," are exactly co-extensive. Movement under the first light extends only as far as Virgil can discern; the first conversion which is preparation for the second conversion extends also just so far. And Virgil's words dismissing Dante from further guidance by him announce that preparation is completed. Preparation, one might ask, for what? Virgil's words themselves give the answer, for he not only declares an attainment, he makes a promise. Beatrice is expected, Beatrice will come at any moment. Dante has now been made ready for her. She is the very goal to which Virgil has brought him. Yet when she comes finally into view, Virgil will no longer be there by Dante's side. Beatrice as the goal to which Virgil has led is quite beyond Virgil. Here, actually, the pattern of meaning reaches beyond our perspective of the moment and enters another, soon to be examined. But on the pattern of justification itself, the meaning is clear if measured by the two master patterns. To pass from Virgil to Beatrice must mean to pass from the first natural light to the second, which is supernatural. It means to pass over out of a first conversion into a second, wherein the soul attains to that meritorious justice which is given with sanctifying grace and the infused virtues. On such a test, we see the truth of what was noted at the outset: that we may understand a part of this journey to God only if we see that part within the pattern of the whole. Thus, justification finds its proper and enlightening measure within the whole pattern of the three lights and three conversions, as a part thereof. And by that measure we can understand what the phase of preparation is, as well as what the end moment of completion must be. Perhaps quite the most important thing of all in this is that we see how Beatrice is thus both an end or goal in one pattern of event, and at the same time a beginning of another, within the broader pattern. Where journey with Beatrice begins, there journey to Beatrice ends. It seems a simple truth. Yet where journey to Beatrice ends is precisely where a whole line of event ends the proper name of which in established theology is *iustificatio impii*.

Perhaps enough has already been said of the first conversion with Virgil under the natural light to provide a sufficient view of that phase as "preparation to receive," a first phase in the whole event of justification. But we ought here to face a matter of terminology which can at first cause some perplexity. It would appear, as noted, that Virgil leads his charge to a kind of justice, which is right order in the will, and which implies the dominion of the will over the faculties which are properly subject to it. We must therefore speak of an actual attainment to justice with Virgil. But then, again as noted, Beatrice herself is the further goal, beyond Virgil, and to attain to her means also to attain to justice. Thus, if

justification, in its simplest definition, is a "movement to justice,"
it would appear that Dante has staged a journey to two kinds of
justice, both situated at the summit of Purgatory. We might call
the first, to which Virgil leads, "justice according to the Philosophers," and we might rightly call the second, which is given
with Beatrice, "justice according to the Apostle." [11] But the important point we shall not forget is this: the justice to which Virgil
leads is a preparation for the justice which is given with Beatrice,
because the first conversion leads to the second, even as the first
light leads to the second. The first justice is therefore *ordered to*
the second. This being so, it would seem important to take note
of a name which the second justice, given with Beatrice, may bear,
a name, indeed, which can be one of Beatrice's names when she is
seen as the completion and end of justification according to St.
Paul. That name is "justifying grace" (*gratia justificans*), which
is only to say that Beatrice, as the completion towards which
justification of the ungodly has moved, is Sanctifying Grace.[12]

"Justifying grace": what we gain by realizing that such a name
fits Beatrice at this point is important, as we are soon to see. For,
however much Beatrice's advent may be seen as a justice given
from above and beyond human limits, it will not do to lose sight
of such justice as the *grace* which it is when so given. Such justice
is gratuitous and it sanctifies. This not only serves to keep a proper
focus upon the essential features, in terms of the theology involved; it further makes visible a pattern which we have yet to
consider in its greater extensions of meaning — a pattern, that is,
which consists essentially and simply of a first moment when
justice is attained (as with Virgil), followed by a second moment
when grace is given (as with Beatrice). In this conception, Virgil's
justice is the preparation for grace. And once more we may refer
this to the Aristotelian scheme of *generatio*, now so familiar, which
provides precisely for two such moments: 1) a preparation for
the form, and 2) reception of the form. But we have lingered long
enough with that notion, and it is now time to observe that a saint
who was not at all given to thinking Aristotelian thoughts could
also speak of just such a pattern of event, in which first there is
justice and then there is grace, and the justice is a preparation for

the grace. St. Bernard, in fact, quotes not Aristotle but Holy Scripture in support of such a conceptual pattern, when he preaches to his brethren at Clairvaux in the season of Advent. With this we may now move into a closer focus to witness the event at the summit of the mountain which is the very goal of this journey to justice: the advent of Beatrice.

Notes

1. Aquinas, *Summa Theol.* I–II, q. 113, a. 1, resp.: "iustificatio passive accepta importat motum ad iustitiam." The definition is repeated many times throughout his works. For the concept of justice before the triumph of the Aristotelian scheme, see O. Lottin, *Psychologie et morale au xii⁰ et xiii⁰ siècles* (Paris, 1949), III, 283 ff.

2. Aquinas, *In VII Phys.*, lect. VI, in fine: "Salvantur tamen et hae rationes secundum opinionem Aristotelis. Ad cujus evidentiam considerandum est quod susceptivum aliquod tripliciter potest se habere ad formam suscipiendam. Quandoque enim est in ultima dispositione ad susceptionem formae, nullo impedimento existente nec in ipso nec in alio; et tunc statim ad praesentiam activi susceptivum recipit formam absque aliqua alteratione; sicut patet in aere illuminatio ad praesentiam solis. Aliquando autem susceptivum non est in ultima dispositione ad susceptionem formae, et tunc per se requiritur *alteratio*, secundum quam materia dispositionem acquirat, ut sit propria huic formae; sicut cum de aere fit ignis. Aliquando vero susceptivum est in ultima dispositione ad formam, sed adest aliquod impedimentum; sicut cum aer impeditur ad susceptionem luminis, vel per clausionem fenestrae, vel per nebulas; et tunc requiritur alteratio vel mutatio per accidens, quae removeat prohibens."
See also *Summa Theol.* I–II, q. 113, a. 1 and 7.

3. Albertus Magnus, *In IV Sent.* d. xvii, a. 10 (ed. Borgnet, XXIX, 675–676): "In mutationibus corporalibus oportet esse dispositiones, quae solubiles faciunt privationes a materia sive formas contrarias, in quibus supponitur privatio formae inducendae; sicut patet in aere qui dicitur fieri ignis: oportet enim arefacere humidum quod tenet aerem, antequam depellatur aeritas et induitur igneitas. Et similiter est hic, quod voluntas aversa a Deo, et diligens peccatum, est sibi dispositio tenens peccatum in anima et impediens gratiae inductionem. Sed voluntas mota in Deum et contra peccatum, est sibi dispositio inclinans ad peccati expulsionem et introductionem justitiae et gratiae."

4. *Nicomachean Ethics* V, 11. I have cited the translation of W. D. Ross (Oxford, 1925). In the *versio antiqua* known to Aquinas the passage reads:

"Secundum metaphoram autem et similitudinem est, non ipsius ad ipsum justum, sed eorum quae ipsius aliquibus. Non omne autem justum, sed dominativum, vel dispensativum. In his autem sermonibus divisa est pars animae ad irrationalem in quae utique respiciunt. Et videtur esse injustum ad seipsum, quoniam in his est pati aliquid praeter suiipsius appetitum. Quemadmodum igitur imperanti et imperato, esse adinvicem injustum aliquod et his." This version of the *Ethics* is included in Aquinas, *In Decem Libros Ethicorum Aristotelis ad Nicomachum Expositio* (Turin, 1934).

5. *Summa Theol.* I–II, q. 113, a. 1, resp.: "Justificatio passive accepta importat motum ad iustitiam; sicut et calefactio motum ad calorem. Cum autem iustitia de sui ratione importet quandam rectitudinem ordinis, dupliciter accipi potest. Uno modo, secundum quod importat ordinem rectum in ipso actu hominis. Et secundum hoc iustitia ponitur virtus quaedam. . . . — Alio modo dicitur iustitia prout importat rectitudinem quandam ordinis in ipsa interiori dispositione hominis; prout scilicet supremum hominis subditur Deo, et interiores vires animae subduntur supremae, scilicet rationi. Et hanc etiam dispositionem vocat Philosophus, in V *Eth.*, iustitiam metaphorice dictam. Haec autem iustitia in homine potest fieri dupliciter. Uno quidem modo, per motum simplicis generationis, qui est ex privatione ad formam. Et hoc modo iustificatio posset competere etiam ei qui non esset in peccato, dum huiusmodi iustitiam a Deo acciperet, sicut Adam dicitur accepisse originalem iustitiam. — Alio modo potest fieri huiusmodi iustitia in homine secundum rationem motus qui est de contrario in contrarium. Et secundum hoc, iustificatio importat transmutationem quandam de statu iniustitiae ad statum iustitiae praedictae. Et hoc modo loquimur hic de iustificatione impii, secundum illud Apostoli, Ad Rom. iv. 5, 'Ei qui non operatur, credenti autem in eum qui iustificat impium,' etc. Et quia motus denominatur magis a termino ad quem quam a termino a quo, ideo huiusmodi transmutatio, qua aliquis transmutatur a statu iniustitiae per remissionem peccati, sortitur nomen a termino ad quem, et vocatur iustificatio impii."

6. *Purgatorio* XXIX, 115; XXX, 22 ff.

7. *Purgatorio* II, 122.

8. "Remotio impedimentorum" is, in fact, the standard phrase with St. Thomas. See *In IV Sent.* d. xvii, q. 1, a. 4, sol. 1: ". . . quia secundum genus causae materialis materia est causa formae quasi sustentans ipsam, et forma est causa materiae quasi faciens eam esse actu secundum genus causae formalis. Ex parte autem causae materialis se tenet secundum quemdam reductionem omne illud per quod materia efficitur propria huius formae, sicut dispositiones et remotiones impedimentorum. . . ."

9. See "nota" in *Purgatorio* XI, 34 ff.; "velo" and "nebbia," *Purgatorio* XXX, 3. The terms are out of established theology and refer to what is most commonly called a "macula" or a "detrimentum nitoris."

10. *De Monarchia*, I; and *passim* in the *Comedy*. The same metaphor is present in the term "iustitia civilis" common in St. Thomas and contemporary theology; see *In II Sent.* d. xxviii, q. 1, a. 1, ad 4: "Aliquis potest dici justus dupliciter: vel justitia civili vel justitia infusa. Justitia autem civili potest aliquis justus effici sine aliqua gratia naturalibus superaddita; non autem justitia infusa."

11. See the quotation in note 10 above, wherein the two justices are

clearly envisaged. "Justitia infusa" is the Apostle's justice, "justitia civilis" is Plato's and Aristotle's. And that the latter *disposes* for the former is evident in Thomas' statement in his next paragraph: "Est autem aliud bonum opus etiam virtutem antecedens, quod virtutem acquisitam causat, et ad infusam disponit . . . et talis operatio naturalem perfectionem rationis non excedit, quia tota rectitudo huius operis est secundum regulam rationis."

On St. Paul's conception of justice and justification, see E. Tobac, *Le problème de la justification dans saint Paul* (Louvain, 1908).

12. Aquinas, *Summa Theol.* III, q. 5, a. 4, resp.: "Secundo haec positio repugnat utilitati incarnationis quae est iustificatio hominis a peccato. Anima enim humana non est capax peccati nec gratiae iustificantis, nisi per mentem."

Chapter V

Advent of Beatrice

When Beatrice comes at the summit of Purgatory,[1] in that awesome and splendid procession which is her "triumph," unmistakable signs and suggestions attend her to proclaim that her coming should be seen as an Advent. This is evident even as the procession gradually comes into view, disclosing itself to be, in figure, the coming of the Word of God in history. The reader has been given to expect Beatrice to appear, but before she comes, cries and utterances and yet other signs seem instead to herald an advent of Christ; by deliberate poetic strategy expectation is made ambiguous. There is in all this, of course, no affirmation that Beatrice represents Christ, even in this figure. That, indeed, is quite excluded by the fact that Christ, in this procession, is represented by the Gryphon. Much less, of course, is any sort of equivalence suggested, as if Beatrice might somehow *be* Christ. There is quite another principle at work here, one which a mediaeval poet had reason to think might be less subject to misunderstanding than has proved to be the case. The principle is analogy.

Even as Beatrice comes finally to stand upon the triumphal

chariot at the center of the procession, resolving by her appearance the ambiguity of the expectation that has been aroused, her analogy to Christ is the more emphatically affirmed (in the oblique mode of poets, never directly). For, as she comes into view, the poet chooses to present her to us in the figure of a rising sun [2] — familiar and established figure for Christ's coming. Moreover, at just the moment when she is to appear so, the poet has deliberately brought to mind, by way of yet another figure, the day of the Last Judgment,[3] so that, if the coming of Beatrice is like a coming of Christ, it now appears to be like that which shall be the Last. And so it is in the analogue. Beatrice comes in her own special cloud of glory to stand in judgment on her lover.

As judgment is delivered here, moreover, there is brought to mind by her charges the whole experience of the *Vita Nuova:* how in that earlier work she had shown, in her role in the poet's life, a miraculous resemblance to Christ; how, in fact, she had been seen, in a vision recounted at the center of the work, to die amidst signs which can call to mind no other death than Christ's, and then to rise to Heaven attended by angels and the cry of Hosanna in an ascension which is most like His. In this way it is apparent that the analogy Beatrice-Christ is being extended out of the *Vita Nuova* into the last cantos of the *Purgatorio*. Because of this, Beatrice's coming here in Purgatory can be revealed as a second coming.

So much, to restate briefly what it had been possible to see before.[4] Yet apparently, with this poem, we are never done with seeing. There is always more. It must be that we shall never know enough. And the knowledge we lack is not erudition but awareness — awareness not of scattered facts, but of patterns of thought. To be sure, there is ultimately nothing mysterious in this. The poem is allegorical *and* symbolical *and* analogical.[5] Each and all of these dimensions of the poem involve it in more than a literal meaning, each is a dimension of "otherness." And it is within that common dimension of "otherness" which they together make that we shall see, if we are ever to see at all, the patterns which have determined for the poet what the literal outline of his poem was to be. In the reading of the poem, then, the reverse will prove to be the case: the literal, that is, will summon to mind the shapes that lie in the "otherness." These shapes will arise simply by evocation, by being called to mind.

And there precisely seems to lie the area of our own shortcomings. Much is gone from our minds that Dante had thought could be counted on to be there and hence be called up there. Awarenesses are gone, and gone without our knowing it (the more's the pity), until one day we may happen to be reading (*per diletto*, say!) the Sermons for Advent of a St. Bernard of Clairvaux when, suddenly, we *see*. What we see is a pattern, a mold of thought; we see how it is the pattern which a poet had trusted he would be able to call to his reader's mind. In the illumination of an instant we know this, for a whole scene of the poem comes into sharp focus and in that scene all details become "quiet," because they find their places as functional and contributing parts of a whole design.

At the moment the instance, happily, is more than hypothetical, having occurred. But it seems only right, before going into particulars, to recognize this, first of all, for the familiar and typical thing that it is, and we can hope may continue to be in Dante studies. Familiar instance, this, of new light on the poem [6] and of the way that light can come; and perhaps further, if not very surprising, evidence that we are never through growing up to Dante's *Commedia*.

*   *   *

St. Bernard's *Sermons for the Season of Advent* [7] are seven in number. As is clear from the opening words of the first of them ("Hodie, fratres, celebramus adventus initium") and repeatedly throughout, they must have been preached to his Cistercian brethren, but in what year we do not know, nor does it matter for present purposes. All seven sermons bear clear witness to the predilections and special emphases of doctrine that we associate with the Saint. The Blessed Virgin is especially celebrated, for example, as the way by which the Saviour came to us as well as the way by which we ascend to Him. In this connection, as in yet others, the special devotions of the Contemplative and the Mystic

who qualified in Dante's *Comedy* for the high station and office
that he there occupies are evident enough. But among the several
noteworthy features in these sermons, there is one which is especially striking: Bernard, in preaching the Advent, shows a constant
concern to keep that event in the present tense as well as in the
past. And in this, the verb in Latin which he has occasion of
course to use time and again, *venit*, can serve him well (presenting also an insoluble problem for a translator). When, for instance, the first sermon has come to a certain point along the line
of a quite normal development, Bernard can turn back over the
way treated so far and look forward to that which remains to be
treated, so: "Habetis jam et personam venientis et locum utrumque,
id est, a quo et ad quem venit; causam quoque et tempus non
ignoratis. Unum restat, via scilicet, per quam venit; et haec quoque
diligenter requirenda, ut possimus, sicut dignum est, ei occurrere." [8] Is *venit* here in the past tense or in the present? The
phrase "causam quoque et tempus" would seem to make it the
past. But "ut possimus . . . ei occurrere" seems clearly to cast it
in the present.

What was already becoming evident enough comes wholly clear
as we read on. Bernard is truly at special pains to keep the event
of the Advent in both the past and present tenses, and the verb
in Latin can indeed do a special service for him in this:

> Now just as He came once for all visibly and in the flesh to "work
> our salvation in the midst of the earth," so He comes daily, in spirit
> and invisibly, to save individual souls. Hence it is written, "A Spirit
> before our face is Christ the Lord." And to give us to understand
> that this spiritual advent is secret, the Prophet continues, "Under
> Thy shadow we shall live among the gentiles." It is therefore be-
> coming, if the sick man cannot go forth any distance to meet so
> august a Physician, that he should at least show Him honor on His
> arrival by making an effort to raise his head to the one who comes
> and to sit up in his couch. There is no necessity for thee, O man,
> to cross the seas, or to penetrate the clouds, or to pass over the
> mountains. Thou art not invited to undertake any great journey.
> Even within thine own soul rise to meet thy God. For it is written:
> "The Word is nigh thee, even in thy mouth and in thy heart." Rise
> to welcome Him by compunction of the heart and by confession
> of the mouth, so that thou mayest issue forth in His honor, at least

from the sink of thy miserable conscience; for it would be a grievous crime to introduce hither the Author of all purity. So much concerning this spiritual advent of the Word, whereby He condescends to illumine with His invisible presence the soul of every one of us.[9]

The concern of the Preacher is evident enough: to keep the Advent in the present as well as in the past, to hold to it as to that occurrence which can take place time and again in the soul, to make a special insistence on the *now* of it. "Just as He came once . . . visibly and in the flesh, . . . so He comes daily, in spirit and invisibly."

This stress by Bernard on a "daily" advent in the present (an emphasis which has been noted to be peculiarly Cistercian) [10] brings him, in his third sermon, to insist that the Advent of Our Lord is in fact *triplex*, that there are, so to speak, three advents of Christ to be distinguished and declared. Two of these, he recognizes, are of course well known and manifest to all, i. e., Christ's first coming which has been and His last which shall be. But there is a second or middle advent, as he has already said, which is spiritual and occult, calling for special recognition:

There are three distinct comings of the Lord of which I know, His coming *to* men, His coming *into* men, and His coming *against* men. He comes (came) to all men indifferently, but comes not into all or against all. His coming to men and His coming against men are too well known to need elucidation. But concerning the second advent, which is spiritual and invisible, listen to what He says Himself, "If any man love Me, he will keep My word, and My Father will love him, and We will come to him, and will make Our abode with him.[11]

Affirming thus that the Advent is *triplex*, Bernard proceeds in the next and fourth sermon to preach on the first and the third comings, that which has been and that which shall be. Then, in the fifth sermon, he can come back to that second and middle advent which he is careful to keep always before the attention of the brethren:

In my last sermon I told you, my brethren, that they who have covered their wings with silver must "sleep among the midst of lots." I explained these lots to mean the two advents of Christ, but said nothing concerning the place of sleeping between them. This intermediate place is in fact another advent wherein such as have knowledge thereof enjoy a most pleasant repose. For whereas the other two are known to all, this one is secret. In the first "He [Christ] was seen on earth and conversed with men," when, as He Himself bears witness, "they both saw and hated" Him. In the last "all flesh shall see the Salvation of God," and "they shall look on Him Whom they pierced." But in that which intervenes, He is hidden, visible only to the elect who see Him in themselves, and so their souls are saved. Therefore, in the first He came in the flesh and in weakness, in the second He comes in spirit and in virtue, and in the third He shall come in glory and majesty. For it is through virtue that glory is reached, as the Psalmist sings, "The Lord of virtues, He is the King of glory." And similarly, the same prophet says in another place, "In the sanctuary I have come before Thee, to see Thy virtue and Thy glory." Thus, this intermediate advent is the way, so to speak, by which we must travel from the first to the last. In the first, Christ was our Redemption, in the third He shall appear as our Life, whilst in this second He is our Repose and our Consolation, so that we may "sleep among the midst of lots."

But perhaps what I have been saying about the middle advent may seem fanciful to some of you. Listen, therefore, to the words of Christ Himself, "If any one love Me, he will keep My words, and My Father will love him, and We will come to him, and will make Our abode with him." [12]

As many of his brethren will have known, this second of three advents is no invention of St. Bernard's. Yet Bernard seems to have been known and remembered for his special insistence on it and on that "triple" Advent of which this is the middle one, spiritual and occult. We may note that more than a century later, when St. Thomas Aquinas came to write a special treatise on the Humanity of Christ and the Sacrament of the Redemption [13] and to speak of the Advent in that context, he recalled that it was Bernard who had declared the Advent to be threefold: "We can distinguish a triple advent of Christ, that is, in the flesh, in the mind, and at the judgment: whence Bernard: 'We know of a triple advent of Christ.' " [14] Whereupon he proceeds to quote the passage from Bernard's third Sermon for Advent noted above. Following this, in the same treatise, after many pages in which the first advent, *in carnem*, is treated, St. Thomas comes back to the second advent and again acknowledges Bernard: "But since above, according to Bernard, we recognize that there is a triple advent of Christ, that is, in the flesh, in the mind, and at the judgment; having seen the first, now let us take note of the second. In evidence of which we should know that the advent of Christ in the mind is through sanctifying grace. . . ." [15]

Aquinas has in this way assigned to Bernard's second coming of Christ that name out of theology which Bernard in these sermons never ventures to give it, but which he will surely have taken always for granted: this advent is the advent of Sanctifying Grace (*gratia gratum faciens*) in the soul of the Christian. Even as Bernard maintained and now Aquinas is explicit in affirming, this advent is *occultus et humano sensui investigabilis*.

But if that which comes in the second advent, *in mentem*, can thus bear properly the name of Sanctifying Grace, that is not its only other name. For both Aquinas and Bernard recognize that it can have yet another, *Sapientia*, the name which is, of course, the connecting link in this case between the name of Grace and that of Christ. Surely no "other" name for Christ is more firmly established than *Sapientia*. And since this link will reveal its importance to us later, it may be well to note how it enters the thought of both Bernard and Thomas.

From the naming of the second advent of Christ, *in mentem*, as the advent of sanctifying grace, Aquinas proceeds directly in this treatise to the identification with *Sapientia*:

. . . the advent of Christ in the mind is through sanctifying grace. . . . We are not to understand the advent of God as if He came where He was not already, but that He exists in a new way where He was already. For the new way by which God is in the rational creature is as the known is in the knower and the loved in the lover. For to know God and love God as the object of beatitude is by sanctifying grace: wherefore the advent of Christ in the mind is to be understood as being according to sanctifying grace. Therefore he who was wise desired this advent when he said (Wisd. 9.10): "Send her forth out of Thy holy heavens and from the throne of Thy glory, that being present with me she may toil with me. . . ." The Gloss says: "Whatever we say of the Wisdom of God, we refer to Him Who is our peace, Who made the two one, the power and the wisdom of God and the invisible image of God," . . . as much as to say: "Send forth Christ, the power of God and the wisdom of God, that He may be with me by virtue of sanctifying grace, and that He may toil with me in the joy of uplifting grace, that I may know that I am acceptable to Thee through the splendor of illuminating grace." Therefore he prays for the advent of Christ in the mind.[16]

Similarly, in his third sermon Bernard extended his meditations on this second advent to a recognition that it is the advent of *Sapientia*:

But because the first and the third are known and manifest, listen to what He says Himself of the second, which is spiritual and occult: "If any man love Me, he will keep My word, and My Father will love him, and We will come to him and make Our abode with him." Blessed is the man with whom Thou, Lord Jesus, makest Thy abode! Blessed he in whom "Wisdom hath built herself a house, and hath hewn out her seven pillars!" [17] Blessed is the soul which has become the seat of Wisdom! Shall I tell you whose soul this is? It is the soul of the just man. This is manifest from the words of David, "Justice and judgment are the preparation of Thy throne" (Ps. 88.15).[18]

* * *

No doubt before now we have known that *Sapientia* is one of the several names which Beatrice can bear in the allegory of the *Commedia*, and that another of her allegorical names is Grace. This can be seen in the poem out of more than one perspective. But here, in the thought of a Bernard and a Thomas, it is the way in which precisely those names arise naturally and, one feels, necessarily in the context of their reflections on Advent which is so striking. Before now, too, we noted that Beatrice's advent at the summit of Purgatory is designed to reveal a notable resemblance to that of Christ: to two of Christ's advents, indeed, to the first, which has been, and to the last, which shall be. But, until we came across the pattern of it in Bernard and again in Thomas, we had not thought to look upon the advent of Beatrice for the resemblance which it might reveal to *three* advents of Christ. Now we do see, being aware of the pattern. Beatrice comes as Christ *came*; the signs of that are unmistakable. Beatrice comes as Christ *shall come* — in glory, to judge; again a poet's intention that this should be disclosed in her advent is clear beyond any doubt.[19] And now we know that the Advent is *triplex* and we look for yet a third. May it not be that Beatrice comes as Christ *comes*? But what shall the signs of that advent be? The signs of the first and last of Christ's comings are known to us because they are public and visible to all. But this second advent of His is *in mentem*, occult and *investigabilis*. Moreover, as Bernard recognized in preaching before his brethren, this middle advent is far less known than the others, and calls for special explanation, since it has other and more familiar names. This fact alone serves to distinguish it from the other two advents. For those advents, public and historical as they were and shall be, may not be so translated to other terms.

Or perhaps an essential difference may better be seen in yet another way. Bernard's three advents are, first of all, distinguishable on a principle of time: the first in the past, the last in the future, the middle one in the present. Yet, unlike the other two, the middle advent does not occur once only but many times; and if it be insisted that its time is in the present, then this is that ever-present which is the over-and-over-again present. When does this second advent take place? Bernard has answered the question: *whenever* the individual soul of a Christian is prepared for it — that is, when justice prevails in any soul.

In this way we are brought to recognize that if Beatrice's advent is to disclose a resemblance to that second and middle advent of Christ which is *in mentem*,[20] it will have to do this in a different dimension from the other two. For Beatrice comes, and the poet can guide us, by the recognizable signs and utterances, to see that her coming resembles Christ's first advent, which was. Beatrice comes and the poet can also guide us, again by the known sign, to see that her coming reveals a resemblance to Christ's last advent, which shall be. In both cases the resemblance holds on a difference in time. Not so, clearly, in the case of the middle advent. In that, Beatrice's coming *now* must disclose a resemblance to Christ's advent *now*. But how, then, can there be the resemblance of analogy when there is no longer a distinction in time? Must not the absence of that very basis of distinction mean that the possibility of such a resemblance is lost?

Again the answer has been given us by Bernard and by Thomas. It arises from the fact that this present advent of Christ can bear, indeed must bear, other names: Wisdom and Grace. When Christ comes, in Bernard's middle advent, it is Wisdom who comes with her seven pillars, it is Sanctifying Grace that comes attended by all the virtues, the *infused* virtues. In this mystical advent, these are Christ's *other* names. This, when the tense of the advent is the present tense, must be the basis on which the analogy holds.

It is thus apparent what the light of understanding is that can come from certain Sermons on Advent to illuminate the whole of the design which a Christian poet was concerned to establish at the center of his poem. "Triplicem enim ejus adventum novimus." Beatrice's advent mirrors that triple advent in its three dimensions in time. But it is only because her advent bears within it the signs of Christ's first and last advents that we are guided to see that her coming also discloses its analogy to that advent of Christ which is *now*. Without those signs at the beginning and at the end, we should hardly see that the analogy prevails and is valid at the middle as well. Nor would it be possible for us to see, as clearly as we may now see, what Beatrice is in her other names when she comes. It is the whole of this pattern which illuminates the poem. Beatrice's other names in this advent in the present are the same as Christ's other names when His advent is *now*: Wisdom and Grace. Beatrice is not Christ. The suggestion of any such identity would be sacrilege indeed; moreover, in the procession, Christ is represented by the Gryphon. Nor may we turn it around and think that somehow Christ is Beatrice. The one figure may not replace the other, taken either way.[21] But in their advents in the present tense, the other names for Christ and the other names for Beatrice are the same names.

Thus it is that the figure of a rising sun by which Beatrice comes at last to stand upon the triumphal chariot is the most revealing image which the poet might have found not only to affirm the analogy of her advent to Christ's in the present tense, but to stress, in so doing, the very basis upon which that analogy rests: the advent of Light. Grace comes as light, for so Christian theology has conceived it in a very long tradition, with the result

that the instances of that image are indeed legion. One such may
be remarked in that same treatise of Thomas Aquinas on the
Humanity of Christ from which we have been quoting:

> We should know that the grace of union precedes habitual grace
> in Christ, not in order of time, but of nature and intellect: where-
> fore it is said in Isaiah 12: "Behold my servant, I will uplift him,"
> which pertains to the grace of union; and then it is said: "And I will
> place upon him my spirit" which pertains to the gift of habitual
> grace. . . . Grace is caused in man by the presence of the Divinity,
> even as light in the air by the presence of the sun; whence it is said
> in Ezechiel 43 that "the glory of the God of Israel came forth out of
> the East . . . and the earth shined with His glory." [22]

Thus an entire conceptual pattern comes into clear view, with
the parts falling into place in a manner that is delightful to witness. In reading the words of Aquinas above, is it not so? Do
they not bring to mind Beatrice's coming as a rising sun, and that
whole procession which is her triumph as it advances out of the
East to meet the wayfarer at the summit of the mountain? "Gloria
Dei Israel ingrediebatur per viam orientalem . . . et terra resplen-
duit a majestate eius." It is like a clarion note heralding her procession out of the East, in Eden.

And so it is throughout, in so many respects. Relevance is
everywhere apparent. As we watch Bernard's thought pass from
Christ's second advent to the name of Wisdom and her seven
pillars, those words must call to our mind Beatrice as she comes
attended by her seven handmaids who are the seven infused Virtues, maidens who explicitly declare that they were "ordered to
her" as her *ancillae* even before she came into the world. And this
being so, who would Beatrice be, if not Wisdom and Grace? [23]

One has only to look back over the few quotations from Bernard and Thomas which we have had before us to note point
after point that cries its relevance to some feature in Dante's staging of Beatrice's coming. Beatrice comes to judge her lover (in the
aspect of the third coming) and the charges which she so sternly
pronounces against him all readers will recall. When she has
spoken them, Beatrice insists that the man before her acknowledge
the truth of these accusations, even to the angels who know this,

knowing the truth with God. Dante must here confess before
Beatrice. And his confession before her follows upon an over-
whelming sense of contrition.[24] Thus, once again, when we heard
Bernard in his sermon speak of that second advent which is *in
mentem* and invisible, through the detail of his statement there
came the light of relevance:

> It is therefore becoming, if the sick man cannot go forth any dis-
> tance to meet so august a Physician, that he should at least . . .
> [make] an effort to raise his head to the One who comes and to sit
> up in his couch. There is no necessity for thee, O man, to cross the
> seas. . . . Even within thine own soul rise to meet thy God. . . .
> Rise to welcome Him by compunction of the heart and by confes-
> sion of the mouth, so that thou mayest issue forth . . . from the sink
> of thy miserable conscience.[25]

A close scrutiny of the whole design in its full detail may not
be undertaken here. Let one more aspect of it be considered, however, so that the sure confirmation of it may be acknowledged
beyond further doubt. This concerns what Bernard declares to
be the seat and preparation for that middle advent of Wisdom,
building her house of seven pillars.

> Blessed is the soul which has become the seat of Wisdom! Shall I tell
> you whose soul this is? It is the soul of the just man. This is manifest
> from the words of David, "Justice and judgment are the preparation
> of Thy throne." . . . Who among you, my brethren, desires to pre-
> pare in his soul a throne for Christ? . . . *Justitia et judicium prae-
> paratio sedis tuae*.[26]

The *judicium*, as we have but now recalled, is delivered by
Beatrice herself, before Dante may cross the stream to the far
shore (*beata riva*, it is called) [27] and be admitted to her presence.
But in this matter of *justitia*, of the *anima justi*, as Bernard has put
it: has the poet built according to the recognizable pattern in this
respect as well?

The answer is written large indeed into the structure of the
journey as it attains to the summit of Purgatory. For when at last
Virgil has brought his charge up the long way to this point, he
turns to Dante to speak the words that dismiss him from his further guidance, dismiss by declaring that Dante needs Virgil no

more, that he has now come to that goal to which he, Virgil, could lead him. The attainment is *justice*. And the very words which proclaim it announce that Beatrice will now come. *Justitia praeparatio sedis tuae!*

Notes

1. *Purgatorio* XXIX–XXX.
2. *Purgatorio* XXX, 22–33.
3. *Purgatorio* XXX, 13–18.
4. For a detailed analysis of these views, up to this point, see *Dante Studies 1*, pp. 45–60.
5. *Dante Studies 1* is concerned precisely with these several dimensions of meaning in the poem.
6. It may be well to declare at once that I am here concerned not to prove an "influence" of St. Bernard on Dante, but rather with recognizing a pattern of thought which Dante clearly did not need to get from Bernard or from any one theologian in particular, as it was the common property of so many. That the particular pattern here singled out connects theologically with the Sacrament of the Eucharist will be evident, but the strict relevance of that point remains open to question.
7. The Sermons are given in *PL* 183.35 ff. My references are to this text, although I have actually cited from the critical text published in *Xenia Bernardina: Sanctii Bernardi Sermones de Tempore, etc.* (Vienna, 1891), I, 3–31.
8. *PL* 183.39.
9. *Ibid.*, cols. 39 f.
10. Thomas Merton, "Le Sacrement de l'Avent dans la spiritualité de saint Bernard," in *Dieu Vivant*, no. 23 (1953), pp. 23–43. The article is mainly a digest of the Sermons for Advent, and came to my attention, I may add, only after I had come across the ideas hereafter indicated in Bernard and Aquinas. See p. 24: "Une chose en particulier, au suject de l'Avent, a toujours impressionné les Cisterciens: l'Avent est le mystère de la *Presence* de Dieu dans Son monde. . . . Les Cisterciens mettent un accent spécial sur la descente du Christ *hic et nunc*, dans l'âme individuelle."
11. *PL* 183.45.
12. *Ibid.*, cols. 50 f.
13. Opusc. 53, *De Humanitate Jesu Christi.* It may be further noted here that Hugh of St. Victor also makes mention of a triple advent (*Quaestiones in Epistolas Pauli, PL* 175.587): "*In adventu eius*, scilicet Domini. Quaeritur in quo adventu. Solutio. Triplex est adventus Domini, unus in carnem, unus in spiritu, unus in carne. In carnem venit factus homo. In spiritu venit quando

Spiritum suum spiritui nostro infundit ipsum sanans et justificans. In carne veniet in judicio. Occulte etiam venit unicuique in morte, vel ut eos purget, vel ut januam regni aperiat: ut eos puniat."

This last named advent, indeed, brings them to *four*, as Innocent III in his *De Miseria Humanae Conditionis* observes (ed. M. Maccarrone, p. 78), under the rubric "De adventu Christi ad diem mortis cuiuslibet hominis": "Quatuor namque leguntur adventus Christi. Duo visibiles: in carne primus, ad iudicium secundus. Et duo invisibiles: primus in mente per gratiam, unde: 'Ad eum veniemus et mansionem apud eum faciemus'; alter in obitu uniuscuiusque fidelis, unde Johannes: 'Veni domine Jesu.'"

14. Opusc. 53, *De Humanitate Jesu Christi.*

15. *Ibid.*, a. 24, "Sequitur de secundo adventu."

16. *Ibid.*

17. Prov. 9.1: "Sapientia aedificavit sibi domum, excidit columnas septem."

18. *PL* 183.45.

19. For a full analysis of the detail of the two advents, first and last, as they are reflected in Beatrice's advent, the reader is again referred to my *Dante Studies 1*, pp. 45 ff.

20. As all students of Dante will recall, Beatrice is called "la gloriosa donna della mia mente" in the opening words of the *Vita Nuova*, when her very first appearance to the poet is spoken of. It will also be remembered, in connection with her handmaids, the Virtues, in her triumph in Purgatory, that in that early work also (IX, 2) she is named "regina delle virtudi."

21. A fundamental part of this analogy also rests on a most essential distinction of *Sapientia increata* and *Sapientia creata* (Beatrice), which extends a similar distinction between *caritas creata* and *caritas increata* already discernible in the *Vita Nuova*. See my *Essay on the Vita Nuova* (Cambridge, Massachusetts, 1949), p. 76.

22. Opusc. 53, *De Humanitate Jesu Christi.*

23. Thomas Aquinas, *Summa Theol.* I–II, q. 110, a. 3, resp.: "Sicut igitur lumen naturale rationis est aliquid praeter virtutes acquisitas, quae dicuntur in ordine ad ipsum lumen naturale; ita etiam ipsum lumen gratiae quod est participatio divinae naturae, est aliquid praeter virtutes infusas, quae a lumine illo derivantur, *et ad illud lumen ordinantur.*" (Italics mine.)

24. *Purgatorio* XXX, 76–78, 85–99; XXXI, 4–15. It may be noted that Grandgent, as a consequence of his view that Beatrice is the *Church* here exercising Her functions, tries to follow herein the pattern of the *sacrament of penance* which involves *satisfactio operis* following upon *contritio cordis* and *confessio oris* (his edition of the poem, Argument to *Purgatorio* XXX–XXXI). But here *satisfactio operis* is not to be found in that succession. This is instead, I submit, the pattern of *justificatio.* Nor is Beatrice the Church. The chariot is that.

25. *PL* 183.39 f.

26. *PL* 183.45.

27. *Purgatorio* XXXI, 97.

Chapter V I

Justification in History

In the shape of the literal event, this climb to the top of a mountain and Beatrice's coming there, we see, as in a mirror, the reflected outline of other events strangely resembling this. In Beatrice's advent is disclosed the image of Christ's Advent in no less than three dimensions of time, in triple aspect: as it was, as it is, and as it shall be.

If St. Augustine could have read this poem and could have seen how the poet constructed this part of the work he called his *Comedy*, he would no doubt have recognized the essential truth of Dante's conception. For it was Augustine who had noted that one may speak of three dimensions of time existing somehow in the soul, and they are just such dimensions as Dante appears to have envisaged in deliberately causing the coming of Beatrice, in its literal and poetic present, to show forth Christ's coming in three times:

> Perchance it might be fitly said, "There are three times: a present of things past, a present of things present, and a present of things

future." For these three do somehow exist in the soul and otherwise I see them not: present of things past, memory; present of things present, sight; present of things future, expectation.[1]

We may note in particular the first of these: "present of things past, memory." It is, for Augustine, a question of the *where* and the *how* of the past as it exists in the present. The past must somehow be present in the soul or otherwise we know it not. *Memoria*: for a Christian, *memoria* will be above all *memoria Christi*. We recall how essentially Augustinian in this respect is a famous hymn sometimes attributed to St. Bernard, the *Jesu dulcis memoria*. Nor shall we forget how *memoria Christi* shines at the center of the *Vita Nuova*.[2] To be sure, in that earlier work, such a "memory" is not given in the manner of allegory, whereas in the *Comedy* it is, taking on there the nature of one of the senses of Scriptural allegory.

Thus, in Beatrice's advent there is *memoria*, there is remembrance of that great Event in history which marks the dividing line on our calendar. That Event, which is Christ's Advent, reveals its *presence* in the literal happening taking place in 1300 A.D. The literal may be said to "remember," and, in remembering, to "commemorate." It is for us now to see that what is remembered so is not only the Advent of Christ in itself, but an entire outline of providential history which culminated in that event.

There is also the "presence of things present" in the event at the summit of the mountain. With the help of St. Bernard and St. Thomas, we have seen this: in the literal coming of Beatrice is disclosed that advent of Christ which is *present*, when He comes to any soul prepared to receive Him. And in this same literal event we are to take notice of the "presence of things past." The time of the two *presences* is distinct, the respective stage on which the action takes place is in each case different. Christ's advent now (in that present which is a "whenever") is advent in the individual soul, and is hidden, seen by no man; whereas Christ's advent in the past, His first, took place on the great open stage of history, and once only. There and then He came to all men, to justify. This was justification in history, and on the grandest scale. In this action in history the "agent" (as Dante would have called him),[3] the protagonist, is not a single individual, but the entire human race. Christ came in the fullness of time to justify all men, even as He comes daily "now" in the soul to justify an individual.

What we have to see is what Dante has so well realized as poet: that justification as it took place in history, and justification as it takes place now in the soul, are strikingly alike in essential outline. In the one, in justification in the soul, there are two basic features, as we know. First there is preparation, then there is that for which preparation has been made. Or, in the Aristotelian scheme of generation, we may say that a "matter" is prepared to receive a "form." Thus, Virgil guides to the top of the mountain and his guidance is preparation. Virgil leads to justice, whereupon the "form" is given: Beatrice as sanctifying grace.

It cannot be clear how this line of event resembles the great line visible in history until we know that two such phases are also distinctly discernible in the latter case: that there was a time of preparation preceding Christ's first advent. The stage changes now, the actors change. Replacing the individual Dante (or "whoever") is the human race as a whole. Replacing Beatrice (or Christ in His hidden advent) is Christ in His first advent, coming to justify all men. In this historical order, Dante figures mankind, and Beatrice Christ. This leaves Virgil and a time of preparation. Transposed thus to the stage of history, what does Virgil represent? May we speak of a preparation for Advent, of guidance towards Advent, in *history*?

Keeping our eye on the literal event which must support such a pattern in history and provide the first answer to the question, we should note that Virgil, in his role as guide through Purgatory, presents something of a problem for the reader who has not glimpsed the requirements of the allegory in the background. We come to take Virgil for granted, of course, and find it nearly impossible to conceive that any other figure might replace him. Yet why should Virgil have been chosen to guide in this most Christian place, this middle realm where sin is purged away and souls are made worthy of rising to the final beatitude? Pagans are excluded from Purgatory; and if we think of the great exception of

Cato, then why should Cato not serve as guide here, in a realm which is said to be his, rather than Virgil? Or we might give thought to another possibility: why not Aristotle as guide instead of Virgil, if it must be some other pagan than Cato who guides here?

Through the *Inferno*, of course, question as to Virgil's qualifications does not arise. He had made the journey down that way before, to the very bottom of Hell. Yet, at once, when Virgil comes into this new realm of Purgatory, he declares that he does not know the way.[4] Time and again, in the long climb to the summit from terrace to terrace, he must ask the way up the mountain. Is one who must do this a proper guide for the wayfarer?

In the choice of Virgil as the one who guides to Beatrice we may glimpse the answer to the question raised above, concerning Virgil's meaning in the historical line and the phase of preparation which took place therein. It is nothing less than a requirement arising out of a pattern of history which determines the choice of Virgil. For in that justification which came about on the stage of history, it was the Roman people who brought the world to justice, even as Virgil brings Dante to justice; and this justice to which Rome led proved to be the very preparation for Christ's coming to all men.

When we have found the meaning of Virgil's guiding to justice in this line of historical allegory, then all figures in the action fall into their proper *other* meanings. Dante is mankind, Beatrice is Christ and Virgil is Rome leading to that justice which came finally under Augustus Caesar and which was the preparation. As for Virgil's qualifications in this role, surely we may say that no other figure out of that time in history could serve as well as he does to represent Rome: Virgil, poet of Empire.

* * *

As every reader of the *Convivio* and the *De Monarchia* will recall, Dante had written earlier of God's great design in history, of the preparation which led up to Advent. He had appealed, in the latter treatise especially, to this notion as the very foundation of his thesis on monarchy. In this there are two points of special interest for us. First, it must be noted that Dante speaks of the whole process in history in terms now familiar: of a "preparation" or a "disposition," and of *justice* as such a preparation; and furthermore, that thought of Virgil and the prophecy of the Fourth Eclogue occurs to Dante in this context of ideas. It was Virgil himself who had seen that the world was best *disposed* in justice, the justice under Caesar Augustus:

> Moreover, the world is best disposed when justice is most potent therein; whence Virgil, in praise of that age which was visibly rising in his own day, sang in his *Bucolics*: "Iam redit et Virgo, redeunt Saturnia regna." By "Virgin" he meant Justice, who was also called Astraea. By "Saturnian kingdoms" he meant the best ages, which were also called the golden.[5]

Here is justification in its first phase: the world is "disposed" in justice under Rome's rule.

In this same passage of the *De Monarchia*, Dante advances the claim that monarchy or world empire is required for the best disposition of the world. Only with universal empire as it was under Rome can there be perfect justice, and the world is best "disposed" when it is in a condition of perfect justice. Whereupon, not forgetting that line of literal event in the poem in which Virgil guides, we think of his last words to Dante, crowning and mitering him over himself. Is this not a "coronation" which must bring to mind the figure of that Emperor who, as Dante hoped, would come to sit in supreme rule over the world and through whom right order must prevail?

> Justice is most potent only under an Emperor. Therefore for the best possible disposition of the world it is necessary that there be Monarchy or Empire. In evidence of which let it be known that justice is a certain rectitude or rule which casts off the oblique on either side.[6]

As for the manner in which the literal event in the *Comedy* supports the allegory in this respect, it is noteworthy that Dante proceeds in the next chapter of the *De Monarchia* to speak of freedom of the will. Thought of justice evidently brings thought of freedom in this sense: justice in the state and freedom in the will. From the stage of history we pass to the stage of soul. It is so in the poem. Virgil dismisses Dante, "crowning" him and at the same time telling him that he has now regained the freedom of his will:

> "Libero, dritto e sano è tuo arbitrio,
> e fallo fora non fare a suo senno:
> perch'io te sovra te corono e mitrio."
> *Purgatorio* XXVII, 140–142.

"Your will is free, straight, and whole, and it would be wrong not to do as it discerns, therefore I crown and miter you over yourself."

Justice, right order, freedom of will: such are the conditions in which the soul, or the world,[7] is best disposed to receive. To receive what? In the literal action it is Beatrice who comes to the man made ready to receive her. In the moral allegory it is Christ, in his hidden advent in the soul. And now we must know that, in the order of history, it was Christ in His first Advent. It was for His coming that preparation had been made. Not only this, but we must also know that it was none other than Virgil himself who had prophetically proclaimed that Christ must come to that justice which Rome had established as a preparation for Him. Virgil had himself lived into the time of that justice, so that when he wrote of it in the verses of the Fourth Eclogue, this much was less prophecy than fact. But his verses go on to make the promise that a "nova progenies" is to come to such a golden time, "a child." Virgil did not live to know the real meaning of this promise. By ever so brief an interval of time its truth was kept from him. Virgil died but nineteen years before Advent. We turn back to the literal event of the poem to note how the poet has provided even for this detail: when Beatrice appears, in the procession at the summit, Virgil does not see her. He has quit the scene but a moment before "advent." Thus even the personal history of Virgil is reflected here in the literal narrative and has determined a particular detail of its outline.

The peace and justice which Virgil had proclaimed in the famous verses had indeed proved to be that very "fullness of time" which the Gospels and the Apostle record. In the conclusion of the first book of *De Monarchia*, Dante is concerned to point out this truth. The world was "disposed," was made ready to receive the Christ, and when it was made ready, He came to it. Never, since the Fall, had there been such a perfect "disposition":

> All the reasons set forth above are attested by a memorable experience; namely, of that state of mortal things which the Son of God, when about to become man for man's salvation, either awaited, or, when he would, produced. For if we go through all the states and periods of man, even from the fall of our first parents, which was the point at which we turned aside in our wanderings, we shall find that the world was never quiet on every side except under divus Augustus, the monarch, when there was a perfect monarchy. And that in truth the human race was then blessed in the tranquillity of universal peace is witnessed by all the historians, witnessed by illustrious poets. To this the scribe of the gentleness of Christ has likewise deigned to bear witness; and finally Paul has called that most happy state the "fullness of time." Verily the time and all temporal things were full, for no ministry to our happiness was then vacant of its minister.[8]

In the *Convivio*,[9] too, Dante expressed such notions respecting monarchy and justice under monarchy as the most perfect condition of human society. There he wrote of this same great plan discernible in the order of history as being the supreme confirmation of the fact. Following upon the perfect justice to which Rome had brought the world, it was Christ's advent to that justice, as to a place prepared, which had put a seal upon this design. There, in history, was the clear outline of a great movement towards justice and man's redemption. Rome had been the instrument through which "preparation" had been effected, even as God in His providence had ordained that it should be.

* * *

Here is Virgil, in the literal line of the poem, summoned from Heaven to guide this man to a justice which prepares for Beatrice's coming to him. Nor must we overlook one further point here, if we are to perceive the perfect correspondence between the three lines of meaning which have become visible in the structure: the literal event, the event in soul, the event in history. In the event in soul, in moral allegory, we were concerned to see this journey to God as a progression by way of three lights, and we saw that the first of the three was a natural light. Thus, in the literal line it was a pagan Virgil's guidance through the first area which supported this meaning in the other, the moral line. And now, in the historical line, we note again the correspondence. It was a pagan people, it was Rome, that had brought the world to justice and a perfect disposition to receive.

In all lines of meaning it is always a matter of help from Heaven, of God's providence, of *auxilium Dei* or *misericordia Dei*, as Thomas and Albertus termed it. Beatrice is sent and "harsh judgment is broken above," [10] and she comes first to Virgil, not to Dante. The heaven-sent assistance, in the first phase, respects the bounds of the natural, is given within the proportion of human nature. And so we must understand it to have been with the Romans: God's guiding hand was there, but He chose to direct them only by the *natural* light. And they did not know the way on which they were moving, nor the true goal of the Christian revelation, to which they were being guided.

It is clear that we thus have three distinct lines of event to keep in mind if we would read this journey to Beatrice in its full range of meaning, and it may be that in this a simple diagram can help. Let such lines be shown as parallel, as coextensive, and in a mounting progression, since this, in the literal sense, is a mountain climb. And let the line of the literal be a solid line, of course, since that line is primary and from it the others derive; which other lines shall be shown as broken, for that reason, being there only because the literal is there in the particular outline which it bears.

The structure, as an achievement in poetry, is impressive, to say the least. (1) In the literal event of a climb up Purgatory Mountain, Virgil brings Dante to Beatrice. And, if we are such readers as Dante expected us to be, we shall see, in this shape of the literal, a pattern of action which is moral, (2) a movement towards justice and advent: Virgil's guidance is a first movement of preparation under the natural light, and following upon this there is advent, when sanctifying grace is given. Inner justice is attained, and to this Christ comes in His hidden advent in the soul made ready to receive Him. Then there is still another outline of event reflected in the literal, (3) one taking place on the broader stage of history, whereon it is Rome that guides to justice and it is Christ who comes in His first advent.

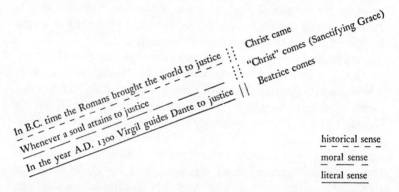

historical sense
moral sense
literal sense

In such a diagram there must be provision for another feature present in all three lines of meaning. This is given first, in the literal sense, by the river which cuts across Dante's path at the top of the mountain and which for a while separates him from Beatrice. It is a stream which Virgil may not cross. On its far bank, called a "blessed shore," Beatrice comes. Now such a line projects out of the literal to cross the other two lines of meaning, the moral and the historical, in a most significant way. In each of them it serves to mark that all-important line of division between a natural order and a supernatural. In the moral line, we know that this point must be understood in terms of two lights, a natural light succeeded by a light of grace; or, in terms of two conversions, a first turning to God which is entirely within the natural order, followed by a second turning made possible from above the natural. In the historical pattern, this same line, cutting across the progression, serves also to mark the primary and essential limits, to separate a first phase when the Romans, who were pagans, led the world to justice within a natural order, from the great moment of Advent which then came to such justice from above the natural order.

The structure in allegory is thus somewhat complex. It declares the number three, among other things, and there is much beauty in it — or so the poet must have felt. Yet it is safe to guess that many a reader of the kind we so readily call "modern" will not share in the poet's feeling, even when such a structure is made visible to him in its broad outlines and several dimensions. With thought of such a reader, one might digress a moment to note our tendency to invoke his name whenever we wish to impute to the Middle Ages something which we sense is no longer to our taste, and note, too, that this "modern" is essentially a child of the Renaissance. It was in the time to which we give that much-debated name, a time (in Italy, at least) following so closely on Dante's poem, that such relations as Dante has here affirmed in his three-fold structure were discredited as mere figments of the imagination. Dante's poem means to be an imitation of reality, mirroring the true nature of the real world wherein there are actual relationships between orders of existence. Man does not put those relationships there, projecting them into reality out of his own mind. They are there, and man perceives them. But there came a time when the reality of such relations, as existing in any truly objective sense, was doubted. Or, perhaps the doubt was a methodical way of doing away with them, the method being a way of seeing orders of existence as separate and discreet rather than as connected.[11] Men come who aspire to clear the physical order of all its affirmed connections with the spiritual order, and others come who wish to separate the historical order from the moral.[12] Things (through our deliberately *thinking* them so) are to be reduced to the status of things merely, they must not be more than themselves and point beyond their own orders of existence. Things in nature are things, events in history are simply events, and that is that. Symbolism must go and allegory must go, which are but two different ways of seeing how things are more than just things and how one event can mirror another. And analogy must go — analogy which is a way of knowing how orders of existence and events on different stages and in different times are *alike.*

This is not simply a matter of a falling away of modes of thought and imagination that are necessarily or primarily mediae-

val. We may give thought to the great metaphor and analogy lying at the heart of Plato's *Republic*, the affirmation of a resemblance between the soul and the state, between order or disorder
in the soul and order or disorder in the state. Surely we do not
have to call the mind which can think in such terms a "mediaeval"
mind. It is simply that the mediaeval mind remains open to such
a way of thought, confident of its validity because deeply persuaded of the reality of the relations which prevail between
separate orders of existence.

The central analogy of Plato's *Republic* is in fact still actually
present in the main line of action of the *Purgatorio*. Only, with
Dante, the structure has become more complex than in the *Republic*, involving elements understandably alien to Plato's thought,
elements historical and Christian, of course. Yet, with due allowance made, and to view the matter simply as a mode of thought,
Dante's poem is closer to Plato and more in touch with Plato's
ways of thinking than is the Renaissance, or than are we, its children, whenever we fall into Renaissance perspectives of thought
— which is most of the time.

This is not a matter of the merging of separate orders of existence. They remain, as orders, separate and distinct. It is simply
a matter of there being bridges, so to speak, between them; there
are affinities and bonds between. They remain in touch with one
another, and this on the great principle of a relationship through
analogy, so that in our thoughts we may pass from one order
to another, knowing the affinity and the resemblance they display,
seeing how one declares the other out of a real and abiding likeness. From order in the soul, Plato can pass quite naturally to
order in the state. In the same way Dante and mediaeval thought
generally can deal with history, finding the bridge between an
event in soul and an event in history. Such a bridge is nothing
but their resemblance. Thought crosses from one order to another
constantly and with ease, confident that the bridge is real.

We may come back to that specific pattern in Christian history
which is our present concern, and find striking confirmation of
these sketchy observations by focusing upon the manner in which
a poet, writing almost a thousand years before Dante, had used this
bridge of analogy. Aurelius Prudentius was a contemporary of

Augustine and of Paulus Orosius who also had born witness to
that outline of history in which the justice of Rome had proved
to be the preparation for Advent.[13] Orosius, however, is not concerned with such a pattern in history in other than historical
terms, whereas it does not surprise us that Prudentius, author of
the *Psychomachia*, does show such concern. What we shall remark in this passage from his *Reply to Symmachus* is the natural-
ness and ease of his transition from the order of history to the
inward order of the individual soul (a point scored by my italics).
Let it be noted, as we read, that here also are two of St. Bernard's
three advents of Christ: the first which has been and the second
which is now, in the soul, where Christ comes daily whenever
justice is established there: *iustitia praeparatio sedes tuae*!

> But I see the instances of ancient valour which move you, Sym-
> machus. You say the world was conquered on land and sea, you
> recount every success and victory, and recall a thousand triumphal
> processions one after another, with their loads of spoil passing
> through the midst of Rome. Shall I tell you, Roman, what cause it
> was that so exalted your labours, what it was that nursed your glory
> to such a height of fame that it has put rein and bridle on the world?
> God, wishing to bring into partnership peoples of different speech
> and realms of discordant manners, determined that all the civilised
> world should be harnessed to one ruling power and bear gentle
> bonds in harmony under the yoke, so that love of their religion
> should hold men's hearts in union; for no bond is made that is
> worthy of Christ unless unity of spirit leagues together the nations
> it associates. Only concord knows God; it alone worships the bene-
> ficent Father aright in peace. The untroubled harmony of human
> union wins his favour for the world; by division it drives Him
> away, with cruel warfare it makes Him wroth; it satisfies Him with
> the offering of peace and holds Him fast with quietness and broth-
> erly love. In all lands bounded by the western ocean and lightened
> by Aurora at her rosy dawning, the raging war-goddess was throw-
> ing all humanity into confusion and arming savage hands to wound
> each other. To curb this frenzy God taught the nations everywhere
> to bow their heads under the same laws and become Romans — all
> whom Rhine and Danube flood, or Tagus with its golden stream, or
> Great Ebro, those through whose land glides the horned river of the
> western world, those who are nurtured by Ganges or washed by the
> warm Nile's seven mouths. A common law made them equals and
> bound them by a single name, bringing the conquered into bonds of
> brotherhood. We live in countries the most diverse like fellow-citi-

zens of the same blood dwelling within the single ramparts of their native city, and all united in an ancestral home. Regions far apart, shores separated by the sea, now meet together in appearing before one common court of law; in the way of trade in the products of their crafts they gather to one thronged market; in the way of wedlock they unite in legal marriage with a spouse of another country; for a single progeny is produced from the mixed blood of two different races. Such is the result of the great successes and triumphs of the Roman power. For the time of Christ's coming, be assured, was the way prepared which the general good will of peace among us had just built under the rule of Rome. For what room could there have been for God in a savage world and in human hearts at variance, each according to its different interest maintaining its own claims, as once things were? *Where sentiments are thus disordered in man's breast, agreement upset, and faction in the soul, neither pure wisdom visits nor God enters.* But if a supremacy in the soul, having gained authority to rule, checks the impulses of refractory appetite and rebellious flesh and controls all its passions under a single order, the constitution of life becomes stable and a settled way of thought draws in God in the heart and subjects itself to one Lord.

Come then, Almighty; here is a world in harmony; do Thou enter it. An earth receives Thee now, O Christ, which peace and Rome hold in a bond of union. These Thou dost command to be the heads and highest powers of the world. Rome without peace finds no favour with Thee; and it is the supremacy of Rome, keeping down disorders here or there by the awe of her sovereignty, that secures the peace, so that Thou hast pleasure in it.[14]

When Prudentius wrote this Reply, Rome had not yet fallen. The peace and universal order which had come under Augustus still prevail, as he sees it; only that peace and order now bear the confirming seal of the Coming which Virgil had foretold but had never really known. Prudentius was writing these verses in the first years of the fifth century[15] and stood thus much nearer in time to the first advent of Christ than Bernard or Dante; and unlike them, he lived in a time which he could confidently proclaim as golden. Christ had come four centuries before; yet are we not struck by the way this poet, in his closing apostrophe, can turn from that first coming to pray that Christ come *now*, to a world in harmony, as if He were to come again, now, at any time, today? What is finally most evident is the ability of this early Christian poet to hold two orders together, that of history and that of soul, seeing that an event in the one "repeats itself" in the other. Advent in history, advent in soul — and in each instance advent follows upon a justice which is the preparation.

All of which can help us to realize that in writing his *Comedy*, almost a thousand years later, Dante was not constructing a poem on any new design nor spinning novel webs out of his own imagination.

Notes

1. *Confessions* XI, 20.
2. For the *Jesu dulcis memoria* and the notion of *memoria Christi* in the *Vita Nuova*, see my *Essay on the Vita Nuova*, pp. 116 and 166.
3. As, for example, in speaking of himself in the *Epist. ad Can. Gran.*, 6. One gets the proper view of this notion often in Augustine. Thus, in the *De Vera Religione* VII, 13: "Huius religionis sectandae caput est historia et prophetia dispensationis temporalis divinae providentiae, pro salute generis humani in aeternam vitam reformandi atque reparandi"; and *ibid.*, XXV, 46: "Quoniam igitur divina providentia, non solum singulis hominibus quasi privatim, sed universo generi humano tanquam publice consulit; quid cum singulis agatur, Deus qui agit itaque ipsi cum quibus agitur sciunt. Quid autem agatur cum genere humano, per historiam commendari voluit, et per prophetiam." The figure of Adam is, of course, in the background of such conceptions (*ibid.*, XXVII, 50): ". . . sic proportione universum genus humanum, cuius tanquam unius hominis vita est ab Adam usque ad finem huius saeculi, ita sub divinae providentiae legibus administratur, ut in duo genera appareat."
4. *Purgatorio* II, 63 — and frequently thereafter.
5. *De Mon.* I, 11.
6. *Ibid.*
7. For the "crown" bestowed by Virgil and the analogy with the justice established by Rome, see *De Monarchia* II, 10: "Quis igitur adeo mentis obtuse nunc est, qui non videat sub iure duelli gloriosum populum coronam orbis totius esse lucratum? Vere dicere potuit homo Romanus quod quidem Apostolus ad Timotheum 'reposita est michi corona iustitie.' "
8. *De Mon.* I, 16,
9. *Convivio* IV, 5: "Non è maraviglia se la divina provedenza, che del tutto l'angelico e lo umano accorgimento soperchia, occultamente a noi molte volte procede, con ciò sia cosa che spesse volte l'umane operazioni a li uomini medesimi ascondono la loro intenzione; ma da maravigliare è forte, quando la essecuzione de lo etterno consiglio tanto manifesto procede

con la nostra ragione. E però io nel cominciamento di questo capitolo posso parlare con la bocca di Salomone, che in persona de la Sapienza dice ne li suoi Proverbi 'Udite: però che di grandi cose io debbo parlare.'

"Volendo la'nmensurabile bontà divina l'umana creatura a sè riconformare, che per lo peccato de la prevaricazione del primo uomo da Dio era partita e disformata, eletto fu in quello altissimo e congiuntissimo consistorio de la Trinitade, che'l Figliuolo di Dio in terra discendesse a fare questa concordia. E però che ne la sua venuta nel mondo, non solamente lo cielo, ma la terra convenia essere in ottima disposizione; e la ottima disposizione de la terra sia quando ella è monarchia, cioè tutta ad uno principe, come detto è di sopra; ordinato fu per lo divino provedimento quello popolo e quella cittade che ciò dovea compiere, cioè la gloriosa Roma. E però che anche l'albergo dove il celestiale rege intrare dovea convenia essere mondissimo e purissimo, ordinata fu una progenie santissima, de la quale dopo molti meriti nascesse una femmina ottima di tutte l'altre, la quale fosse camera del Figliuolo di Dio: e questa progenie fu quella di David, del qual nascette la baldezza e l'onore de l'umana generazione, cioè Maria. E però è scritto in Isaia: 'Nascerà virga de la radice di Jesse, e fiore de la sua radice salirà'; e Jesse fu padre del sopra detto David. E tutto questo fu in uno temporale, che David nacque e nacque Roma, cioè che Enea venne di Troia in Italia, che fu origine de la cittade romana, sì come testimoniano le scritture. Per che assai è manifesto la divina elezione del romano imperio per lo nascimento de la santa cittade che fu contemporaneo a la radice de la progenie di Maria. E incidentemente è da toccare che, poi che esso cielo cominciò a girare, in migliore disposizione non fu che allora quando di là su discese Colui che l'ha fatto e che'l governa; sì come ancora per virtù di loro arti li matematici possono ritrovare. Nè'l mondo mai non fu nè sarà sì perfettamente disposto come allora che la voce d'un solo, principe del roman popolo e comandatore, fu ordinato, sì come testimonia Luca evangelista. E però che pace universale era per tutto, che mai più non fu né fia la nave de l'umana compagnia dirittamente per dolce cammino a debito porto correa. Oh ineffabile e incomprensibile sapienza di Dio che a una ora, per la tua venuta, in Siria suso e qua in Italia tanto dinanzi ti preparasti! E oh stoltissime e vilissime bestiuole che a guisa d'uomo voi pascete, che presummete contra nostra fede parlare e volete sapere, filando e zappando, ciò che Iddio, che con tanta prudenza hae ordinato! Maladetti siate voi, e la vostra presunzione, e chi a voi crede!"

10. *Inferno* II, 96.

11. One thinks of Descartes, for instance, and *res cogitans* vs. *res extensa*.

12. Galileo and Machiavelli come to mind.

13. *Seven Books against the Pagans*, trans. I. W. Raymond (New York, 1936). See pp. 116, 316 ff.

14. *Contra Orationem Symmachi* II, 578–638. I have given the translation by H. J. Thomson in the Loeb edition, II, 53–57.

15. See Thomson's remarks in the preface to the above edition.

Chapter VII

The Goal at the Summit

"**W**hy do you not climb the delightful mountain which is the principle and cause of every joy?" It is Virgil's first question to the man struggling before the beasts that beset his path and block his way up the slope.[1] Virgil, of course, knows the answer. The question is rhetorical, but it serves at least as a first pointer to the fact that this is something more than a mere mountain. And since it is a mountain to be climbed, it must be that the joy here spoken of is somehow at the summit, something to be attained there.

Then, at that summit where Beatrice comes to this man, speaking to him at first so sternly, her words again point to the same *other* meaning for the mountain:

> "Guardaci ben, ben son, ben son Beatrice!
>   Come degnasti d'accedere al monte?
>   Non sapei tu che qui è l'uom felice?"
>
> Purgatorio XXX, 73–75.

> "Look at me well, I am, I am indeed Beatrice! How did you dare to come up the mountain? Did you not know that man is happy here?"

We know, by the time Beatrice speaks these words, that here at the top of the mountain is found nothing less than Eden itself, where our first parents lived so briefly in perfect happiness, so that the affirmation "man is happy here" takes on thereby a deeper meaning. Man *was* happy here, and now there is a return to this place. Happiness must surely be the allegorical meaning of this summit, the goal of this mountain climb.

There is further confirmation of this in the words which Virgil speaks to Dante as they arrive here, ascending the last flight of steps. The third night of the journey up the steep way is now over, and it is early morning. Dante has just awakened from his sleep and stands ready to climb again. Whereupon Virgil, clearly to inspire him with a greater will to be up and on the way, makes a promise that the goal is to be reached "today"; and this, as Virgil puts it, is a goal sought not merely by Dante but by all mortals:

> "Quel dolce pome che per tanti rami
>   cercando va la cura de' mortali,
>   oggi porrà in pace le tue fami."
>   *Purgatorio* XXVII, 115–117.

"That sweet fruit which the concern of mortals seeks on so many branches will today set your hungers at rest."

And upon such a promise, Dante hurries the remaining steps to the summit.

What, if not happiness, can this sweet fruit be that all mortals seek in so many ways? Have not philosophers and theologians all agreed that it is happiness? Indeed, there is such a general agreement on this that there can be no doubt about it. As the Philosopher himself observed, all who think about this matter concede that happiness is that which all desire as something for its own sake, the final goal of all striving. Yet, while this is true, while all agree that happiness is that object, there are many differing conceptions of what happiness actually is. Some men insist that the highest happiness lies in riches, others in pleasure, others in honor, to name but a few of the divergent notions.[2] And we note a phrase in Virgil's statement providing for this truth as well: the sweet fruit is sought by mortals "on so many branches."

By Dante's time, of course, Aristotle's inquiry into the nature of happiness, in the *Nicomachean Ethics*, was familiar to all philosophers and theologians. As for Dante, we know from the *Convivio* in particular that he accepted the final ruling of the Philosopher in this matter as the most certain truth. Aristotle had concluded his review of the whole question with the definition which Dante repeatedly cites in that earlier work: happiness is "operation according to perfect virtue." [3]

Now if the goal at the summit of Mount Purgatory is happiness, can it be happiness on such a definition by Aristotle? In putting the question so, it is well to pay special attention to the key term in the definition: "operation." Operation is activity, but specifically an *inner* activity, one which may be said to "abide in the agent" rather than pass into outward matter. The latter is the activity of art, concerned with ends lying outside of man, whereas the operation which is happiness has its end within. It is *agere* as distinguished from *facere*, in short. [4] Happiness, that which we seek for its own sake, lies therefore in inner activity, in the life of the soul, where the virtues reside. Such was Aristotle's conclusion, and it rests on a more general principle: namely, that all creatures desire their own perfection above all else. [5] That perfection, for man, must lie in "operation according to perfect virtue." Evidently, happiness, on such a definition, is something which can fit very well into a pattern of moral allegory, since such allegory is always in terms of *agere*, of action or movement in the soul.

It is important to recall in this connection that Aristotle had decided in favor of action or operation in this sense as the proper goal, rather than rest from action. Man will be most happy in doing, in operation. [6] And if it is held that man must rest, in some sense, when he attains to a goal, then such rest will be a resting in operation itself, for its own sake, in activity according to the best within a man. Only so, in operation according to perfect virtue, can a man come to the full perfection and true fulfillment of his nature. With Aristotle, moreover, we must conceive of movement towards such a goal in terms of *generatio*, of movement from potency to act, from matter to form.

In the *Ethics*, the Philosopher had proceeded from such first principles to distinguish three kinds of activity for man. There is the life aimed at pleasure, there is another, the active political life, and there is yet a third, the life of the philosopher, in speculation or contemplation. And of these three, which is the highest or most perfect kind of operation? Not the life of pleasure, surely, since such a life is not according to that which makes man what he is and sets him apart from animal nature, namely his reason. Animals all seek pleasure, but such a goal as a final goal is beneath man and unworthy of the best within him. On the other hand, the other two kinds of life do stand the test. Both are quite proper to man: the active life of politics and the life of speculation.

And of these two, which is the better kind of life? The Philosopher comes to that searching question and major issue at the very end of the *Ethics*, and there he would seem to feel some hesitation as he faces up to it. Man is a social animal and the active life of the *polis* is surely the social life par excellence. How then should the active life not be preferred, being that way of life which is more properly human? Is there not something distinctly unsocial in the life of pure speculation? Is it not a life somewhat *above* that which is proper to man, since those who pass their days in contemplating enduring truth are clearly engaging in an activity proper to the gods? And if this is so, and if we say that man ought to choose such a life above all else as the highest form of happiness known to mortals, then are we not saying that man should aspire to an activity higher than any which is specifically and properly *human*? [7]

However, for all his apparent hesitation in making the choice, Aristotle comes to a clear decision on this point, putting his seal of approval on the life of contemplation as that to which man should ultimately aspire, even though it is a life "higher than man":

> But such a life [the contemplative] would be too high for man; for it is not in so far as he is man that he will live so, but in so far as something divine is present in him. . . . If reason is divine, then, in comparison with man, the life according to it is divine in comparison with human life. But we must not follow those who advise us, being men, to think of human things, and, being mortal, of mortal things, but must, so far as we can, make ourselves immortal, and

strain every nerve to live in accordance with the best thing in us; for even if it be small in bulk, much more does it in power and worth surpass everything. This would seem, too, to be each man himself, since it is the authoritative and better part of him. It would be strange then, if he were to choose not the life of his self but that of something else. And what we said before will apply now; that which is proper to each thing is by nature best and most pleasant for each thing; for man, therefore, the life according to reason is best and pleasantest, since reason, more than anything else *is* man. This life therefore is also the happiest.

But in a secondary degree the life in accordance with the other kind of virtue [the active life] is happy; for the activities in accordance with this befit our human estate.[8]

In both the *Convivio* and the *De Monarchia* Dante shows himself familiar with all such major points in Aristotle's doctrine in this question of happiness, and fully persuaded of their truth. And from both treatises it is quite clear that the Philosopher's preference of the contemplative life as the higher goal is one most firmly adopted by Dante. Happiness may be attained along both "branches," but the more perfect happiness is in the contemplative life, even if the full perfection of the contemplative is not to be had in this life.

But, be it known, in this life we may have two kinds of happiness, according to two different paths, one good, the other best, which lead us thereto: the one is the active life, and the other the contemplative. Which latter (although by the active life we arrive, as was said, at a good happiness) leads us to the best happiness and blessedness, as the Philosopher proves in the tenth of the *Ethics*. And Christ affirms it with his mouth in the Gospel of Luke, speaking to Martha, and answering her: "Martha, Martha, thou art anxious and dost trouble thyself about many things; verily one thing only is needful," that is to say, "the thing which thou art doing." And he adds: "Mary hath chosen the best part, which shall not be taken from her." And Mary, as is written before these words of the Gospel, sitting at the feet of Christ, showed no concern for the management of the house, but listened only to the words of the Saviour. For if we would expound this morally, our Lord meant therein to show that the contemplative life was the best, although the active life was good. This is manifest to whoso will think on the Gospel words.[9]

In *De Monarchia*, Dante is even more radically Aristotelian in

setting up the proper goal of human life. Man is a being endowed
with a certain nature, he has innate capacities to be realized. The
proper goal lies in the realization of those capacities.[10] The goal
is therefore an "operation" in the Philosopher's sense, that is, a
function. Now all exists for some purpose in Aristotle's teleological universe and in Dante's: else we should have to think that
nature makes something in vain, that is, idle, inoperative, without
purpose — and this is repugnant to reason. Man must exist for a
purpose, and that purpose must be the full actualizing of his nature, which is that of a rational being.[11] Man's rational nature
must be fully realized, and this can be only in an activity of the
highest level, that is, in contemplation. Moreover, it must be possible to say what the goal of human civilization as a whole is.
Again, it is a question of teleological function. Why, for what
purpose, for what ultimate goal, does God by His art (which is
Nature) bring the human race into being? When Dante reaches
the end of his quest along these lines, the goal as the proper (because intended) function for the human race stands clear: it is
"to keep the whole capacity of the potential intellect constantly
actualized, primarily for speculation, and secondarily (by extension and for the sake of the other) for action." And we should
note his statement carefully as he continues here:

> And since it is with the whole as it is with the part, and it is the
> fact that in sedentary quietness the individual man is perfected in
> knowledge and in wisdom, it is evident that in the quiet or tran-
> quillity of peace the human race is most freely and favorably dis-
> posed towards the work proper to it (which is almost divine, even
> as it is said, "Thou hast made him a little lower than the angels").[12]

Peace is a prerequisite and first condition, a "disposition" which
makes possible that activity by which man realizes his nature.
From this first principle Dante moves on into his thesis respecting
universal monarchy. Universal peace, his argument runs, is possible only if a single monarch rules over the world. There will
then be peace, because then and only then will there be justice,
which is right order among the parts of the world. All here is
syllogistic, all follows in strict reasoning according to first principles. One must ask *why*: why does man exist? Man exists in

order that he may achieve his nature in its highest capacity, that is, in contemplation. But such a goal can be attained only on a condition: justice and peace must prevail. Thus the argument runs back from the end to those things which are for the sake of the end. But in any movement towards attainment of the end the order is of course the reverse. If the end is contemplation and the means to the end is justice and peace, then we shall come first to justice and peace, and then to contemplation. Justice or right order is the disposition which prepares for the higher thing, contemplation.[13]

We must recall that Dante, in the context of this argument in the *De Monarchia*, appeals to that pattern in history which we have studied and which proves to be the confirmation of this order of things in the attainment of the goal. For so it was in history: first the Romans had brought the world to peace and justice, and to this "disposition" of the world Christ came. And so too in the matter of justification in the soul: first justice, then advent of grace, as to a place prepared. What seems different now is only that the argument out of Aristotle would put *contemplation* at the end of the whole event rather than "advent" in some form or other. But there is here no final difficulty, as we are to see. Contemplation in a Christian sense can be synonymous with Wisdom (Sapientia). In which case we have again the familiar sequence: justice as the disposition or preparation for what then follows, be it Christ, or Sapientia, or Contemplation, or Light of Grace. Beatrice, in fact, can bear more names than one in the allegory of the poem.

* * *

It is well to come back to the poem to consider the import, in the matter of the goal at the summit of the mountain, of an event which precedes immediately Virgil's promise of the "sweet fruit." This is a dream which comes to the wayfarer Dante in the hours just before the dawn of the fourth day of his climb.[14] Other dreams have come in each of the two preceding nights spent on the slope of the mountain and in just those hours when dreams are most prophetic. And each of these dreams then, in the subsequent action, has in fact proved to be prophetic.[15] Must not this third dream be like the other two in this respect? Will it not be fulfilled somehow in the climb?

We see that this is in fact the case when we understand, first of all, that this third dream is a dream about the goal at the summit. Immediately, when Dante awakens, it is Virgil's promise that the sweet fruit sought by all mortals will be plucked *today*. And so it is with this dream: it too makes a promise, and like Virgil's, it is the promise of happiness to be attained "today," which must mean here, at the summit of the mountain.

This third dream is about a familiar pair of Old Testament figures, Leah and Rachel. Taken together and seen in the light of what is declared of them, they are an allegory which the poet was confident would be quite evident in its meaning. In a sense it might as well have been a dream of that other New Testament pair, Martha and Mary, which we have noted Dante citing in the *Convivio*. In either case we have to do with an allegory standing for two ways of life, the active and the contemplative. For Martha "was cumbered about much serving" and came to the Lord to protest that Mary her sister had left her to serve alone, sitting all day at Jesus's feet to hear His word. And to her the Saviour answered, saying: "Martha, Martha, thou art careful and troubled about many things: but one thing is needful: and Mary has chosen that best part which shall not be taken away from her." If we understand, as we should, that Mary here signifies the contemplative life, then we may note, even as Dante did, that Jesus agrees with Aristotle: contemplation is the better part.

As for Leah and Rachel, the former was productive, the latter sterile. And more importantly, for the meaning of the dream in Purgatory, we remember the succession: how Jacob had labored first for Leah and obtained Rachel only after he had got her sister. Thus, in allegory, the active life comes first and is for the sake of the contemplative. Indeed, it is this particular feature of the Old Testament allegory which makes it more meaningful here than any dream of Martha and Mary would have been. Leah *leads to* Rachel.

In the dream it is Leah who appears alone. She is seen to walk about a meadow picking flowers. She sings as she goes, and her song declares her own name, that there may be no mistake about the meaning. She gathers flowers to weave a garland to adorn herself; whereas her sister Rachel, as her song goes on to say, sits all day long before her mirror, never turning away from it, being enamored of her own eyes. Then, in its last verse, Leah's song leaves no doubt as to the allegory: "She (Rachel) is content with seeing, I with working."

> Nell'ora, credo, che dell'oriente
>   prima raggiò nel monte Citerea,
>   che di foco d'amor par sempre ardente,
> giovane e bella in sogno mi parea
>   donna vedere andar per una landa
>   cogliendo fiori, e cantando dicea:
> "Sappia, qualunque il mio nome dimanda,
>   ch'i' mi son Lia, e vo movendo intorno
>   le belle mani a farmi una ghirlanda.
> Per piacermi allo specchio qui m'adorno;
>   ma mia suora Rachel mai non si smaga
>   dal suo miraglio e siede tutto giorno.
> Ell'è de' suoi belli occhi veder vaga,
>   com'io dell'adornarmi con le mani:
>   lei lo vedere, e me l'ovrare appaga."
>   *Purgatorio* XXVII, 94–108.

At the hour, I think, when from the east Cytherea, who with fire of love seems always burning, first beamed upon the mountain, I seemed in a dream to see a lady, young and beautiful, going through a meadow gathering flowers, and, singing, she was saying: "Let him know, whoever asks my name, that I am Leah, and I go moving my fair hands about to make me a garland. To please me at the mirror I do here adorn me, but my sister Rachel never turns from her mirror, and sits all day. She is fain to look at her fair eyes, as I to adorn me with my hands. Her, seeing, and me, doing satisfies."

There has been no difficulty in understanding the meaning of the dream in itself, of course. Leah and Rachel must signify respectively the active and the contemplative life. The problem is rather how the dream applies in the subsequent action of the poem, in what happens to Dante who has the dream. If the dream is prophetic, as it must surely be, then just how is it so? We may think of the dream that came during the second night, of the "old witch" as she is called, how she was subsequently "met" in the upper terraces of the mountain after being presented in the dream.[16] It must be that Dante is somehow to "meet" Leah and Rachel in a similar way, having had this dream about them. Will this be at the summit which now is so near? Are we to understand, for instance, that Beatrice is the fulfillment of the figure of Rachel or the contemplative life? And if this be so, then wherein are we to see the corresponding fulfillment of the figure of Leah, the active life? Dante studies do not appear to have come to any very sure view of the answers on these points.

We first get our bearings in recognizing that, like Virgil's words about the sweet fruit to be plucked today, this dream makes a promise. Therein lies its "prophetic" character. And even as Virgil's, this promise made by the dream concerns the summit of the mountain and the goal there. In fact, the two promises are essentially one and the same. At the summit is happiness as the goal which is sought by all mortals. And the dream in its way is saying what such happiness, what *true* happiness is. It will not be rest, it will be operation, even as the Philosopher had decided. It will be an inner activity, an action abiding in the agent (*agere*), and of such activity there are two kinds proper to man: the active and the contemplative.

We must also see that the particular manner of the dream affirms yet other aspects of the traditional meaning of Leah and Rachel in their allegory: for one thing, the fact that Leah must come first. In the dream, Leah alone appears, and Rachel remains off-stage. By this a certain order of progression or sequence is denoted: the wayfarer must first come to Leah. So it was with Jacob, as allegorists who use the two figures are always prepared to point out. Jacob toiled first for Leah, and then for Rachel. Perfection in the active life must precede perfection in the contemplative. It is a matter of a progression from a lower to a higher kind of life. And so it must be on the mountain, as the wayfarer moves upward. In the fulfillment of the dream, he will come first to Leah, and then to Rachel.

We glimpse thus two moments or phases in the attainment at

the summit. Nor shall we forget that this has proved to be the
case in other patterns of meaning based on the Aristotelian scheme
of *generatio*. The two moments were visible in the line of moral
allegory and again in the line of historical allegory, except that
in these two latter cases, it was clearly a matter of attaining first
to *justice*, which was the completion of the first phase and the
requisite preparation for what came next. So that the question
quite naturally comes: in the fulfillment of the dream, are we
meeting this same pattern again? Do we have here also the close
correspondence of analogy? If so, then to attain to Leah must mean
in some sense to attain to justice. But Leah is surely the active
life. Can the perfection of the active life, then, also mean justice?

*   *   *

A mystic and contemplative who is given a high station among
the *sapienti* of the *Paradiso*,[17] and whose work was well known
to Dante, can tell us that Leah is "justice." Richard of St. Victor
makes the point in a work best known by the short title of
Benjamin Minor.[18] Yet for present considerations its longer title
is the more significant: *De praeparatione animi ad contemplationem*; for if the active life precedes the contemplative and is a
preparation for it, from such a title it would seem that Richard's
work is about Leah, the preparation. It is in fact about both of
Jacob's wives, as is evident in its opening words. At once the
reader is struck by the fact that Richard understands Leah as
justice, and Rachel as wisdom. Such terms as these for the familiar
pair may throw some light on the prophecy of the dream in Purgatory as it applies to the summit and the goal.

> Now, even as you read, Jacob is known to have had two wives,
> one called Leah, the other Rachel. Leah was fecund but blear-eyed;
> Rachel quite barren, yet of striking beauty. But let us see what these
> two wives of Jacob are, so that we may more easily understand who
> their children are. Rachel is the science of truth, Leah the discipline
> of virtue. Rachel the devotion to wisdom, Leah the desire of jus-
> tice.[19]

Richard's particular terms for the allegory of the two figures
can indeed prove enlightening for our reading of the third and

last dream of the Purgatory. *Studium sapientiae*, as the meaning of Rachel, applies very well indeed, since in the dream Rachel is said to sit all day before her mirror, enamored of her own eyes. In *studium* an activity is clearly implied. And matching this is *desiderium justitiae* for Leah, wherein again an operation is denoted, as in the dream, by Leah's activity in walking about and adorning herself with flowers.

The *Benjamin Minor* is about the "preparation of the soul for contemplation," that is, the preparation for Rachel. Leah is that preparation, and Richard naturally has much to say about her and her offspring in this treatise, though he does not cease to speak of Rachel as well. Therefore, if Leah is justice, or better, the desire of justice, we have to consider that such justice is a matter of an inner condition. Justice is in the will, first of all, the perfection of volition. Justice is right love. So begins the second chapter of the *Benjamin*:

> Now of justice we shall speak likewise. Now equally we all desire to be just, but it chances that we cannot be just. Assuredly all could be just if all desired perfectly to be just. For to desire justice perfectly is to be just already.[20]

For Richard, justice is primarily a matter of the will, of right order in the will, as is evident when he goes on to speak thus allegorically of Jacob's two wives. Leah stands in fact for the affective life:

> Yet we may inquire more diligently of these two wives of Jacob. . . . One [Rachel] is reason, the other [Leah] is affection: reason by which we discern, affection by which we love; reason for truth, affection for virtue.[21]

We may turn from the *Benjamin Minor* to the Christian tradition generally to note that the active life is usually seen in such an inward sense rather than in that of the outward political life, as in Aristotle's view. Even so, this is not a focus alien to the *Ethics*, since *operatio* is above all a kind of action abiding in the agent. Aristotle is still closely in touch with Plato, for whom right order in the state and right order in the soul must be seen together. It is only a matter of accent. And in the Christian tradition the accent is of course on soul.

Among the many who expounded the meaning of Leah and Rachel in allegory, none is more quoted than St. Gregory, who in his Commentaries on Ezekiel and on Job was ever alert to interpretations in the line of moral allegory. And it is typical of Gregory that, whenever he writes of the pair, he never fails to make the point that Jacob took Leah first and Rachel after Leah, that is, the active life comes first and is a preparation for the contemplative. We move, in due order, from the active to the contemplative. To get Rachel it is necessary first to take Leah.[22]

In the Christian tradition, moreover, there is a particular stress on one matter which we cannot expect to find in Aristotle: namely, an insistence that we inherit a corrupt nature through Adam's fall, that all mortals now suffer the consequences of this fallen condition. Having lost the justice with which Adam had been endowed, we are now constantly tossed on a storm of disordered passions. And we all yearn, however much in vain, for the quieting of that storm, for the peace that can only come with a will made "straight and free and whole" again, with right order within, with justice in the soul.[23] Verses in the *Paradiso* bearing the familiar figure of such "waves" come to mind; for the storm is in the disordered will and bears the name of "cupidity":

> O cupidigia che i mortali affonde
>   sì sotto te, che nessuno ha podere
>   di trarre li occhi fuor de le tue onde.
> *Paradiso* XXVII, 121–123.

Oh cupidity, drowning mortals so beneath thyself that no one has the power to lift his eyes from thy waves.

Cupidity is the contrary of justice, and to lift one's eyes from its waves means to enter into the desire for justice. One thinks of the first simile of the *Comedy*, of the swimmer who struggles from the deep to look back upon that "pass that never left anyone alive," [24] and we may recall a metaphor in the *Paradiso* which gives us Dante as one now saved from "the sea of crooked love." [25] Of *cupidigia* Dante wrote many times in metaphor and out of metaphor, in the *Comedy* and in the earlier works. Cupidity is the chief opponent of justice, as we are told in the *De Monarchia*, where Aristotle's fifth of the *Ethics* is cited in confirmation. Greed "clouds the disposition of justice" whereas right love brightens it; and at the end of the treatise Dante returns to the common metaphor of that storm-tossed sea of disorder in the will when he speaks of the goal or goals of human life as ordained by God's providence. The goal is a "port," a haven of rest out of these waters.

> And since none, or few (and these with extremest difficulty) could reach such a port were not the waves of seductive cupidity quieted and the human race left free to rest in the tranquillity of peace. . . .[26]

It is justice, that right order prevailing under a universal monarch, which will be such a disposition. Or, in the soul, it is justice prevailing in the will which is the preparation and necessary first condition for contemplation.

The raging sea of the passions derives, of course, from the corruptible body which we inherit through Adam's sin. That storm within us is a constant reminder of the fall, of the justice and right order of man's first condition lost through sin, a point on which we may again listen to St. Gregory:

> For the mind of the righteous man, in that his way is directed to the realms above, is sore beset by a grievous war arising from the corruptible body . . . for temptation constrains every man to mark from whence and whereunto he is fallen, who after he has forsaken the peace of God feels a strife rise up against him from out of himself.[27]

Let the inner tempest of the disordered passions first be stilled, let there be inner peace, that we may "lay hold of the summit of perfection" and occupy the "citadel of contemplation": first justice, then contemplation, first Leah, then Rachel, even as with Jacob:

> For the season of action comes first, for contemplation last. Whence it is needful that every perfect man first discipline his mind in virtuous habits, and afterwards lay it up in the granary of rest. . . .

Hence it is that Jacob serves for Rachel and gets Leah, and that it is said to him, "It is not the custom to give the youngest before the first-born." [28]

There is, in this way, a striking agreement to be noted between Aristotle and Christian doctrine as to the life that is proper to man and man's highest goal in this life. That goal is a summit of perfection in both the active and the contemplative orders of life, the contemplative being the higher of the two and the "final" goal. There, at the summit, is true happiness to be found. The summit has two peaks, and one peak is higher, the contemplative. First we reach the lower peak of the active life that we may move from it to the higher one. We must come first to justice, the perfection of the active life.

The dream thus makes a promise of true happiness to be attained by the wayfarer "today," even as does Virgil's promise of "sweet fruit"; and we may now interpret the dream with better understanding, seeing how it is realized in the action beyond it. If Leah is the desire for justice and justice resides in the will, then it must be that Virgil leads to Leah. Outside the dream, in the event of the poem, there is no figure to represent her. There is only the full attainment under Virgil of that which Leah signifies.

At Virgil's encouraging promise Dante hastens up the remaining steps of the way. Then, in the moment when he attains the summit, he is told that he has now come as far as Virgil may lead, to a condition of justice in the will. Virgil has thus led to Leah, for it is to her that we must come first. She is the perfection of the active life, she is justice and from her the wayfarer can pass to her sister Rachel, that is, to contemplation. Leah is the disposition for the higher life beyond. First justice, then contemplation. A dream is fulfilled at the summit, and when we are able to see the terms of its fulfillment we note once more the familiar pattern of the two phases, the first a preparation, a doorway, to the second.

At the summit of the mountain is Eden. Dante literally regains the Earthly Paradise. Should we not see also that he regains, in the moral and inner sense, that condition which Adam enjoyed before the fall? We have much to learn about human nature, as it was at first, before we can give the right answer to that question with all the precise distinctions required by the doctrine of Dante's day. And yet, with justice in mind, and contemplation as the final goal at the summit of the mountain, and with the reminder that Eden is situated there, we take note of how, in a sense, Dante may be said to return to Adam's first condition.

In insisting, in the *De Monarchia*, that man was created for a purpose, namely, that he might attain to contemplation in the fullest measure possible, Dante was in no sense advancing an original theory respecting man's goal in this life as ordained by God. One has only to realize that this truth is evident in the creation of the first man. God made Adam for both the active and the contemplative life, but He made him above all for the contemplative or higher order, as St. Thomas and many another theologian of his century can teach us. Thomas even uses the metaphor of "the high peak of contemplation" (*summum fastigium contemplationis*) as that for which man was created, in speaking of Adam in his first condition which was one of perfect rectitude, an original justice.[29] But, for Adam to hold to that peak whereon he was placed it was necessary that the lower passions and powers of his soul be kept in perfect subjection: the prerequisite is right order in the soul, a disposition for that higher activity of contemplation for which man was made.

The journey to the summit means journey to Beatrice. Contemplation is one of Beatrice's names. A Virgil who leads to justice may be said to prepare for Beatrice, or, in terms of the dream, to prepare for Rachel in leading to Leah. In the journey with Virgil through Purgatory, right order is restored in the passions and lower powers. If we keep these aspects of meaning in mind, we may see how both the promise of the dream and Virgil's promise of sweet fruit are kept.

Here at the summit "man is happy," as Beatrice says. She might also have said that man is happy when he attains to her, as her very name signifies: Beatrice, bearer of beatitude.

Notes

1. *Inferno* I, 77–78. There may well be a conscious echo here of precise words of Aristotle respecting happiness (*Eth. Nic.*, in the *versio antiqua* known to Aquinas, I, 12): "Nobis autem manifestum ex his quae dicta sunt, quoniam est felicitas honorabilium et perfectorum. Videtur autem ita habere et propter esse principium. Huius enim gratia reliqua omnia omnes operantur. *Principium autem et causam* bonorum honorabile quid, et divinum ponimus." (Italics mine.)

2. *Nicomachean Ethics* I, 4. The argument of Aristotle is given many times by Aquinas. The following is typical, and may be noted especially because of Dante's term "sweet fruit": "De ultimo fine possumus loqui dupliciter: uno modo, secundum rationem ultimi finis; alio modo, secundum id in quo finis ultimi ratio invenitur. Quantum igitur ad rationem ultimi finis, omnes conveniunt in appetitu finis ultimi, quia omnes appetunt suam perfectionem adimpleri, quae est ratio ultimi finis, ut dictum est. Sed quantum ad id in quo ista ratio invenitur, non omnes homines conveniunt in ultimo fine: nam quidam appetunt divitias tanquam consummatum bonum, quidam vero voluptatem, quidam vero quodcumque aliud. Sicut et omni gustui delectabile est dulce, sed quibusdam maxime delectabilis est dulcedo vini, quibusdam dulcedo mellis, aut alicuius talium. Illud tamen dulce oportet simpliciter esse melius delectabile, in quo maxime delectatur qui habet optimum gustum. Et similiter illud bonum oportet esse completissimum, quod tanquam ultimum finem appetit habens affectum bene dispositum." (*Summa Theol.* I–II, q. 1, a. 7, resp.) See also especially the *Summa c. G.* III, 31, 33, and *passim*.

3. *Convivio* IV, xvii, 8: ". . . sì come dice lo Filosofo nel primo de l'Etica quando deffinisce la Felicitade, dicendo che 'Felicitade è operazione secondo virtute in vita perfetta' "; and *passim* in the same work.

4. The distinction of these two kinds of activity is quite fundamental. The whole of the moral allegory of the poem is in the line of *agere*, of course. Students of Aquinas know how often he refers to the distinction, out of Aristotle. A typical passage is the following (*Summa Theol.* I–II, q. 3, a. 1, ad 3): "Sicut dicitur in IX Metaph., duplex est actio. Una quae procedit ab operante in exterioram materiam, sicut urere et secare. Et talis operatio non potest esse beatitudo, nam talis operatio non est actio et perfectio agentis sed magis patientis, ut ibidem dicitur. Alia est actio manens in ipso agente, ut sentire, intelligere et velle, et huiusmodi actio est perfectio et actus agentis. Et talis operatio potest esse beatitudo."

And that the latter kind of activity is precisely that represented by the moral allegory is evident everywhere in the many and divers statements by Thomas, e. g. *In III Sent.* d. xxxv, q. 1, a. 2, sol.: "cum enim vita humana

ordinata . . . consistat in operatione intellectus et rationis, habeat autem in-
tellectiva pars duas operationes, unam quae est ipsius secundum se, aliam
quae ipsius est secundum quod regit inferiores vires; erit duplex vita humana:
una quae consistit in operatione quae est intellectus secundum seipsum,
et haec dicitur contemplativa; alia quae consistit in operatione intellectus
et rationis secundum quod ordinat et regit et imperat inferioribus partibus,
et haec dicitur vita activa. Unde secundum Philosophum (in 6 Ethic. cap. 5
et 6), agere proprie dicitur operatio quae est a voluntate imperata, in ipso
operante consistens, non in materiam exteriorem transmutandam transiens:
quia hoc esset *facere*, quod est operatio mechanicae artis. Morales enim
virtutes quae in vita activa perficiunt, circa agibilia dicuntur." Dante's awareness of the distinction is most evident in the *Convivio* (IV, ix, 5–6, and
passim).

5. Cf. the opening words of the *Convivio*: "Sì come dice lo Filosofo
nel principio de la Prima Filosofia, tutti li uomini naturalmente desiderano
di sapere. La ragione di che puote essere ed è che ciascuna cosa, da provi-
denza di propria natura impinta, è inclinabile a la sua propria perfezione;
onde, acciò che la scienza è ultima perfezione de la nostra anima, ne la
quale sta la nostra ultima felicitade, tutti naturalmente al suo desiderio semo
subietti." See Thomas Aquinas, *Comm. Metaph.*, Proem.: "Omnes autem
scientiae et artes ordinantur in unum, scilicet ad hominis perfectionem, quae
est eius beatitudo."

6. In a typical statement by Aquinas we may read (*Summa Theol.* I–II,
q. 3, a. 2, resp., "Utrum beatitudo sit operatio"): "Secundum quod beatitudo
hominis est aliquid creatum in ipso existens, necesse est dicere quod beatitudo hominis sit operatio. Est enim beatitudo ultima hominis perfectio." It
is in the first book of the *Ethics* of course that Aristotle distinguishes between an end considered as an *activity* and an end considered as the *result*
of an activity. In ch. 10 of that book the decision is reached that happiness
must be an *activity*.

7. Time and again Aquinas will echo "the Philosopher" on this point and
proceed to make the adjustments required by Christian doctrine; as, for
example (*De Virt. Card.* q. 1, a. 1, resp.): "Cardinalis a cardine dicitur, in
quo ostium vertitur: . . . unde virtutes cardinales dicuntur in quibus fundatur vita humana, per quam ostium introitur; vita autem humana est quae est
homini proportionata. In hoc homine autem invenitur primo quidem natura
sensitiva, in qua convenit cum brutis; ratio pratica, quae est homini propria
secundum suum gradum; et intellectus speculativus, qui non perfecte in
homine invenitur sicut invenitur in Angelis, sed secundum quamdam participationem animae. Ideo vita contemplativa non est proprie humana, sed
superhumana; vita autem voluptuosa, quae inhaeret sensibilibus bonis, non
est humana, sed bestialis. Vita ergo proprie humana est vita activa, quae consistit in exercitio virtutum moralium; et ideo proprie virtutes cardinales
dicuntur in quibus quodammodo vertitur et fundatur vita moralis, sicut in
quibusdam principiis talis vitae."

8. *Nicomachean Ethics* X, 7 and 8 (Ross translation).

9. *Convivio* IV, xvii, 9 ff.; see also IV, xxii, 10 ff.

10. See *Convivio* I, v, 11: "Ciascuna cosa è virtuosa in sua natura che
fa quello a che ella è ordinata; e quanto meglio lo fa tanto è più virtuosa.

Onde dicemo uomo virtuoso che vive in vita contemplativa o attiva, a le quali è ordinato naturalmente; dicemo del cavallo virtuoso che corre forte e molto, a la qual cosa è ordinato."

11. The basic assumption runs through the whole argument of the *De Monarchia*, of course, and becomes explicit at several points, as at the outset (I, iii, 1–3): "Nunc autem videndum est quid sit finis totius humane civilitatis: quo viso, plus quam dimidium laboris erit transactum iuxta Phylosophum ad Nicomacum. Et ad evidentiam eius quod queritur advertendum quod, quemadmodum est finis aliquis ad quem natura producit pollicem, et alius ab hoc ad quem manum totam, et rursus alius ab utroque ad quem brachium, aliusque ab omnibus ad quem totum hominem; sic alius est finis ad quem singularem hominem, alius ad quem ordinat domesticam comunitatem, alius ad quem viciniam, et alius ad quem civitatem, et alius ad quem regnum, et denique ultimus ad quem universaliter genus humanum Deus eternus arte sua, que natura est, in esse producit. Et hoc queritur hic tanquam principium inquisitionis directivum. Propter quod sciendum primo quod 'Deus et natura nil otiosum facit,' sed quicquid prodit in esse est ad aliquam operationem."

12. *De Mon.* I, iv. 2,

13. "Justice" and "peace" become synonymous on this argument. One may compare a typical statement by Aquinas in this (*In IV Sent.* d. xlix, q. 1, a. 2, sol. 4): "Sicut dicit Augustinus, 19 de Civit. Dei (cap. 13), pax omnium rerum est tranquillitas ordinis: ex quo patet quod ex hoc ratio pacis assumitur quod aliquid non impeditur a recto ordine: tranquillitas enim perturbationem impedimenti excludit. Pax autem praecipue respicit illum ordinem quo voluntas in aliquid ordinatur: unde et tunc dicimus hominem pacem habere quando nihil est quod impediat ordinem suae voluntatis in aliquid; et similiter dicimus pacem esse in civitate, quando nihil est quod perturbet rectum ordinem civitatis, qui est ex voluntate gubernatoris civitatis, etc."

14. *Purgatorio* XXVII.

15. *Purgatorio* IX, XIX.

16. We are guided to see that the "strega" is met in the form of the sins of upper Purgatory by Virgil's words preceding the dream (XVII, 136–139):
   "L'amor ch'ad esso troppo s'abbandona,
      di sovra a noi si piange per tre cerchi;
      ma come tripartito si ragiona,
   tacciolo, acciò che tu per te ne cerchi."
The dream is an aid to the understanding, and is fulfilled in the actual experience of what it represents.

17. *Paradiso* X, 131–132, where a verse praises him especially as excelling in the contemplative life (*considerare*):
      . . . Riccardo
   che a considerar fu più che viro.

18. PL 196.1 ff.: *De Praeparatione Animi ad Contemplationem. Liber Dictus Benjamin Minor.*

19. *Ibid.*, col. 1: "Duas namque, ut legitis, uxores Jacob habuisse cognoscitur. Una Lia, altera Rachel dicebatur: Lia fecundior; Rachel formosior. Lia fecunda, sed lippa; Rachel fere sterilis, sed forma singularis. Sed jam,

quae sint istae duae uxores Jacob, videamus, ut qui sint earum filii facilius intelligamus. Rachel doctrina veritatis, Lia disciplina virtutis. Rachel studium sapientiae, Lia desiderium justitiae."

20. *Ibid.*, col. 2: "Numquid de justitia similiter dicimus. Numquid aeque justi omnes esse volumus, sed justi forte esse non possumus. Imo omnes utique justi esse potuissent, si esse justi perfecte voluissent. Justitiam enim perfecte diligere, est jam justum esse."

21. *Ibid.*, col. 3: "Sed libet adhuc de his duabus uxoribus Jacob diligentius inquirere, et quidquid inde animus suggerit manifestius aperire. . . . Una est ratio, altera est affectio: ratio qua discernamus, affectio qua diligamus; ratio, ad veritatem, affectio ad virtutem."

22. Gregory the Great, *Moralium in Job Lib. VI*, PL 75.764: "Hinc est quod Jacob pro Rachel servit, et Liam accipit, eique dicitur: 'Non est consuetudinis in terra nostra ut minores ante tradamus ad nuptias quam majores' (*Genes.* xxix, 27). Rachel namque visum principium; Lia autem laboriosa dicitur. Et quid per Rachelem, nisi contemplativa; quid per Liam, nisi activa vita desinatur? . . . Post Liae ergo complexus ad Rachelem Jacob pervenit, quia perfectus quisque ante activae vitae ad fecunditatem jungitur, et post contemplativae ad requiem copulatur." Gregory continues here to speak of Martha and Mary. See also his *Homiliarum in Ezechielem Lib. II*, PL 76.953 ff.

Gregory is often remembered by later writers on the subject. Aquinas cites him frequently in treating of the matter, as, e.g., in his question comparing the contemplative and active life, *Summa Theol.* II–II, q. 182, a. 1, ad 2: ". . . unde patet quod vita activa non directe praecipit vitae contemplativae; sed, disponendo ad vitam contemplativam, praecipit quaedam opera vitae activae, in quo magis servit vitae contemplativae quam dominetur. Et hoc est quod Gregorius dicit."

23. See Chapter XIII below, on the consequences of the Fall and loss of original justice. And for the accepted view, making the active life a pursuit of inner rectitude (justice), see Aquinas, *Summa Theol.* II–II, q. 182, a. 3, resp.: "Vita activa potest considerari quantum ad duo. Uno modo, quantum ad ipsum studium et exercitium exteriorum actionum. Et sic manifestum est quod vita activa impedit contemplativam, inquantum impossibile est quod aliquis simul occupetur circa exteriores actiones, et divinae contemplationi vacet. — Alio modo, potest considerari vita activa quantum ad hoc quod interiores animae passiones componit et ordinat. Et quantum ad hoc vita activa adiuvat ad contemplationem, quae impeditur per inordinationem interiorum passionum. Unde Gregorius dicit in VI Moral. 'Cum contemplationis arcem aliqui tenere desiderant, prius se in campo per exercitium operis probent.'" Dante's allegory of the active life and attainment by it concerns the second kind here. Aquinas puts the matter, moreover, in terms of *generatio*, so that the contemplative life becomes the *form* and the active the preparation (*ibid.*, a. 4, resp.): "Aliquid dicitur esse prius dupliciter. Uno modo, secundum suam naturam. Et hoc modo vita contemplativa est prior quam activa, inquantum prioribus et melioribus insistit. Unde et activam vitam movet et dirigit. . . . Alio modo, est aliquid prius quoad nos, quod scilicet est *prius in via generationis* [my italics]. Et hoc modo vita activa est prior quam contemplativa, quia disponit ad contemplativam.

. . . Dispositio enim in via generationis praecedit formam, quae simpliciter et secundum suam naturam est prior."

24. *Inferno* I, 22–27.

25. *Paradiso* XXVI, 62–63:
   tratto m'hanno del mar dell'amor torto
   e del diritto m'han posto alla riva.

26. *De Mon.* III, xvi, 11.

27. *Moralium Lib. VI*, PL 75.757.

28. *Ibid.*, col. 763.

29. *De Malo* q. 5, a. 1, resp.: "Est enim homo compositus ex anima et corpore, et ex natura intellectuali et sensibili; quae quodammodo si suae naturae relinquantur, intellectum aggravant et impediunt, ne libere ad summum fastigium contemplationis pervenire possit. Hoc autem auxilium fuit originalis justitia."

See Chapter XIII below, on this point.

Chapter VIII

Lady Philosophy
or Wisdom

Whatever the pattern in allegory, among the several noted, one feature is seen to be constant and common to all: the journey, in passing from the goal to which Virgil leads to that further goal which Beatrice is, moves out of one order into another, higher order. The fact was first evident in an examination of the two master patterns of that major line of moral allegory which extends throughout the poem. In the pattern of three lights, to pass from Virgil's guidance to Beatrice's means transition from a natural to a supernatural light, the light of faith and sanctifying grace. In the pattern of three conversions, this same transition means that the will turns from a first orientation which is natural and within the proportion of our human nature, to another with Beatrice which is above that proportion, being a conversion which is made possible by grace and charity.

Many are the signs and signals in the poem of this fundamental fact. Among others, there is, as noted, the verb *trasumanar*: "to go beyond the human," to pass beyond a human order which is natural to an order which is above nature. Such, along all lines of meaning, is the significance of transition from Virgil to Beatrice. And even in the subordinate patterns of justification, whether taking place in the individual soul or in history, that same dividing line between these two orders is evident. Virgil's justice is justice as the "philosophers" had understood it, it is justice according to Aristotle and Plato; whereas justice with Beatrice is quite beyond their conceptions and is the justice of which the Apostle speaks, the justice Christ brought to sinful man for his redemption. So had it been in history, for the justice to which Rome had brought the world had proved to be the preparation for Christ's advent and His justice.

Now that we have seen how the goal at the summit, as envisaged through a dream and a promise made by Virgil, is happiness (on a definition by Aristotle), we may further note, in this particular line of meaning, the same transition: a *trasumanar*. The dream of Leah and Rachel is fulfilled at the summit: Leah is attained when that justice is reached to which Virgil guides; and Rachel, who is contemplation, is attained in Beatrice. And yet, no sooner have we said as much than we are obliged to recognize, in the matter of Leah as the active life and as justice, that Leah is really attained, in final perfection, with Beatrice. Thus, if she is justice or, as Richard of St. Victor had said, the "desire for justice," then in this again we face the familiar feature: the complete fulfillment of the dream is with Beatrice, not with Virgil. Not with Virgil but with Beatrice is that justice of the active life had *in its full perfection*.

The unmistakable sign of this is to be seen in the fact that there are virtues of the active life attending Beatrice when she comes, that with her, indeed, come virtues of both the active and the contemplative operations. The two groups as such are easily recognized in the procession, even before Beatrice has appeared on her chariot. They come, four at the left wheel of the *carro*, and three at the right wheel. The four on the left are surely the cardinal virtues, also called the moral virtues, and these are of the active life. As such they were known to the pagan philosophers.

Indeed it was they who had first distinguished them and named them, and Virgil as well as the other virtuous *savi* dwelling in Limbo may be said to have known these four and to have had them in life. Moreover, these four moral virtues must be thought to be present in the condition of rectitude of the will to which Virgil brings Dante at the summit. And yet we are in no way told that the four are with Virgil at that point. Instead, we see them come with Beatrice.

As handmaids attending Beatrice, the four can only represent the cardinal virtues in an order which is quite beyond Virgil, a "transhuman" order unknown to the philosophers because unknowable by the natural light. And this the very color of their attire declares. All four partake of the red of charity. They are therefore the four *infused* moral virtues, prudence, temperance, fortitude, justice, and are not the acquired virtues which bear these same names with the pagans.[1]

The four maidens who represent these virtues are the first to receive Dante when he crosses the stream to Beatrice — when Virgil, be it remembered, has departed the scene. They declare themselves to be *ancelle* to Beatrice, affirm that they are "ordered to her." They lead Dante to the other group of three, the theological virtues which are faith, hope, and charity; and with the three, Dante is made able to look deeply into Beatrice's eyes, beholding there a vision of truth above the human order.

Now these three are virtues of the contemplative life, even as the four are of the active; and the very fact that the four come first to lead Dante to the three is surely the way in which the poet is meeting a fact now known to us, that the active life does come first and leads to the contemplative.

But if we are remembering the prophecy of the dream and Virgil's promise of the sweet fruit of happiness at the summit, how then are we to understand the fulfillment of both dream and promise? The problem becomes most evident with respect to the four maidens, the virtues of the active life, who are not seen on Virgil's side of the stream at all, but only on Beatrice's side. For if the virtues of the active life attend Beatrice, along with those of the contemplative, how then may we see Beatrice as the fulfill-

ment of the figure of Rachel merely? Must we not think that Leah
is somehow Beatrice, across that stream over which Virgil may
not pass?

We know now how such a question finds its answer. We are
simply confronting here the familiar feature of that transition
from Virgil to Beatrice which is a passing from one order to another, from what is human and may be known by the natural
light (known to a Virgil and the philosophers) to what is beyond
a human order and can be known only by the higher light of grace
and faith (and therefore known only to the "saints" in this life).
This being so, Leah, or the active life as a justice which prepares
for contemplation, must be thought of as attained on both sides
of the stream which flows between Virgil and Beatrice: on Virgil's
side, this will be the Leah or the justice which the philosophers
who lived before Christ had discerned, whereas on Beatrice's side,
Leah or justice will be justice as only the Christian saints know it,
through Christ. For it was Christ who first brought this higher
justice to men, when He came in the fullness of time, even as it
is He who brings such justice daily when He comes to the soul
in His hidden advent.

The virtues of the active life come thus with Beatrice in *their
Christian perfection*, and are seen to lead to the higher three,
accessible only in the time of grace and unknown generally to the
pagans. These are the virtues of contemplation. Their colors are
white, green, and red, signifying faith, hope, and charity respectively. It should be observed, moreover, that these colors
which are *their* colors inform the whole procession and are also
the colors of Beatrice's dress and crown. Surely, in this latter
aspect, they are there to declare that the lady so dressed is, above
all, Contemplation, that through these three virtues attending her
we may rise to the celestial Athens above, even as Dante had said
in the *Convivio*.[2]

One thing, however, must be evident: if Beatrice is thus attended by the virtues of both the active and the contemplative
life, and is therefore the fulfillment of the dream and of Virgil's
promise of happiness, she is also something more than the sum
merely of those virtues. They are "ordered to her," they serve

her as handmaids. The colors of her dress affirm that in her is contemplation in its perfection. As such Beatrice is Rachel, that contemplative life in which Aristotle had placed man's highest happiness. Yet these virtues were not known to an Aristotle, nor could a Virgil have discerned them to be any part of the sweet fruit of happiness as conceived by the natural light.[3]

All signs declare indeed that if Beatrice is happiness and as such is the goal at the summit of the mountain, she is a happiness lying quite beyond the natural light of the philosophers. They had not discerned so far, and Virgil's words "più oltre non discerno" meet this very point. And yet, in a sense, Aristotle's definition of happiness does apply here; to attain to Beatrice is to attain to "operation according to perfect virtue," and such is happiness according to the Philosopher — except that the virtues attending Beatrice are simply more perfect than any which Aristotle might have conceived. Or again, if happiness be an operation in terms of action and contemplation, then the dream of Rachel and Leah is fulfilled beyond the stream, with Beatrice; and in this Aristotle's requirements are met, even his point at the end of the *Ethics* that the contemplative is above the active, along with his further point that the contemplative life is above the human order, is higher than man. Aristotle too had seen the contemplative life as a *trasumanar*. And so it is in the poem, as journey with Beatrice begins. But here again is the familiar feature of the transition: this *trasumanar* with Beatrice is one that Aristotle could not have known, for attending her are perfect virtues, those contemplative theological virtues of faith, hope and charity, far above the acquired intellectual virtues of which Aristotle had spoken. These are Christian virtues *par excellence*. They are *given*, from above and beyond a human order. So, also, is the Lady whom they attend: Beatrice is given from above. In so far as she comes to fulfill the prophecy of the dream, and above all the figure of Rachel, Beatrice may be seen as Contemplation. But such a name will not do her full justice in all those aspects of meaning that are revealed when Virgil is no longer on the scene. We need other names for Beatrice, since she is something other than the virtues. Perhaps we should call her Lady Philosophy, that Lady who had brought comfort to Boethius, for Boethius had called her *magistra omnium virtutum*.[4] Or, since Wisdom is another name for such a figure, perhaps a better name for Beatrice is Sapientia.[5] Such names for her in any case would in no way alter the basic fact we have been noting, the wayfarer's transition from one order to another when he leaves Virgil and comes to Beatrice. The two names might indeed be useful, to register a distinction. From Virgil's side, that is, where we discern by the natural light given to the philosophers, Beatrice may be seen as that Lady Philosophy who was in fact known to them. Indeed Virgil himself sees Beatrice so, as we are now about to observe. But then at the summit, when Beatrice comes and Virgil is gone, she is seen in a splendor surpassing by far the natural light, and her name must rather be Wisdom, Sapientia, in the fullest Christian sense of the word. For Beatrice is a Wisdom *de sursum descendens*. She is that Sapientia which is given from above. And that is why the virtues which attend her must also be those virtues which are *given*, not those which are *acquired* by human effort.

*   *   *

"O donna di virtù, sola per cui
 l'umana spezie eccede ogni contento
 di quel ciel c'ha minor li cerchi sui."
                              Inferno II, 76–78.

With these words Virgil recognizes Beatrice in Limbo, where she comes to send him to the rescue of her "amico." Such is her way of speaking of the man fighting the losing struggle before the beasts on the mountain slope: "l'amico mio e non della ventura." There is good reason, as we shall see, to give close attention to such a turn of phrase. As for Virgil's words to Beatrice, they are clearly words of recognition. Virgil knows her at once, and in just such terms. Literally he is saying: "O Lady of Virtue, through whom alone mankind goes beyond all that is contained within that heaven which has its circlings least." And we have only to get our cosmological bearings to understand what he is saying. The heaven referred to must be that of the moon, since the sphere of the moon is, in its circumference, the smallest of the nine spheres of the planets and stars which, in Dante's universe, circle the earth. The "contento" of the sphere of the moon must be its "contenuto," that which is contained by it. To speak of all that is within the sphere of the moon is but another way of denoting what is commonly referred to as all that lies beneath the moon, especially whenever the notion of rising above and beyond the moon's sphere enters in, as it must do here with the verb *eccedere*. Virgil's words thus speak of mankind as "exceeding," that is, "rising above" the sublunar world by means of this lady of virtue, and by no other way. Such, in the literal sense, is Virgil's recognition of Beatrice when she comes to him in Limbo.

We may note, too, that in having Virgil recognize Beatrice in such terms as these, the poet has dealt with what could otherwise have been something of a special problem: how, that is, might a Virgil, born *sub Julio*, be thought able to recognize a Beatrice born in Florence so many centuries later, a woman (apart from what could be known of her in the *Vita Nuova* and the *Convivio*) having no claim whatever to any kind of public recognition? The poet has here met this difficulty by having Virgil know Beatrice as he might in fact have known her — as a Lady Philosophy, a familiar figure to those pagans who had come before Christ and had lived by the natural light alone.

We may see this more clearly if we recall that the notion of an ascent of the mind or the soul to a region above the circle of the moon was familiar enough to the pagans, was perhaps at least, as old as Pythagoras.[6] Central to that notion is the conception of a major dividing line built into the actual structure of the universe, a line traced precisely by the sphere of the moon. Above that line all is conceived to be permanent, impassible, not subject to change. There "aether" is in place of air and there are those eternal bodies, the stars and planets. None of the four elements is there at all. But beneath the moon, all is different. Here are the four elements in their endless shuffle of combinations and recombinations, here is the world of generation and corruption, of mutability, of impermanence, the world of *becoming*.

Such a conception was long in disappearing from men's thoughts. Galileo, for instance, was still concerned to get rid of it as one of the greatest obstacles to the advance of his new science of the heavens. Typically, this great dividing line in the regions above bore with it a symbolic value as well — indeed it was because of this that Galileo found it so difficult to dispel. There were religious overtones to the notion; man and man's proper destiny were involved. Man is born into this lower sublunar realm, this transitory region of generation and corruption where earth is. But will man be content to stay here below, where nothing abides, where flux itself is the only constant condition, where all is a becoming? Can happiness be found in this lower region of impermanence? Or must man not seek to rise above this lower sublunar place, rise up to permanence and the changeless which is above and beyond the moon?

Ancient philosophy had been rather unanimous in its answer to the question. One thinks first of all of the Platonic myth which had insisted on the desirability of such an ascent to "being" out of "becoming," and in this Augustine would find his Plato and the Platonists to be so near his Christian truth. The Stoics also had agreed, stressing the notion that the wise man through *virtue* ("O donna di virtù") will rise above the lower realm of Fortune where all is mutability.[7] And we may think of Aristotle's decision that man must seek to live a life of contemplation, which life is above the human.

Seen in and through this line of thought, it is evident that the verses spoken by Virgil to Beatrice serve simply to declare who she is. They give her a name. She must be Contemplation, in some sense, since only in contemplation can we ascend beyond, to the region where "divine things" are. And Beatrice's role in the poem, as we later know, confirms this. In fact, what Beatrice actually does, her role as later revealed, is the best possible gloss to Virgil's words. Dante rises with Beatrice to those spheres which lie above the moon, where no change is. That realm is somehow Beatrice's, being the area through which she serves as guide.

Below the line of the moon's sphere is Fortune's realm. And this is a point not to be overlooked, as we consider Virgil's words to Beatrice in their immediate context in the poem. There is a familiar opposition in the pair of terms, "contemplation" and "fortune," attaching precisely to the notion of the sublunar as that region where Fortune holds sway. And we must note that such an opposition is rather clearly suggested by Beatrice's words to Virgil which speak of the man to be rescued as "l'amico mio e non della ventura." *Ventura* means "fortune," and in the context of Beatrice's words there is the merest suggestion that *ventura* here means Fortune personified. Thus one lady, Beatrice, is claiming this man as hers and, in her desire to save him, spurns any claim that a rival lady, Fortune, might have on him.

Dante had already written of such a figure as Beatrice here appears in terms of Virgil's recognition. Her name in the *Convivio* was not Beatrice, it was Filosofia and Sapienza, and in that pair of names we recognize already something of the ambiguity which we now must note in the figure of Beatrice in the *Comedy*. In the earlier work, this Lady Philosophy, who is also Sapienza, bears, with the latter name, a burden of Christian meaning extending quite beyond the scope of a Lady Philosophy as known to the ancients or as represented by Boethius. Only, in the *Convivio*, no clear distinction is drawn between what Christian theology knows as *uncreated wisdom* on the one hand, and as *created wisdom* on the other. But such a treatment, in any case, is quite in line with a tradition originating in those very Sapiential books of Scripture which give rise to this figure of a "lady," a Sapientia personified, who is somehow to be identified with Christ who is Himself Sapientia.[8]

In the *Comedy* clearer lines of distinction are drawn in this respect, as we have already seen in various perspectives and patterns of meaning. In the figure of Beatrice as she is in the *Comedy* we come finally to see that we confront a lady who, in allegory, is *created* Sapienza, bearing through analogy a relation and resemblance to that uncreated Sapienza who is Christ. Yet such meanings do not attach to Beatrice until Virgil has quit the scene of the action; whereas, when Beatrice comes to Virgil in Limbo, we see her through his eyes (since he is reporting the event there), we know her in his perspective and *by his light*. Virgil's is the perspective of ancient thought which did not know Christ; Virgil sees by the natural light and does not therefore see Beatrice in meanings which are peculiarly Christian. To Virgil, Beatrice is that lady through whom alone man ascends to the realm above the moon, she is Philosophy or Contemplation. But to him she is not and cannot be Sapientia in the Christian sense, nor Grace, names and notions unknown to him. In these aspects of meaning she is revealed to us only when Virgil is no longer there to see her.

We have to do here, in short, with the matter of Virgil's having a perspective in the poem and of the poem "seeing" with him. When we see Beatrice through his eyes we see her within the limits of his awareness as a pagan, in terms which in no way exceed the frame of an ancient *pagan* notion. Indeed, must we not also note that Virgil's "point of view" is respected by Beatrice herself when, addressing him in Limbo, she refers to the man to be helped as "l'amico mio e non della ventura?" The realm of Fortune is the whole sublunar region; Contemplation is the means, the sole means, according to Aristotle, of rising above her realm. It is a manner of speaking, a way of phrasing which a Virgil might be expected to understand. In this way, Beatrice (since she speaks first) is already telling Virgil who she is, helping him to recognize her, as he does forthwith.

We may not say that Virgil is unaware that Beatrice transcends his limits of vision and of understanding. More than once he will bring an argument to a point beyond which he cannot discern and thereupon will refer it on to Beatrice, since it is a "matter of faith." Virgil knows his limitations now, in all such respects, as he could not have known them in life. Yet he actually *sees* Beatrice only once, in Limbo, and when he does, he knows her in terms which hold to the limits of what was known of such a lady by the natural light, before Christ's advent.

*   *   *

Sapientia aequivoca est. St. Thomas had had occasion to make the point many times.[9] It all depends on the point of view from which we may happen to speak. That is, we may see with an Aristotle, and we may thus conceive of man's highest activity, whether we call it contemplation or speculation, as an ascent of the mind to the knowledge of divine things. But if we do so speak, we must not forget that this knowledge of divine things is only such as can be had by the natural light. Man has such knowledge through things, as we have been told, knowing God by the things which are made, rising through them to a sphere above the human: a *trasumanar* which is "natural." The movement, even though it does attain to regions "above the human," is never more than a movement out of a purely human center, is always by man's natural powers and within the proportion of his nature. Such is speculation or contemplation, according to the philosophers; such is Wisdom as they knew it.

Then, there is Wisdom in the Christian view which they did not know. And the first and most searching test of the difference between the two is the matter of the source or origin of each of them. Sapientia, on the Christian view, is something *given*, first of all. It is a gift of God, of a personal Christian God, it descends from above. By it is man uplifted, even as by grace. Indeed, there is no clear way, ultimately, of distinguishing between this Wisdom and the Grace which sanctifies. Charity will be present, in any case, as will all the other *infused* virtues. *Sapientia* is thus one of the ways by which God may be present in a rational creature. As such, Wisdom is something which is *created*, and is a participation, on the part of the creature, in that uncreated Wisdom which is the Son. There are, one sees, sound theological reasons why a Beatrice who comes as created Wisdom, *de sursum descendens*, should reveal such a resemblance to Christ as she does reveal.[10]

What further distinguishes Wisdom, in this Christian sense, from anything which the pagan philosophers could have known, is something again which is given representation in Dante's poem. Aristotle had not conceived that *love* would enter into the ascent of speculation. Contemplation, for him, is a matter of pure intellection; the affective part of man is not really thought of as primarily engaged in it. Thus it matters very much here again, as St. Thomas so frequently points out, whether we are speaking according to the Philosopher or according to Christian theology, because Sapientia in the Christian conception touches the will and the affective life most profoundly. Such, of course, is bound to be the case, since Christian Wisdom is always attended by charity and the other virtues, even those *infused* virtues of the active life, as Aristotle's contemplation is not.[11]

One readily sees from this how Sapientia, in the Christian sense, must be one of the names which Beatrice can bear in allegory. Indeed it would appear to be the one name which can do most justice to her when she comes in triumph at the summit of the mountain. Beatrice *descends* to that place, she is a light given from beyond the bounds of nature. She is also a *love* descending and given from beyond. A conversion takes place with her advent and an elevation of man's nature to a dignity which makes him acceptable (*gratum*) to God. Through her a man becomes again an "adopted son" of God.[12] This it is which sets Christian Sapientia at such far remove from the pagan conception. In the ascent of the mind in contemplation, on Aristotle's view (or on Plato's, for that matter) God does not adopt the man who "rises above."

On passing from Virgil's guidance to Beatrice, the wayfarer leaves a natural light to attain to a light grace. But the noteworthy point is this: Beatrice is beheld according to one and then the other light, in the poem. *Contemplatio aequivoca est.* The poem is seen to agree with St. Thomas in this, and provides for the equivocation in its very structure. There is on the one hand the contemplation of the "philosophers," by the natural light, the ascent by natural powers; and there is, on the other, the contemplation of the "saints" by the light of faith, the ascent made possible by a power (*virtù*) which comes from above the human. In the poem the wayfarer moves from the first to the second in moving from Virgil to Beatrice.

But what shall we make of this transition in yet another sense? Must we think that contemplation by the natural light *ceases* when that by faith and grace takes over? Does the first movement end where the second begins? Does the light of grace do away with the light which is natural? In the allegory it might seem so. Virgil's guidance does end, Virgil leaves the scene of the action. Virgil had led to justice, to "Leah" in a certain sense, as to a justice which prepares for contemplation, for sister Rachel beyond. But if Virgil's justice is that which is according to the philosophers, must not the "sister" contemplation for which it prepares be of the same order, contemplation by the natural light? Or is the pattern simply not maintained in this respect?

Such questions may be taken to St. Thomas for their answers, and these will be such as Dante himself would surely have given. In fact, there is *one* answer, and every student of Thomas knows how large it is written into his philosophy: *gratia non tollit naturam sed perficit*, grace does not abolish nature but perfects it.[13] And we have only to bring this principle to bear on the allegory of Dante's poem to understand what the meaning must be when at the summit a Contemplation comes which is that of grace and not that of the natural light. We must see that the dream of Rachel and Leah is fulfilled in Christian terms with Beatrice's advent, when Virgil is gone. But the light by which Virgil had guided is not thereby swept away. It remains, it is perfected. Virgil leads to a justice which the philosophers had discerned and he leads no further. Then beyond the stream, with Beatrice, come the four virtues which are the true perfection of the active life, that is, true justice. A Leah who is *perfected* Leah thus comes with Beatrice.

So must it be with contemplation. The Beatrice who actually comes at the summit does not deny the Beatrice recognized by Virgil in Limbo; nor, in fulfilling the dream, does she deny the "natural" Rachel who would be the sister of a Leah known by the natural light. The Beatrice who comes as the goal at the top of the mountain simply perfects the Beatrice recognized by Virgil; and perfects the Rachel forecast by the dream, even as the light of grace perfects the natural light. In Beatrice there comes a Wisdom which includes Lady Philosophy but transcends that Lady by being her perfection.

Notes

1. On this whole matter of the distinction betwen the acquired and the infused virtues, see below, Ch. X. For the four cardinal virtues attending Beatrice in her allegorical meaning of "Wisdom," see Wisd. 8.7: "Et si justitiam quis diligit, labores huius magnas habent virtutes: sobrietatem enim et prudentiam docet, et justitiam et virtutem."

2. *Convivio* III, xiv, 15: "Per le quali tre virtudi si sale a filosofare a quelle Atene celestiali, dove gli Stoici e Peripatetici e Epicurii, per la luce de la veritade etterna, in uno volere concordevolmente concorrono."

3. On this particular point the following remarks by Aquinas are most relevant (*In III Sent.* d. xxiii, q. 1, a. 4, sol. 3): "In omnibus quae agunt propter finem oportet esse inclinationem ad finem, et quamdam inchoationem finis: alias nunquam operarentur propter finem. Finis autem ad quem divina largitas hominem ordinavit vel praedestinavit, scilicet fruitio sui ipsius, est omnino supra facultatem naturae creatae elevatus. . . . Unde per naturalia tantum homo non habet sufficienter inclinationem ad illum finem; et ideo oportet quod superaddatur homini aliquid per quod habeat inclinationem in finem illum, sicut per naturalia habet inclinationem in finem sibi connaturalem: et ista superaddita dicuntur virtutes theologicas ex tribus. — Primo quantum ad objectum; quia cum finis ad quem ordinati sumus, sit ipse Deus, inclinatio quae praeexigitur consistit in operatione quae est circa ipsum Deum. Secundo quantum ad causam: quia sicut ille finis est a Deo nobis ordinatus non per naturam nostram, ita inclinationem in finem operatur in nobis solus Deus: et sic dicuntur virtutes theologicas, quasi a solo Deo in nobis creatae. Tertio quantum ad cognitionem naturae, inclinatio in finem non potest per naturalem rationem cognosci, sed per revelationem divinam: et ideo dicuntur theologicae, quia divino sermone sunt nobis manifestatae: *unde philosophi nihil de eis cognoverunt.*" (Italics mine.)

4. *De Cons. Phil.* I, pr. 3.

5. That "Philosophy" and "Sapientia" are interchangeable as names for the Lady is evident throughout the *Convivio*. See in particular III. xi. 5 and Aquinas, *Comm. Metaph.* I, lect. 3, no. 56: "Cum enim antiqui studio sapientiae insistentes sophistae, idest sapientes, vocarentur, Pythagoras, interrogatus quid se esse profiteretur, noluit se sapientem nominare sicut sui antecessores, quia hoc praesumptuosum videbatur esse, sed vocavit se philosophum, id est amatorem sapientiae. Et exinde nomen sapientis immutatum est in nomen philosophi et nomen sapientiae in nomen philosophiae."

6. See J. Carcopino, *Virgile et le mystère de la IVe eglogue* (Paris, 1930), p. 82: "Dès le premier tiers du premier siècle av. J.-C., les doctrines du néopythagorisme sur les générations humaines et le destin des âmes s'étaient amplement propagées, grâce surtout à l'enseignement de Posidonius d'Apamée

(135-51 av. J.-C.). En établissant une distinction radicale entre l'Autre et l'Un, c'est à dire entre la Nature et Dieu, entre le monde sublunaire, qui est le domaine de la nature, et le monde éthéré, où baignent les astres, qui est le lieu de l'Unité divine; puis, en affirmant que l'âme immortelle émane de Dieu et préexiste à la Nature dans laquelle il s'incorpore, Posidonius a réhabilité le dualisme de Pythagore au centre du Portique, et professé à son tour que les âmes tombent du ciel dans la génération, pour remonter ensuite, selon le *credo* de la secte, vers les sphères éternelles, leur patrie divine. . . . Le dogme avait circulé déjà chez les auteurs qui ont immédiatement précédé Virgile."

7. Cicero, *De Re Publ.* VI, 17, 17: "Infra autem lunam nihil est nisi mortale et caducum, praeter animos deorum hominum generi datos, supra lunam sunt aeterna omnia." Macrobius is one of the most important spokesmen for this notion, of course. See further notes on this point in the *Seventy-fourth Annual Report of the Dante Society* (Cambridge, Mass., 1956), pp. 36-38.

8. Aquinas, *Summa c. G.* IV, 9: "Quod autem dicitur sapientia *esse creata*: primo quidem potest intelligi, non de Sapientia quae est Filius Dei, sed de sapientia quam Deus indidit creaturis."

See also Augustine, *Confessions* XII, 15.

9. Typically, in *In Sent. III* d. xxxv, q. 2, a. 1: "Utrum sapientia sit donum," one finds the "objection" stated so: "Praeterea nullum donum habetur per acquisitionem. Sed sapientia habetur per acquisitionem; quia Philosophus Philosophiam primam sapientiam nominat, quae per doctrinam habetur. Ergo sapientia non est donum." The reply to this is to be noted for the particular distinction: "Aequivocatio est in sapientia, ut dictum est." For a slightly fuller statement, see *Summa Theol.* II–II, q. 45, a. 1, for instance, in a "reply" (ad 2): "Sapientia quae ponitur donum Spiritus Sancti differt ab ea quae ponitur virtus intellectualis acquisita. Nam illa acquiritur studio humano; haec autem est 'de sursum descendens,' ut dicitur Jac. III, 15. Similiter et differt a fide. Nam fides assentit veritati divinae secundum seipsam, sed iudicium quod est secundum veritatem divinam pertinet ad donum sapientiae. Et ideo donum sapientiae praesupponit fidem quia 'unusquique bene iudicat quae cognoscit,' ut dicitur in I Ethic."

The verse in James 3 reads: "Non est enim ista sapientia de sursum descendens, sed terrena, animalis, diabolica."

10. Beatrice, as *goal* at the summit, as *happiness*, and as *Sapientia*, can be seen in all such aspects through such statements in theology as the following, Aquinas, *Summa c. G.* III, 50: "In quo etiam satis apparet quod in nullo alio quaerenda est ultima felicitas quam in operatione intellectus: cum nullum desiderium tam in sublime ferat sicut desiderium intelligendae veritatis. Omnia namque nostra desideria vel delectationis, vel cuiuscumque alterius quod ab homine desideratur, in aliis rebus quiescere possunt: desiderium autem praedictum non quiescit nisi ad summum rerum cardinem et factorem Deum pervenerit. Propter quod convenienter Sapientia dicit, *Eccli.* XXIV, 7: 'Ego in altissimis habitavi et thronus meus in columna nubis.' Et *Proverb.* IX dicitur quod 'Sapientia per ancillas suas vocat ad arcem.' Erubescant igitur qui felicitatem hominis, tam altissime sitam, in infimis rebus quaerunt."

Both quotations from Scripture here are most relevant, for Beatrice is, after all, on the high summit, she appears in a cloud (of flowers), and her *ancelle* (the virtues) "invite" to her, bringing Dante to her.

On Wisdom as participation in the uncreated Wisdom (and Charity as such), see Aquinas, *Summa Theol.* II–II, q. 23, a. 2, ad 1: "Ipsa essentia divina caritas est, sicut et sapientia est et bonitas est. Unde sicut dicimur boni bonitate quae est Deus, et sapientes sapientia quae est Deus, quia bonitas qua formaliter boni sumus est participatio quaedam divinae bonitatis, et sapientia qua formaliter sapientes sumus est participatio quaedam divinae sapientiae."

11. On the essential distinction, see Aquinas, *Summa Theol.* II–II, q. 19, a. 7, resp.: "Cum autem sapientia sit cognitio divinorum . . . aliter consideratur a nobis et aliter a philosophis. Quia enim vita nostra ad divinam fruitionem ordinatur et dirigitur secundum quandam participationem divinae naturae, quae est per gratiam; sapientia secundum nos non solum consideratur ut est cognoscitiva Dei, sicut apud philosophos; sed etiam ut est directiva humanae vitae, quae non solum dirigitur secundum rationes humanas, sed etiam secundum rationes divinas, ut patet per Augustinum, XII *De Trin.*"

Or one may note, on this same point, the distinctions as stated by Alexander of Hales (*Summa Theol.*, Introd., q. 1, cap. 1): "Theologia igitur, quae perficit animam secundum affectionem, movendo ad bonum per principia timoris et amoris, proprie et principaliter est sapientia. Prima Philosophia, quae est theologia philosophorum, quae est de causa causarum, sed ut perficiens cognitionem secundum viam artis et ratiocinationis, minus proprie dicitur sapientia. Ceterae vero scientiae, quae sunt de causis consequentibus et causatis, non debent dici sapientiae, sed scientiae. — Unde secundum hoc dicendum quod doctrina theologiae est sapientia ut sapientia; philosophia vero prima, quae est cognitio primarum causarum, quae sunt bonitas, sapientia et potentia, est sapientia sed ut scientia."

Or see Aquinas, *In III Sent.* d. xxxv, q. 2, a. 1, sol. 3: "Sapientiae donum eminentiam cognitionis habet, per quamdam unionem ad divina, quibus non unimur nisi per amorem, ut qui adhaeret Deo, sit unus spiritus cum eo. . . . Et ideo sapientiae donum dilectionem quasi principium praesupponit, et sic in affectione est. Sed quantum ad essentiam, in cognitione est."

12. Aquinas, *Super Epist. S. Pauli* 703–4, on the verse, "Quos praescivit conformis fieri imaginis Filii eius, hos praedestinavit": "Praedestinavit nos in adoptionem filiorum Dei. Primo quidem in iure participandae haereditatis, sicut supra dictum est v. 17: 'si filii et haeredes, haeredes quidem Dei, cohaeredes autem Christi.' Secundo, in participatione splendoris ipsius. Ipse enim est genitus a patre tamquam splendor gloriae eius, Hebr. I, 3. Unde per hoc quod sanctos illuminat de lumine sapientiae et gratiae, facit eos fieri conformes sibi." See also his *Summa Theol.* II–II, q. 45, a. 6, resp.

13. The axiom, so frequently repeated in Aquinas, comes in the *Summa Theol.* near the beginning (I, q. 1, a. 8, ad 2): "Utitur tamen sacra doctrina etiam ratione humana, non quidem ad probandum fidem, quia per hoc tolleretur meritum fidei, sed ad manifestandum aliqua alia quae traduntur in hac doctrina. Cum igitur gratia non tollat naturam, sed perficiat, oportet quod naturalis ratio subserviat fidei, sicut et naturalis inclinatio voluntatis obsequitur caritati. Unde et Apostolus dicit, *II ad Cor.* X, 5: 'In captivitatem redigentes omnem intellectum in obsequium Christi.' Et inde est quod etiam auctoritatibus philosophorum sacra doctrina utitur, ubi per rationem nat-

uralem veritatem cognoscere potuerunt; sicut Paulus, *Act.* XVII, 28, inducit verbum Arati, dicens: 'sicut et quidam poetarum vestrorum dixerunt, genus Dei sumus.' " A passage in the Commentary on Boethius (*In Boetium de Trin.* q. 2, a. 3) is even more closely relevant to this point as it applies to the allegory of the *Comedy*: "Dona gratiarum hoc modo naturae adduntur quod eam non tollunt, sed magis perficiunt; unde et lumen fidei quod nobis gratis infunditur, non destruit lumen naturalis cognitionis nobis naturaliter inditum. Quamvis autem lumen naturale lumen mentis humane sit insufficiens ad manifestationem eorum quae per fidem manifestantur, tamen impossibile est quod ea quae per fidem nobis traduntur divinitus sint contraria his quae per naturam nobis sint indita: oportet enim alterum esse falsum, et cum utramque sit nobis a Deo, Deus esset nobis auctor falsitatis, quod est impossibile; sed magis cum imperfectis inveniantur aliqua imitatio perfectorum, quamvis imperfecta, in his quae per naturalem rationem cognoscuntur, sunt quaedam similitudines eorum quae per fidem tradita sunt. Sicut autem sacra doctrina fundatur super lumen fidei, ita philosophia super lumen naturale rationis; unde impossibile est quod ea quae sunt philosophiae sint contraria eis quae sunt fidei, sed deficiunt ab eis." Moreover, in view of the evident fact that Beatrice, when attained, represents a first *beatitude* attained in the journey, such statements as the following in the *Summa Theol.* (I. q. 62, a. 7, resp.) should be noted: "Manifestum est autem quod natura ad beatitudinem comparatur sicut primum ad secundum; quia beatitudo naturae additur. Semper autem oportet salvari primum in secundo. Unde oportet quod natura salvetur in beatitudine. Et similiter oportet quod in actu beatitudinis salvetur actus naturae."

PART TWO · RETURN TO EDEN

Chapter IX

A Lament for Eden

And the Lord God planted a garden eastward in Eden and there he put the man whom he had formed. Where is eastward? Where on this earth was Eden planted? At least the words *ad orientem* gave a relative indication, however vague. But to make the matter still more uncertain, the Vulgate version eliminated even those words, preferring *a principio* in their place; and thus even that particular pointer to the direction in which Eden lay disappeared from the Latin Bible.[1]

There were, to be sure, other pointers left in the text of Genesis which one might have thought would help in determining the location of the Garden, if Eden might indeed be thought to continue to exist on this earth. According to all versions of the text, four streams flowed out of Eden from a single source, and the names of two of these streams were those of the familiar pair, Tigris and Euphrates. Furthermore we read that the Tigris flowed toward the Assyrians. Now these two rivers and the region around and between them had long been known to topographers, yet no Garden of Eden had been found thereabout. It was known, moreover, that the two rivers did not rise from a single source. What then could the answer be to the puzzling question? St. Augustine, for one, had been perplexed by this, but had happily come up with what seemed a plausible answer, and one which, on his authority, became generally the accepted one. The four streams of Eden, he thought, must indeed rise from a single source, since the text of Genesis is quite clear on this. But if Eden is situated in some remote unexplored region of the earth (and so it must be, since no man had yet found it), then we should conceive that the Tigris and Euphrates, as we know them (as well as the Nile and Ganges, which Augustine took the other two rivers to be), must flow out from the Garden and then pass somehow underground to come up again where we know them in fact to rise, at what may thus appear to us to be their several separate sources.[2] It is evident that Augustine not only holds that Eden once had real physical existence, but also tends to believe that somewhere on this earth Eden must still exist. Indeed, the attempts of Philo and Origen to read the whole account of Genesis as allegory, and in that way to place in question the reality of the Garden, were met and adequately answered by Augustine in his treatise *De Genesi ad Litteram*.[3]

The remarks of St. Thomas Aquinas on the location of the terrestrial paradise may be taken as representative of opinions generally held by Dante's time:

> The situation of paradise is shut off from the habitable world by mountains or seas or some torrid region which cannot be crossed; and so people who have written about topogaphy make no mention of it.[4]

But if Eden continued to exist somewhere on the face of the earth, a further question could be asked respecting this, the question *why*. Why should this be, since we know that Adam and Eve were expelled from the Garden following their sin, and that Eden would thus be an uninhabited and therefore useless place? For this "doubt" there were also answers; and again the one Aquinas found, to precisely such an objection as this, can serve to represent them:

Paradise did not become useless through being unoccupied by man after sin, just as immortality was not conferred on man in vain, though he was to lose it. For thereby we learn God's kindness to man, and what man lost by sin. Moreover some say that Enoch and Elias still dwell in that Paradise.[5]

The relevance of such pronouncements as these to Dante's conception of Eden and its location on the globe is evident. The poet, too, would have it that the Garden was still in existence, at least as late as the year 1300, and with every prospect and promise of being there for a much longer time. His Eden, moreover, is inhabitated, though not by that immortal pair named by St. Thomas. And Dante, too, would have held, indeed did hold (in the way of poets), that Eden continued to exist "for the sake of signifying." Precisely what it did, in that sense, was to point to "God's kindness to man and what man lost by sin," if we may recall and fix in our minds the words of St. Thomas just noted. But that Dante did this we shall see better only after some further examination of his whole treatment of the subject.

To take yet another example of notions commonly held regarding the location of the terrestrial paradise and the nature of things therein, the opinion of Peter Lombard may be chosen as typical; and one turns to him in particular, among the many who might be cited, with the thought of the many times his words were studied and glossed by the theologians who came after him.

Wherefore some hold that the paradise is in an eastward region, separated from the regions that are inhabited by man by a long interjacent expanse either of sea or of land, and situated in a lofty place reaching all the way to the circle of the moon: wherefore the waters of the flood did not reach there.[6]

There were some who could not accept as a literal truth the latter point respecting the high altitude of Eden. And yet a dissenter could find some reason in such a belief, since the opinion did in fact reflect a truth respecting the condition of that place. Thus Albertus Magnus allows this notion of Eden's lofty situation to enter into his *Summa* as an opinion to be rejected, then proceeds, with a note of obvious caution, to express his dissent thus:

Respecting the next point, it may be said (always allowing for some better judgment in this) that Paradise in its altitude does not reach to the lunar sphere, but is said to reach there in participating in the properties of the moon. That is, from the moon upward is the fifth essence which, as the natural philosophers say, is a region of incorruption and of immortality . . . no clouds are there, nor rain, nor thunder, nor anything of the like. But immediately beneath the moon begins the sphere of what is active and passive. And in respect to these properties, paradise is said to reach all the way to the sphere of the moon. For in paradise nothing is mortal, nothing corruptible, nothing tempestuous: and in so far as paradise partakes of these properties it is said to reach to the lunar globe, not because of the altitude of the place. I say this however without prejudice to a better judgment, because in certain very old books I have found that the first author of the above opinion, which is attributed to Bede and Strabo, was the apostle Thomas, namely, that paradise is of such an altitude that it reaches to the globe of the moon.[7]

Again, as with Thomas, we note Albert's thought of the immortality of things in Eden coming into the context of such speculations with a kind of inevitability. As for this particular opinion of Albert's, it must strike a reader of Dante as being very close to the poet's conception. Dante, in fact, agrees with Albert. His Eden is not so high as to reach to the moon, yet it has about it those qualities that are properly assigned to the lunar and translunar region of the universe. It is situated on a lofty place, on what must surely be the highest mountain peak on the earth. Moreover, the one who comes there in Eden to meet him and to guide him upward beyond the moon is that Beatrice whom Virgil, when she had come to him in Limbo, had recognized at once as that "Lady of virtue through whom alone mankind ascends above that heaven which has its circlings least," [8] i.e., the moon. Thus, when he has "returned" to Eden, Dante begins in some sense to participate in that condition which man had enjoyed there before the Fall: the experience of immortal things, of what is above the realm of generation and corruption. In the Garden everywhere are the signs of immortality, of what does not fall into decay. Here, as in the region above the moon, the warring of the elements ceases. There is no disturbance even in the weather, and the gentle morning breeze which Dante feels against his face is "sanza mutamento in se." [9]

In his depiction of the terrestrial paradise, its nature and its whereabouts, Dante has paid his respects to an established body of opinion, and this is a fact certainly of no surprise to us. His Eden is therefore situated in a remote part of the earth, atop the highest mountain and "with a long interjacent stretch of water," as Peter Lombard had it, separating it from the regions inhabited by man. In fact, in the geography of the *Comedy*, Eden is literally as remote as may be from the inhabited part of the earth, if we take the measure of its distance from what was held to be the center of that region. That center is Jerusalem, and for this there was good Scriptural authority.[10] Eden, moreover, in Dante's conception, is located in a "southern" hemisphere of water, as distinguished from a "northern" hemisphere of land. Eden, indeed, is at the exact center of its hemisphere, even as Jerusalem is at the center of the other. Thus the mountain which has Eden on its summit is directly opposite Jerusalem on the globe of the earth.

In "finding" Eden situated in such perfect antipodal balance to Jerusalem, the poet's eye was no doubt delighted with the order that was thus apparent not only in the geography of the earth, as God in His wisdom had established it, but in man's history and in the drama of salvation as well. In this way Eden, the place of man's first happy condition of perfect righteousness and of his first sin, could be seen to be counterbalanced on the other side of the earth, as in a great pair of scales, by Jerusalem, that place of man's redemption from his first sin and of righteousness restored.[11] And an even greater wealth of meaning could be seen in this whole picture if one might think that Satan, when he fell headlong from Heaven, fell in fact on the southern side of the globe, causing the earth to shrink back from him and producing, as by displacement, this very mountain of Eden as well as the hemisphere of water all about it.[12] There is thus "measure, number and weight"[13] even in the drama of man's sin and salvation, which for Dante is synonymous with man's history. And such things can all be seen to be "for the sake of signifying."

It can easily occur to us to think, in the matter of such symmetry and perfect balance on the grandest scale, that a poet was here simply making use of that margin of freedom left him by a tradition which had managed to locate Eden only in the vaguest way. Yet if one reads further in the traditional exegesis of the Book of Genesis, some doubt may well come as to whether Dante's locating of Eden directly opposite Jerusalem is, in fact, an instance of a poet's indulgence in the freedom left him in this sense. That doubt can indeed arise when we note that no less an exegete of Genesis than St. Augustine had understood the sacred text to affirm that when Adam was expelled from Eden for his sin he was placed "opposite" Eden. However, since any excursion into this particular point or further speculation along this line could well seem an instance not unfamiliar in Dante studies of an erudition quite without relevance to Dante's poem, it is necessary first to consider certain verses of the *Comedy* which such a fact might possibly serve to clarify.

*   *   *

The verses in question have proved to be among the most perplexing of the whole poem. They come at the beginning of the second canticle; and, however dimly we may glimpse their meaning, it is clear that they give voice to a lament respecting four stars, which Dante looks up to see for the first time in that southern hemisphere where Eden is:

> I' mi volsi a man destra, e puosi mente
> all'altro polo, e vidi quattro stelle
> non viste mai fuor ch'alla prima gente.
> Goder pareva il ciel di lor fiammelle:
> oh settentrional vedovo sito,
> poi che privato se' di mirar quelle!
>
> *Purgatorio* I, 22–27.

I turned to the right and attended to the other pole and saw four stars never seen except by the first people. The heavens seemed to rejoice in their shining: Oh northern widowed clime since thou art deprived of seeing them!

From vantage points further along in the poem itself we are made certain (as we shall see) that these four stars are, in their allegorical meaning, the four cardinal virtues. But what these six verses may mean in allegorical terms is a question that should wait until their literal meaning has been examined. It is always well to begin at the level of the literal sense (even as Dante himself advised us to do) [14] to see just how much meaning can be had on that level.

The sense of the first of these two terzine comes clear at once on the literal level if we but keep in mind the situation of Eden in Dante's geography, as well as the outline of his journey. In his journey at this point, Dante has been brought by Virgil from the bottom of the pit of Hell where Satan is, having gone first down, then up, on the very body of the Demon, passing through the center of the earth, to come forth on its surface and to see the stars again in the half-light preceding dawn. Dante and Virgil step out of the dark passageway to stand on the lowest slope of the mountain island of Purgatory which bears Eden on its summit. These southern skies, therefore, and these four "holy" stars, look down on Eden, and were thus most certainly visible to those who dwelt there, the "prima gente" of these verses. What must strike the attention particularly is the emphatic insistence that these stars were never seen by any excepting the "prima gente." The "mai che" is all-exclusive: "never seen except by the first people." Of course we must conceive at once that there is, in this moment at least, one exception to this sweeping affirmation, that being Dante himself. We realize too that the souls in Purgatory who may also look up at these same stars do not count. The statement has reference only to the living, and Dante is indeed the unique exception known to us (from the poem) — unless it be Ulysses.[15] Who else among the living had ever passed this way before? Not Aeneas, who descended to the nether regions of Hades and Elysian fields; not St. Paul, who was caught up to Heaven.[16] Dante is the first living man to see these stars since the "first people" saw them here in this southernmost quarter of the sky. But Dante is such an exception that he does not count either in this statement. The verse means that no living human beings ever saw these stars except those who may be counted as the "first people."

Then comes that emphatic note of poignant lament in the second terzina, a note pulling strongly, almost irresistibly, in the direction of the allegorical. For, clearly, four stars such as these

may be ever so beautiful as stars, yet the lament that comes here
is too forceful and too all-engulfing to find a sufficient justification
in that fact alone. We note that two words bear the burden of the
sentiment of this lament following the first signal of the exclama-
tory "Oh!" These are the two words "privato" and "vedovo."
These indeed are the words that alone make this unmistakably a
lament. Immediately there comes, at the sight of these four stars,
the thought of a privation, of a bereavement. It must be that there
has been a loss somehow of something most precious. Again, with
that thought, it is hard not to pass to the question of an allegorical
meaning and to say, or try to say, what that something might be,
in terms other than literal. Still it is well to press the question
further, as far as it may be taken in strictly literal terms, keeping
in mind all the while the central affirmation here and the basis it
gives to the lament: that only a "first people" was ever privileged
to look upon these four stars. Holding, thus, to the essential frame
of the literal sense, we may come to that point in St. Augustine's
reading of Genesis that would seem to promise some illumination
of our way.

However, and to repeat, one must be certain of having one's
bearings here in that literal way. We must have clearly in mind
that, in the geography of the poem, the mountain on which Eden
is situated is in the exact center of the "southern" hemisphere of
water and is directly antipodal to Jerusalem; that anyone, therefore, standing on this island that lies so far to the south (somewhere, say, in our South Pacific) may quite literally see stars that
are never visible to those who dwell in the northern hemisphere
of land, the "settentrional sito" of these verses. And since it is also
true, in Dante's geography, that all living human creatures now
dwell in the "settentrional sito," it evidently follows that the sight
of these particular stars near the "other" or south pole is denied
to all the living. The lament, then, in this sense is all-inclusive.
To address a "northern clime" means to address the whole human
race.

Now to attach to this "sito" or hemisphere thus directly addressed the adjective "settentrional," is to speak straightforwardly,
distinguishing it simply from the other, the "meridional sito," for

there are only two hemispheres, of course, and they divide between them the face of the earth. But we must note the other adjective "vedovo" in its position of stress, made the more evident by the fact that the whole following verse comes as a clause in direct dependence on that adjective, in order to account for it: "O northern *widowed* clime," widowed, that is, "since (i.e. because) thou art deprived of seeing those stars." And clearly the word of stress is a word of commiseration. The northern hemisphere is bereaved. It must be that the whole human race, we the living, are now deprived of something seen or had by those who lived, once upon a time, under these southern skies.

But does the lament envisage only a present situation and one merely geographical? Or does not the tone of "widowed" especially suggest questions of time as well as of space, history as well as geography? For an element of time most surely comes in with the note of a "prima gente." And if a "prima gente," that is, a people in a first time in history, were able to see these stars, that "people" must mean our first parents dwelling here in Eden, even if it means no one else. We begin to take stock of a meaning in historical terms; and we realize at once that, of course, there was a time, a *first* time, when what is now the northern inhabited hemisphere was itself an uninhabited region, and that (in the *very first* time) was when the entire human race consisted of two persons only, Adam and Eve in Eden. Whereas the situation now is exactly reversed as to man's habitation in one or the other hemisphere. Now the whole human race dwells only in the North, whence no eye could possibly see stars that lie as close as these four do to the southern pole. And now it is the southern hemisphere which is the "world without people," as Ulysses calls it.[17]

To come into this particular focus of meaning is to feel questions arise which the poet, alas, did not answer for us. Or should we cry "alas"? Was it not rather part of Dante's wisdom as poet to leave certain questions without direct explicit answers; indeed, to leave the questions unasked, for that matter, except for their latent presence by inference, as here at the beginning of the *Purgatorio*? The questions, in any event, are these: What happened to Adam and Eve when they were driven forth from

the Garden? Are we to think that they continued to live for some
time on the steep slopes of this mountain island? Or were they
somehow transferred to the hemisphere of land in the North
(which had been there since Satan's fall) [18] thus removed from
the southern hemisphere itself, which would mean, of course,
removed from the possibility of seeing these skies over Eden and
these stars? Questions of the kind may indeed appear so idle that
it would be embarrassing to put them into words if we did not
sense that they must and do arise when we try to understand
verses speaking of a "prima gente" and a northern hemisphere
that is "widowed" with respect to stars shining down on Eden.

Dante nowhere answered the questions. Therefore it is time to
come to that promised point in St. Augustine's reading of Genesis
which can so strongly suggest what Dante could well have held
to be the answers, out of a certain background conception of
these first events in human history which he would have felt
deserved the greatest credence.

*   *   *

St. Jerome had noted that, at the end of the third chapter of
Genesis, the Hebrew version was at variance with the Septuagint
version of that particular book of Scripture; or, at least, that the
latter offered a reading telling more about Adam and his expulsion
from Eden than did the Hebrew.[19] And because Jerome here as
elsewhere in his translation chose to accept the reading of the
Hebrew text, we know the last verse of that chapter of Genesis
in our Vulgate so:

> Ejecitque Adam, et collocavit ante paradisum voluptatis Cherubim
> et flammeum gladium atque versatilem ad custodiendam viam ligni
> vitae.

> And He thrust forth Adam and placed before the paradise of delight
> Cherubim and a flaming sword that turned, to keep the way of the
> tree of life.

Jerome's translation from the Hebrew version is literal. On the
other hand, the Septuagint version of Genesis at this point has a

fuller reading, one known in the West through the older translation of that Bible into Latin, the so-called *Vetus latina*:

> Et ejecit Adam, et collocavit eum contra paradisum voluptatis;
> et ordinavit Cherubim et flammeam romphaeam quae vertitur custo-
> dire viam ligni vitae.

> And He thrust Adam out and placed him opposite the paradise
> of delights and he established there Cherubim and a flaming weapon
> which turned to keep the way of the tree of life.

The two versions thus differ significantly only in what must
have appeared to Jerome to be a spurious interpolation by some
scribe: those words telling *where* the Lord had placed Adam
when he expelled him from the Garden. *Contra paradisum*, "opposite paradise." What would that mean anyway? Jerome rejected the words, with the result that their message is quite unfamiliar to most readers of Genesis. But for all Jerome's harsh
dealing with them, they are words that remained familiar to many
in the Middle Ages, and understandably: St. Augustine himself,
in his writings on Genesis, had chosen to follow, not Jerome's
version, but that which Jerome had rejected, the older Latin
translation from the Septuagint.[20] And we must conceive that even
if Augustine knew of Jerome's version,[21] he must still have preferred that older one, because to him it made good sense. These
words about Adam and how he was placed opposite Eden when
he was expelled therefrom were rich in meaning for Augustine.
They reported a fact, first of all, but the fact had in turn a
spiritual meaning. Augustine may be reading his Genesis according
to the letter, even as the title of his most famous treatise declares,
but he remains ever alert to meanings that go quite beyond the
letter, to facts that are both facts and are also "for the sake of
signifying." Thus, in that work of his, the *De Genesi ad Litteram*,
which was destined to become so well-known to the Western
Christian world and so authoritative, we find Augustine citing
the older Latin version and commenting on those words which
the Hebrew text did not offer:

> Et ejecit Adam et collocavit eum contra paradisum voluptatis. Et
> hoc significandi gratia factum est, sed tamen factum, ut contra para-

disum, quo beata vita etiam spiritaliter significabatur habitaret peccator utique in miseria.[22]

And He thrust Adam forth and placed him opposite the paradise of
delights. And this was done for the sake of signifying, and yet it
was done, that the sinner should live in misery opposite paradise,
by which the blessed life is signified also spiritually.

And elsewhere, in other works, Augustine comes back to that
same version of Genesis:

Propter hoc etiam de paradiso dimissus Adam, contra Eden habita-
vit, id est, contra sedem deliciarum: ut significaret quod in laboribus,
qui sunt deliciis contrarii, erudienda esset caro peccati, quae in
deliciis obedientiam non servavit antequam esset caro peccati.[23]

Furthermore, because of this Adam was driven from paradise and
lived opposite Eden, that is, opposite the place of delights, that it
might be signified that in labors, which are opposed to delights, the
flesh of sin should be instructed, which had not observed obedience
in the midst of delights and before it was the flesh of sin.

In this way, through Augustine's repeated use of the older
Latin translation of the Septuagint, it remained a matter of common knowledge [24] that Genesis affirmed that Adam, when he
was thrust from the Garden, was placed by God opposite Eden,
and that this signified placed "in misery"; for, on the authority of
Augustine's interpretation, this was done "for the sake of signifying," and "yet was done," and yet was literal historical fact. But
we are obliged to note that Augustine, though alert to protect
the literal and historical sense of Genesis, as is evident in that last
phrase, did nowhere remember to say just what *contra paradisum*
could mean actually, i. e. geographically, in a literal sense. Where
would such a place be anyway? It must have troubled Jerome and
helped him perhaps in his decision to delete the words and to
follow the "Hebrew truth" of his text.

All of which can suggest to the reader of Dante's poem that the
poet too was familiar with that text telling where Adam had been
placed after sin; and that Dante, as poet, simply made bold to say
where that place opposite Eden would be in literal geographical
fact. To be placed opposite Eden in his geography meant to be
placed in those Old Testament lands that have Jerusalem at their

center. For it is there, of course, that one conceives the unfolding of history to have taken place in the first times, following the Fall. Or better, to turn it around: If those regions of the northern hemisphere are in fact where one conceives the early progeny of our first parents to have lived and continued to sin until the Deluge, and if Adam was placed in those regions of the earth following his expulsion from Eden (and if not, then how did his progeny get there?), and if, furthermore, this meant *ipso facto* that Adam was thus placed "opposite Eden," then it must follow, in reverse, that Eden is directly opposite this region wherein sits Jerusalem, the holy city, "in medio gentium." Thus a poet's geography may be seen to rest after all on some authority, indeed on quite the best, on words in the Book of Genesis itself.

What I propose is evident: that the now generally forgotten words of the Septuagint version of Genesis not only account for that symmetrical balance in Dante's geography in which Eden is in fact directly "opposite" Jerusalem on the globe of the earth; but that those words may serve as the best gloss, and the gloss we have so much needed, on the verses at the beginning of the *Purgatorio* which carry the lament we have been noting. For why a lament? Because the focus is precisely upon the moment of the expulsion of Adam and Eve from Eden as a consequence and punishment of sin, the focus is therefore upon man's first sin and what was lost through sin. For Eve, of course, must be thought to be with Adam. These two alone therefore are meant by the words "prima gente," these two alone enjoyed the delights of the Garden and the sight of those four beautiful stars in the sky overhead and far to the south.

Then, when Adam and Eve were expelled from the Garden, they were placed, even as that text of Genesis affirmed, opposite Eden. A poet has chosen to construe this literally. Adam and Eve were immediately translated to the northern hemisphere, to a region somewhere in or about Palestine or Mesopotamia, shall we say; placed there in misery, as Augustine says. For dressed now in skins they must live by the sweat of their face and bring forth children in pain and sorrow. And neither they nor their children nor their children's children will ever again see those southern

skies or that Garden of delights. These shall remain things seen
only by the first couple when they themselves, though only two,
were the whole of the human race.

The placing of our first parents in a place opposite Eden was
due punishment for sin; and if they were deprived of delights,
that was a rightful consequence and deserved. There is good
reason for lament. Loss of Eden not only meant loss of a garden of
delights, it meant loss of something so precious that we have
almost forgotten that the human race was originally endowed
with it in Adam: immortality of the body and a perfect inner
rectitude. Rectitude is another name for justice in a special sense,
and immortality of the body was part of the total gift of justice
originally given to us in Adam. Immortality of the flesh was lost
through the first man's sin which is also ours, lost when Eden was
lost, and lost forever. We have already noticed how it was generally held that Eden was a place where all was immortal — like
the region above the moon. Loss of Eden means loss of immortality. Time and again those who meditate upon the fateful moment
of the expulsion come to focus centrally on that fact. And thus
the place "opposite" Eden is a place of mortality, being opposite.
We may heed Albertus Magnus on that point:

> For the necessity of dying requires a place in which there can be
> the necessity of dying, which could not be in paradise [Eden].
> Whence the ejection from paradise is a punishment added to the
> necessity of dying *and the two are considered as one*. [My italics.]
> And Augustine says that in punishment of that sin he was ejected
> from paradise into this place of miseries.[25]

We may note again in a "sed contra" of this same article that the
place of misery and the place of mortality are synonymous.[26]

The ejection from Eden and the necessity of dying are one and
the same thing. Thomas Aquinas had agreed when he maintained
that Eden, though now uninhabited, would still exist on this
earth: immortality or God's kindness to man is the thought that
comes immediately in that connection, and Eden continues to exist
to signify that. This being the case, it was not in vain that either
Eden or immortality was given to man, although he was to lose
them both.[27]

The lament of the verses in *Purgatory* over that northern clime which is widowed and deprived of the sight of these stars must be seen to focus essentially on the Fall and on loss of Eden, in terms which four stars can somehow represent. To be denied the sight of these is to be widowed and in a lamentable situation. And the human race ever since the Fall has found and finds itself so widowed and so situated. But if this be the meaning on the literal level, then, even as Augustine claimed for events and things told of in Genesis, those four stars are there "for the purpose of signifying," and yet "they are there," as he would have said, had Genesis made mention of them. But Genesis has nothing whatever to say of these stars in any of its versions. We must pass to the allegorical level to understand how a lament can arise at the thought that we shall never see those stars again.

Notes

1. The older Latin translation from the Septuagint had the reading *ad orientem*, and the new Vulgate from the Hebrew the reading *a principio*. See *Bibliorum Sacrorum Latinae Versiones Antiquae seu Vetus Italica, etc.*, ed. P. Sabatier (Reims, 1751). The reading *ad orientem*, however, remained familiar to the exegetical tradition generally. Augustine, *De Genesi ad Litteram* V, 4 (*PL* 34.325): "Nam utique postea plantavit Deus paradisum juxta orientem." See Jerome's remarks on the two readings, in *Liber Hebraicarum Quaestionum in Genesim*, PL 23.940. St. Thomas (*Summa Theol.* I, q. 102, a. 1, resp.) comments that it was fitting that the terrestrial paradise should be in the East. Cf. P. Lombard, *Liber II Sententiarum* d. xvii, ch. 5 (ed. Quaracchi): "Quod autem dicimus 'a principio' antiqua translatio dicit 'ad orientem.'" Also, among many others, Rabanus Maurus (*PL* 107.476).

2. Augustine, *De Genesi ad Litteram* VIII, 7 (*PL* 34.378): "An eo movebimur, quod de his fluminibus dicitur, aliorum esse fontes notos, aliorum autem prorsus incognitos, et ideo non posse accipi ad litteram, quod ex uno paradisi flumine dividuntur? cum potius credendum sit, quoniam locus ipse paradisi a cognitione hominum est remotissimus, inde quatuor aquarum partes dividi, sicut fidelissima Scriptura testatur; sed ea flumina, quorum fontes noti esse dicuntur, alicubi iisse sub terra, et post tractus prolixarum regionum loci aliis erupisse, ubi tamquam in suis fontibus nota esse perhibentur. Nam

hoc solere nonnullas aquas facere, quis ignorat? Sed ibi hoc scitur, ubi non diu sub terris currunt."

3. For Philo, see Chapter X. For Origen, one may note Thomas Aquinas' remark (*In II Sent.* d. xvii, q. 3, a. 2, sol.): "Origenes posuit paradisum non esse locum aliquem corporalem, sed omnia quae de paradiso dicuntur, allegorice de paradiso spirituali interpretanda esse: quod pro errore reprobat Epiphanius Cypri Episcopus in quadam epistola per Hieronymum translata. Unde simpliciter concedendum est paradisum locum quemdam corporalem esse in determinata parte terrae situm, temperatissimum, et amoenum, ut homo nullis perturbationis impeditus, spiritualibus deliciis quiete frueretur. Hunc autem locum existimant sub aequinoctiali esse versus partem orientalem, eo quod quidam philosophi locum illum temperatissimum asserunt, ex quo etiam loco Nilus, unus de quatuor fluminibus paradisi fluere videtur."

4. *Summa Theol.* I, q. 102, a. 1, ad 3: "Locus ille seclusus est a nostra habitatione aliquibus impedimentis vel montium, vel marium, vel alicuius aestuosae regionis, quae pertransiri non potest. Et ideo scriptores locorum de hoc loco mentionem non fecerunt."

5. *Summa Theol.* I, q. 102, a. 2, ad 3: "Non propter hoc locus est frustra, quia non est ibi hominum habitatio post peccatum; sicut etiam non frustra fuit homini attributa immortalitas quaedam, quam conservaturus non erat. Per huiusmodi enim ostenditur benignitas Dei ad hominem, et quid homo peccando amiserit. — Quamvis, ut dicitur, nunc Enoch et Elias in illo Paradiso habitent."

6. P. Lombard, *Liber II Sententiarum* d. xvii (ed. Quaracchi, I, 385): "Unde volunt, in orientali parte esse paradisum, longo interiacente spatio vel maris vel terrae a regionibus quas incolunt homines, secretum, et in alto situm, usque ad lunarem circulum pertingentem; unde nec aquae diluvii illuc pervenerunt." See the note by the editors of this edition on the several authorities who had held this opinion.

7. Albertus Magnus, *Summa Theol.* II, tr. xiii, q. 79, in *Opera Omnia*, ed. Borgnet, XXXIII, 112: "Ad aliud dicendum quod, salvo meliori judicio, secundum extensionem altitudinis loci paradisus usque ad lunarem globum non ascendit, sed participando proprietates lunae dicitur ascendere. Verbi gratia a luna supra quinta essentia est, quae, sicut dicunt naturales Philosophi, locus est incorruptionis et immortalitatis . . . nubes enim non sunt ibi, nec pluviae, nec tonitrua, nec aliquid talium. Sed quantum ad has proprietates usque ad orbem lunae paradisus dicitur ascendere. In paradiso enim nihil mortale est, nihil corruptibile, nihil tempestuosum: et quantum ad participationem harum proprietatum dicitur paradisus ad lunarem globum ascendere per participationem similitudinis, non par exaltationem loci. Hoc tamen dico sine praejudicio melioris sententiae: quia in quibusdam libris antiquissimis inveni, quod illius sententiae quae attributur Bedae et Strabo, primus auctor fuit Thomas Apostolus, quod scilicet paradisus tantae altitudinis sit, quod usque ad lunarem globum ascendat."

8. See above, p. 128.

9. All of the relevant points are found, of course, in the description in *Purgatorio* XXVIII.

10. Ezek. 5.5: "Haec dicit Dominus Deus: Ista est Jerusalem, in medio gentium posui eam, et in circuitu ejus terras."

11. *Inferno* XXXIV, 112–115:

> E se' or sotto l'emisperio giunto
> ch'è opposito a quel che la gran secca
> coverchia, e sotto'l cui colmo consunto
> Fu l'uom che nacque e visse sanza pecca.

12. *Inferno* XXXIV, 118–126. One notes a "forse" (v. 124) in this account which suggests that Dante is not offering it as literal, or at least certain, fact.

13. Wisd. 11.21: "Sed omnia in mensura, et numero, et pondere disposuisti."

14. *Convivio* II, 8: "Et in dimostrar questo, sempre lo litterale dee andare innanzi, sì come quello ne la cui sentenza li altri sono inchiusi, e sanza lo quale sarebbe impossibile ed inrazionale intendere a li altri, e massimamente a lo allegorico."

15. One recalls that Ulysses makes a special mention of the stars of the other pole, yet it may be worth noting that his turn of phrase attributes the seeing of those stars to the "night," not to himself:

> Tutte le stelle già dell'altro polo
> vedea la notte.
>
> *Inferno* XXVI, 127–8.

16. *Inferno* II, 13–33 and *passim*.

17. *Inferno* XXVI, 117.

18. *Inferno* XXXIV, 121–126.

19. In his *Liber Hebraicarum Quaestionum in Genesim* (PL 23.943) Jerome noted on this verse 24 of the third chapter: "*Et ejecit Adam, et habitare fecit contra paradisum voluptatis. Et statuit Cherubim et flammeam rhomphaeam, quae vertitur ad custodiendam viam ligni vitae.* Alius multo sensus est in Hebraeo quam hic intelligitur. Ait enim: *et ejecit Adam,* haud dubium quin Dominus: *Et habitare fecit ante paradisum voluptatis Cherubim, et flammeum gladium, qui verteretur et custodiret viam ligni vitae.* Non quod ipsum Adam, quem ejecerat Deus, habitare fecerit contra paradisum voluptatis; sed quod illo ejecto, ante fores paradisi Cherubim, et flammeum gladium posuerit ad custodiendum paradisi vestibulum, ne quis posset intrare."

20. Witness to the fact that the older Latin translation remained familiar to exegetes and theologians is to be had everywhere. Thus, to cite only one example, Rabanus Maurus, in his Commentary on Genesis (I, 20; *PL* 107.500): "*Ejecitque Adam, et collocavit ante paradisum voluptatis Cherubim et flammeum gladium atque versatilem ad custodiendam viam ligni vitae.* Hunc locum antiqua translatio sic habet 'Et ejecit Adam, et collocavit eum contra paradisum voluptatis; et ordinavit Cherubim et flammeam rhomphoeam' etc. Quam si sequimur, et his significandi gratia factum credere debemus; sed tamen factum ut contra paradisum, quo beata vita etiam spiritaliter significabatur, habitaret utique peccator in miseria. Quod autem dicitur collocasse Deus ante paradisum voluptatis Cherubim, etc." Here it is clear, as it is in most instances, that R. Maurus has both his reading and his interpretation from Augustine.

21. Jerome's translation of the Pentateuch was made in the years A.D. 398–404.

22. *De Genesi ad Litteram* XI, 40 (*PL* 34.451), and *passim*.

23. *De Peccatorum Meritis et Remissione* II, 34, (*PL* 44.183). Also in his *De Genesi Contra Manichaeos* II, 22 (*PL* 34.214): "Dimissus est ergo de paradiso suavitatis, ut operaretur terram de qua sumptus erat; id est, ut in corpore isto laboraret, et ibi si posset collocaret sibi meritum redeundi. Moratus est autem contra paradisum in miseria: quae utique beatae vitae contraria est. Nam beatam vitam paradisi nomine significatam existimo." Also *passim* in this work.

24. Walafrid Strabo, in his *Glossa Ordinaria*, cites Jerome's remarks on the two versions of Genesis at this point, as well as Augustine's reading and interpretation of the older Latin version (*PL* 113.97).

25. *Summa Theol.* II, tr. xvii, q. 106, sol. (ed. Borgnet, XXXIII, 279).

26. *Ibid.*: "Ergo a simili etiam a loco debuit ejici, et poni in locum miseriae et mortalitatis."

27. See quotations above from Thomas.

Chapter X

Rivers, Nymphs, and Stars

These four stars over Eden are, allegorically, the four cardinal virtues. Happily, in this poem which rarely declares the *other* sense of things and events so explicitly, that meaning for the four stars is, in this instance, a certainty. It is as if the poet were especially concerned to make this particular meaning clear. Four maidens come in Beatrice's triumphal procession at the summit of the mountain [1] and affirm this, in a quite special way. Here with Beatrice, they say, they are "nymphs," and in the sky they are "stars." Now, in their role as "nymphs," these four come as hand-maids to Beatrice; and because of Beatrice's meaning and the whole context of event in which they appear, there can be no doubt of their allegorical identity. Indeed, the very dress and attributes of these maidens make it evident beyond any possibility of doubt that they are the four cardinal virtues — evident, that is, if we are able to read the signs which the poet put there to affirm this.

These things we have already seen, but we may need to review the whole matter in brief at this point. The virtues commonly spoken of, when viewed together as a group, are seven, of course. Thus in Beatrice's cortège (yet preceding her actual appearance

in the procession) the maidens who come as her handmaids are
seven, arranged in two groups. They come dancing alongside the
wheels of the two-wheeled chariot, three at the right wheel and
four at the left. That very grouping of three on the one hand and
four on the other is an obvious first pointer to what they represent. Then, it is the color of their robes which confirms that first
hint of their meaning. First we see the group of three on the right
(a position of higher station than the left),[2] and we notice that
each of the three maidens wears a different color, and that these
three distinct colors are white, green and red. Now these colors,
as we are expected to realize at once, are the established colors
for the three theological virtues, faith, hope and charity. We may
even note, when the entire procession has advanced into view,
that the colors of these three virtues are the colors of the parade
itself, serving to mark it off into three parts. Moreover, the order
of these colors, serving to divide the procession into so many
sections as it emerges, is the established order in which the three
virtues are always named when taken as a group: "faith, hope,
and charity, these three." Then in the dance of these maidens there
is yet another confirming detail: the one robed in red is seen to
lead the dance of the three;[3] and with this, we have only to
remember that charity is the accepted chief of the three theological virtues to recognize what is being affirmed by this detail. "And
now abideth faith, hope, charity, these three; but the greatest of
these is charity."

The four maidens at the left wheel of the chariot are of a lesser
station, that is, of a lower order, than the three. And so it is in the
traditional appraisal of these virtues. What is seen to be their place
here in the procession declares this and thereby points the more
plainly to their particular meaning. And, of course, once the three
at the right wheel of the chariot have been recognized to be the
theological virtues, there remains little chance of doubt as to what
this group of four on the other side would represent. They, too,
must be virtues, and being four, they must be the cardinal virtues,
prudence, temperance, fortitude and justice. Then, in the dance
of these four, another detail is noted which helps to identify them.
One of these maidens has three eyes, and she it is who leads their

dance. This must be prudence, the discerning virtue, long recognized to be chief among these four.[4]

Prudence, temperance, fortitude, justice: the four maidens must surely be these same familiar virtues. But about their dress, too, there is a particular point: the color of it is most significant. That color, indeed, answers an all-important question that could at once be asked about such a group of cardinal virtues, a question arising out of the fact that Dante, in keeping with theological doctrine of his time (and not his time alone) recognized not *one* but *two* sets of the four cardinal virtues. On the one hand, there were the four cardinal virtues known to the "philosophers" (who were pagans) and by them much discussed. Indeed, it was the pagans themselves who had first assigned names to these virtues. "Their" virtues, therefore, made up one set of cardinal virtues. But these virtues are known and had in Christian times, being accessible through Christ and His sanctifying grace. They come into the soul of the Christian, accompanied by grace and by those virtues, the theological, which are known and had only through Christ. Indeed, whenever the four cardinal virtues are Christian and accompany the three which are *only* Christian, it is their essential nature to be informed by charity, greatest of all.[5]

Now since the pagans (with certain notable exceptions) [6] could not know or possess that first of all the virtues, charity, it followed that there must be a distinction here: one must speak of two sets of cardinal virtues, those known to the pagans, or the *acquired* cardinal virtues; and those known through Christ and informed with charity, the *infused* cardinal virtues. The terms point to the essential distinguishing feature. The three theological virtues with charity chief among them are, par excellence, "infused" virtues and are never "acquired," being always a gift from God. They are part of that gift by which He, through His grace, adopts us as his children, guiding us to a goal of life eternal with Him, a goal far above man's powers of attainment. But if, as part of that "infusion" from above, the four cardinal virtues are also given and partake of that highest infused virtue which is charity, we must certainly recognize and speak of a group of four *infused* cardinal virtues: prudence, temperance, fortitude, justice.

As for the *acquired* cardinal virtues, there is no denying that
the pagans knew and had them. It must be, therefore, that such
virtues lay, and lie, within man's own powers and the proportion
of his nature; for it was the condition of the pagans, coming as
they did in a "time of no grace," [7] that they were obliged to rely
on man's "natural" powers, on whatever strength man has of his
own. The pagans were of course without sanctifying grace and
without those three infused virtues of faith, hope and charity.
And because they were without the all-important virtue of charity, it cannot be that they knew or had the infused cardinal virtues
which are always informed by charity.

Such, then, is the question that can arise respecting the four
maidens who come dancing at the left wheel of Beatrice's chariot.
If they are the four cardinal virtues, which set of these virtues are
they, the acquired or the infused? The question is, in a sense,
already answered as we see that these four come together with
the three theological virtues. For by that token alone they must
be the infused cardinal virtues. Moreover, when we understand
that Beatrice herself comes here, in the allegorical sense, as sanctifying grace, then no doubt whatever remains. Even so, the poet
has been concerned to make the matter clear beyond any possibility of doubt. He has told us, therefore, that the four maidens
are all dressed in the same color, a certain shade of red. We have
only to know that red is the color of charity (and who would not
know this!) [8] to see that the answer to the inevitable question
could not be made clearer. These are the infused cardinal virtues.
Their very color affirms that they partake of charity, that they
are informed by charity, which is chief among all infused virtues
and is never anything if not infused.[9]

The question of the precise identity of the four dancing maidens
dressed in charity's color takes on special importance because of
what they themselves declare later in this episode in Eden where
Beatrice comes. Dante returns to Eden not merely to witness the
magnificent spectacle of Beatrice's triumphal procession, but to be
received by Beatrice and her handmaids when he has crossed
through the stream of Lethe. When he reaches the far side of that
stream, the bank which is called "blessed," it is the group of the

four maidens which is first to receive him. Still dancing, they admit him to their circle, cover him with their arms,[10] and make a declaration about themselves which must not be overlooked if we are to understand who these maidens are. Moreover, these same maidens speak of four stars in the sky, affirming their identity with those stars:

> Noi siam qui ninfe e nel ciel siamo stelle:
>   pria che Beatrice discendesse al mondo,
>   fummo ordinate a lei per sue ancelle.
> Merrènti alli occhi suoi; ma nel giocondo
>   lume ch'è dentro aguzzeranno i tuoi
>   le tre di là che miran più profondo.
> *Purgatorio* XXXI, 106–111.

Here we are nymphs and in the sky we are stars: before Beatrice descended to the world we were ordered to her as her handmaids. We will lead you to her eyes; but the three over there, who see more profoundly, will sharpen your own eyes in the joyous light therein.

The three "over there" are the three theological virtues dancing closer to Beatrice. And what the meaning of the whole action may be in which Dante finds himself led to Beatrice, first by these four cardinal virtues, and then by the three theological virtues, is a question answered by the whole pattern of meaning disclosed in the journey and which we have already examined in several aspects. For the moment, now that we are certain that these four can be none other than the cardinal virtues, and the infused set of such virtues, it is this their own affirmation that they are stars in the sky which calls for attention, referring us back, as it clearly does, to those verses at the beginning of the *Purgatorio* which have already been seen to leave troubling questions in the poem. We must take these maidens to mean what they say. And since they are four, and since those "holy" stars over Eden are four; and since (from the poem, at least) we know of no other special group of four stars here, we must understand that somehow these maidens are those stars. Here, in Beatrice's retinue, they are "nymphs," they say. And in the sky they are stars, four stars. There seems no room at all for doubt. These four maidens must be those same four stars, and those stars must be these maidens. Apparently, being both "nymphs" and "stars," these maidens can and do exist in two aspects or natures; and in one of those aspects it follows that they are those same four stars which were never seen except by a first people — and in this, we remember, there was occasion for lament.

It seems clear that any identity of meaning between nymphs and stars can only be sought at the allegorical level. That, in fact, is why it becomes important to see what the four maidens might mean allegorically. They represent the four cardinal virtues, tinged with charity. Therefore, on their own affirmation of identity, we must understand that the four stars over Eden are those same infused virtues. No doubt that is why they were called "holy" stars when seen there. But now, out of this awareness of a meaning quite precise, it is also clear that the problem of these four stars and of the verses that focus upon them becomes even more perplexing, as we recall the clear affirmation that those stars were never seen except by the "first people." How can that possibly be true, if, allegorically, these stars are the cardinal virtues? For to see these stars or to dwell beneath them, would seem to mean to *have* what they stand for, especially if they stand for virtues. Likewise, to be "bereaved" of them and "widowed" of them, as such virtues, must mean to have those virtues no longer. And here, of course, is the special rub of the whole problem. For even the pagans who lived before Christ and did not know Him had these four cardinal virtues as the acquired virtues. Virgil declares as much in the poem,[11] of himself and all the virtuous pagans who dwell in Limbo. Then, after Christ, in that time of grace which begins with His advent, all who believe in Him and are saved must have sanctifying grace, and not merely four but all seven of the infused virtues.[12] All therefore who have been saved through Christ have had the four infused cardinal virtues and many, surely, who live in the "northern clime" have been so saved. Thus, to understand the four maidens to be these virtues and then, on their own declaration, to take these four stars to be those same virtues, would appear to raise more questions than it can put to rest. One begins to see, having come to this view of the problem, that when those verses in Canto I of *Purgatorio* are said to be among the most perplexing in the whole poem, there is no exaggeration in that statement.

In seeking a solution, in the face of such difficulties, one may perhaps venture to proceed on what must appear to be an article of faith: on the assumption, namely, that, if the meaning of such a detail as that of these four stars is to be comprehended, this is likely to happen when we have made out a whole shape and outline of meaning, within which the four stars as a detail will "fall into place" as a part of that whole. This whole shape in turn may prove to be one that exists in the background of the poem's conception as well as in the foreground of its action; and in either event it may turn out to be a shape which is not so familiar to our eyes as the poet had thought it might be. If such be the case, however, this represents no shortcoming of his poem. It is not Dante's memory that is at fault here, but our own.

There is one further point to be considered regarding these four maidens who come with Beatrice and who are also stars in the sky. We note that the maidens are seven in all, the seven familiar virtues. Yet, of the seven, four only declare that they are stars, and these are the four cardinal virtues. But what then of the other three, are they not also "nymphs here and stars in the sky?" It would seem so. For in the journey up the mountain, when night falls at the end of the first day, Dante looks up at the stars again in that unfamiliar sky over Eden to note that a group of three stars now shines in place of the four he had seen in the early morning light of that same day.[13] The three have replaced the four. Since the four are virtues, these three would also seem to be virtues. Since the four are the cardinal, these three must be the theological virtues, shining now in place of the four, far toward the southern pole. Thus, if the four maidens are both nymphs and stars, then so also must the three maidens be who take over and replace the four and from them receive Dante into their dance. But, unlike the four, the three maidens make no explicit declaration of their identity. Surely there is no need for them to do so, since we so readily understand that they too must be stars as well as nymphs. Still, with an eye on these three stars and on that moment

when Dante looks up to notice them (and this is not only the
first but also the last time in the poem that any notice is taken of
these three stars), we cannot fail to remark that no such lament
arises there as did arise when he looked at the four. But is this
perhaps also a matter which might be assumed to be clear without
specific affirmation? Does the lament concerning the four stars
apply to the three as well? There they are, literally in that same
location, so far toward the "other" or south pole that it must be
with them as with the four: no one living in the northern "site"
could behold them. We must therefore conceive that the northern
clime is bereaved and widowed of these stars, too, and consequently deprived of the virtues which they represent. There seems
indeed no other way in which to understand the matter. Mankind
is deprived of the sight of both groups of stars, i.e., mankind living
in the northern hemisphere is somehow dispossessed of both
groups of the infused virtues, represented by these seven stars.
Whereby, this problem clearly becomes as perplexing as can be.
For these are the seven virtues that are known to abound through
the grace of Christ. But a particular point to remark is this: among
the seven maidens who are also seven stars, it is the group of four
only that is singled out for such special attention. The four come
first in the focus of a lament which arises, as we have seen, at the
thought of loss of Eden. When the three are seen, the lament is
not repeated. This was near the beginning of the journey up this
mountain. Then, at the end of the climb, at the summit where
Eden is, again it is only the four maidens who are heard to affirm
that they are stars in the sky. In short, the plain fact cannot escape
us: if there is lament here over loss of Eden, that loss is represented
primarily by the four stars, not by the seven. Loss of Eden is thus
signified explicitly in terms of the four cardinal virtues, and not
of the three theological. What meaning, if any, can the singling
out of the four have (even if it be tacitly understood that the
three are also involved)? The four cardinal virtues are of a lesser
or lower order than the other three. Why then, if there is lament
concerning a loss, and if one only of the two groups must be
chosen to represent both, should that lament not focus on that
"higher tribe" [14] of three virtues?

It is a question which the poem will not answer in any direct way. And it may well be that we shall not account for such a focus on four stars in connection with Eden and loss of Eden unless we become more familiar with certain particular notions respecting the terrestrial paradise, notions which in their own way will be seen to hold to just such a focus on the number four. To make a beginning with such an excursion, we have to recall, first of all, that according to Genesis the rivers in Eden were four.

* * *

In Dante's Eden, there are two streams, not four. The fact is impressive in itself since such a conception runs counter to the clear statement in Genesis that the streams are four. In Dante's Garden, however, the two streams are not at all to be identified with any two of the four named in Scripture. And yet, the poet's two streams would seem to have in common with the four at least the fact that they, like the four of Genesis, rise from a single source. This source we are told is no natural one; indeed the source of the two streams in Dante's Garden is the grace of God itself.[15] And Dante's streams have a purpose which their names express: the first encountered has the familiar name of Lethe and is a stream which obliterates the memory of sin in those who pass through it, as Dante and Statius are seen to do. This same Lethe is the stream that remains between Dante and Beatrice all the while she so sternly draws from him his confession of sins and back-slidings. When Dante passes through its waters to be reunited with Beatrice, Lethe works the effect to which its name points. Then in company with Beatrice and her handmaids, Dante moves with Statius toward the other stream which also bears a name serving to declare its own corresponding function: Eunoè, which restores the memory of all good deeds.[16] When Dante emerges from its holy waters, he is pure and made ready to rise with Beatrice to the stars.

The presence of Statius throughout this whole episode is important, showing us that the rivers have a function in a process of purgation through which all souls must pass, and not just a certain living man in a most exceptional journey. The poem is clear on this

point: what Statius does in Eden is certain evidence of what all
souls must do when they reach this place. We note that the maiden
named Matelda has an office and function in connection with the
two streams: [17] to lead the souls, as here also the living man,
through the waters, first of Lethe, then of Eunoè.

It becomes clear, in this way, that the two streams of Dante's
Eden have significance by having a function in the process of
man's purgation and redemption from sin. This indeed is so evident
that, for all we can see from the poem, Lethe and Eunoè would
have no function here in Eden if sin had never been. Of course,
since we are following a Dante and a Statius, both of whom move
in a process of purgation and redemption, we come to Dante's two
rivers quite ready to accept them as appropriate features of his
Eden; and quite ready also to forget, perhaps, that in this instance
Dante has chosen to conceive his Eden at variance with the account of Genesis, wherein the four streams bear the names of
Phison, Geon, Tigris and Euphrates. Nowhere in Dante's Eden
are streams so named encountered, nor are we given to understand
that they might be here somewhere to one side or other of Dante's
path through the Garden. The four rivers of Genesis have simply
disappeared from Dante's Paradise.[18] The fact is notable enough in
itself. But there is another equally notable: in Dante's conception
there are four stars shining down on Eden that are nowhere
mentioned in Genesis. And, with that thought, some light would
seem to dawn; we appear to be face to face here with a kind of
mutation or transposition wrought by the poet. One feature has
become another. Could the four streams mentioned by Genesis
have become, in the poem, four stars which Genesis does not
mention? A clear answer is to be had in the affirmative, but for
that we shall have to turn to the traditional allegorical interpretation of the four rivers of Genesis, in order to see that those four
rivers, in an exegetical tradition as old as Philo of Alexandria
(whose time is the time of Jesus Christ), did in fact represent the
four cardinal virtues, even as do Dante's four stars.

In Philo's treatise on Genesis,[19] even the plants that grow in
the Garden are virtues. Indeed, the Garden itself is Virtue, and
in this way Eden expresses the happiness that is to be found there-

in. Man is placed in the Garden "to tend it," that is, to give over his whole mind to virtue. But, for Philo, it is specifically the feature of the four rivers which represents the virtues, and since the rivers are four in number they are, of course, the four cardinal virtues. The very number four would seem to require this. And since Philo's allegory of the four rivers of Eden passed to the West by way of St. Ambrose and St. Augustine, and through them came to be unanimously accepted in a tradition extending down through Dante's time and beyond, it seems well to take some special note of Philo's views on this point and the method of allegorical interpretation which they exemplify.

On Genesis 2.10-14, Philo writes:

"A river goes forth from Eden to water the garden: thence it is separated into four heads: the name of the one is Pheison; this is that which encircles all the land of Evilat, there where the gold is; and there is the ruby and the emerald. And the name of the second river is Geon: this encompasses all the land of Aethiopia. And the third river is Tigris: this is that whose course is in front of Assyria. And the fourth river is Euphrates." By these rivers his [Moses'] purpose is to indicate the particular virtues. These are four in number, prudence, self-mastery, courage, justice. The largest river, of which the four are effluxes, is generic virtue, which we have called "goodness." The four effluxes are the virtues of the same number. Generic virtue takes its start from Eden, the wisdom of God, which is full of joy, and brightness, and exultation, glorying and priding itself only upon God its Father; but the specific virtues, four in number, are derived from generic virtue, which, like a river, waters the perfect achievements of each of them with an abundant flow of noble doings.[20]

It is evident enough that Philo knows and remembers his Plato when he interprets Genesis. This is the more apparent when he goes on here to discuss each virtue separately and in detail. Thus prudence, signified by the first of the four rivers, is the chief of the virtues. And after he has touched on the three rivers, Phison, Geon and Tigris, and the corresponding virtues, Philo notes that it is "worth inquiring why courage is mentioned in the second place, self-mastery in the third, and prudence in the first, and why he [the author of Genesis] has not set forth a different order in the virtues." Whereupon we are told that our soul is threefold, and has one part which is the seat of reason, another which is the seat of high spirit, and another which is the seat of desire, and what the place and abode for each is; wherein even more clearly we feel the presence of Plato's chariot of the soul. But what we may note now that can prove to be of considerable importance later is that it is precisely this Platonic notion of a threefold soul as the seat of three of the virtues that serves to separate them from that fourth river which is justice, signified by the Euphrates. Justice is thus, as a virtue, set somewhat apart from the three. When Philo turns to this fourth river, he continues in the vein of the Platonic philosophy and the familiar myth of the chariot with its horses. But justice means something more general in the soul (even as it does in the *Republic*):

> The fourth river is Euphrates. "Euphrates" means "fruitfulness," and is a figurative name for the fourth virtue, justice, a virtue fruitful indeed and bringing gladness to the mind. When, then, does it appear? When the three parts of the soul are in harmony.

When he came to write his own commentary on Genesis [21] almost four centuries later, St. Ambrose found Philo's method in the allegorical interpretation of Genesis to be on the whole quite acceptable, and particularly acceptable was Philo's allegory of the four rivers as the four cardinal virtues. Of course, for Ambrose, there are meanings in the sacred book which Philo Judeaus might not have been expected to see: the stream, for instance, which rises in Eden to irrigate the Paradise is Jesus Christ, *fons vitae aeternae.*[22] But when this stream is said to divide into the four heads, then these for Ambrose are virtues of the soul,[23] even as for Philo. The specifically Christian increment in meaning is thus evident, and is worth noting in Ambrose's interpretation. The one source of the four streams is thus Jesus Christ, which means also to see it as "Sapientia Dei," even as Ambrose points out. Therefore, if the four streams which derive from this one font are the virtues, they must be virtues specifically Christian — even though Ambrose is not concerned to insist on this obvious point. *Sapientia* simply divides into the four familiar virtues, and for Ambrose their names are the Latin names they will thereafter always have in Christian theology: *prudentia*, *temperantia*, *fortitudo* and *justitia*.

Like Philo, Ambrose then proceeds to examine each of the four rivers in due order and each of the corresponding four virtues. Prudence comes first, receiving quite as high an appraisal as with Philo, being judged chief among the four virtues: "prudentia quae pluribus prosit, ideo prima"; [24] temperance and fortitude are then discussed in what are still (though less clearly) Platonic terms. Last comes the fourth river, Euphrates, which means in Latin "fecundity" and "abundance"; but better, says Ambrose, it means "justice," than which there is no fruit more abounding in virtue. Ambrose notes also what he takes to be a clear signal of this point in the text of Genesis itself, a sign by which this fourth river (i. e., this fourth virtue), is set apart from the other three; for in the case of the first three rivers named, we are told by the sacred text just where each flows when it issues from the Paradise. Not so in the case of the fourth river, the Euphrates. Why should this be? Because, says Ambrose (and we note again Philo's thought), justice is the harmony of all three of the other virtues, "for where justice is, there is concord of the other virtues." Therefore the fourth river is not known by the part of the earth whereto it flows, that is, it is not known *ex parte*, for "justice" is not a part but is as mother of all the virtues, "quasi mater omnium." [25] The latter phrase here in Ambrose, by which justice is singled out as special among the virtues, is worth noting. Ambrose insists on it elsewhere, and it passes from him directly into the tradition to stay.

It was the profound understanding which Ambrose of Milan had of the spiritual meaning of Scriptures, as well as his remarkable ability to make use of that understanding in sermons, that helped no less a catechumen than Augustine to see the light of the truth.[26] It is therefore not at all strange that Augustine himself should have made an allegorical interpretation of Genesis. His first treatise [27] in such a method was directed against the Manicheans, whose custom it was, he says, to deride the Scriptures of the Old Testament which they did not understand.[28] Augustine proposed therefore to begin with the first verse of Genesis and to

proceed to meet those heretics and refute their erroneous and
deceitful interpretations, verse by verse and point by point. The
result was Augustine's treatise in two books, *De Genesi contra
Manichaeos.*

It is at once evident in this treatise that the method of interpretation which Augustine proposes to turn against the heretics
is that allegorical method which he so much admired in Ambrose's
teaching. In fact, Augustine makes a special point of defending
the method. Genesis may not be understood everywhere in a
literal sense, for there are perhaps passages wherein the text must
be recognized to speak "figurate" and "in aenigmatis."[29] Hence,
when he comes to the second chapter of Genesis and the description of Eden, it does not surprise us that we hear from Augustine
what we have heard from Philo and Ambrose. Eden is the soul,
and if Eden is planted in the East (for Augustine, we recall, is
reading Genesis in the Septuagint), East must signify that light
of wisdom (*lux sapientiae*) which was in Eden; and the tree of
life which was planted in the middle of the Paradise signifies
Wisdom itself.[30] Augustine's next chapter on the meaning of the
four rivers of Eden, is also quite in line with the interpretations
of Philo and Ambrose. Since it is Augustine's, however, it is well
to consider the whole of that chapter with closer attention, for
Augustine's views were surely decisive both for the traditional
exegesis of the four rivers and for the general method of allegorical interpretation which they represent:

> The river which flowed out of Eden (that is to say, out of the
> delights and the pleasure and the fatness), a river spoken of by the
> Prophet in the following passage of the thirty-fifth Psalm where he
> says: "And Thou shalt make them drink of the river of Thy pleas-
> ure" (that is to say, in Eden, which in Latin is translated by "pleas-
> ure"), divides into four parts indicating the four cardinal virtues,
> prudence, fortitude, temperance, justice. Now the Phison is said to
> be the Ganges and the Geon the Nile, which can be noted in Jere-
> miah the prophet; for they are called by these other names, just as
> now the river is called Tiber which was previously named Albula.
> But the Tigris and the Euphrates even now keep the same names.
> By which names, as I said, the spiritual virtues are signified, which
> is taught by the interpretation of the names themselves, if the
> Hebrew or Syrian languages be considered: even as Jerusalem,

though it be a visible and terrestrial place, nonetheless signifies spiritually the city of peace; and Sion, although it is a mountain on the earth, signifies speculation nevertheless, and that name in the allegories of Scripture is often to be understood in a spiritual sense. So it is with that one who went down from Jerusalem to Jericho, as our Lord tells, left by thieves along the way, wounded and half-dead. Thus, although they are found historically on this earth, we are obliged to understand these terrestrial places, nonetheless, in a spiritual way.

Therefore, the first of these rivers is prudence which means the very contemplation of truth, alien to every human mouth because ineffable. . . . This prudence therefore compasses the land where there is gold and the carbuncle and the emerald, that is, the rule of our lives, which, as though purged of all terrestrial stain, shines as the purest gold; and truth, which no falsehood conquers, as the shining of the carbuncle which is not overcome by night; and eternal life, which is signified by the emerald because of that vigor which does not wither. And that river which compasses the land of Ethiopia which is very hot and burning, signifies fortitude, prompt and swift in the heat of action. And the third, the Tigris, flows against Assyria and signifies temperance which resists sensuality, which is much opposed to the counsel of prudence, wherefore often in Scripture the term "Assyrians" means "the enemy." Of the fourth river, it is not said what it flows against or what land it compasses, for justice pertains to all parts of the soul because it is the very order and equity of the soul, by which the three others are bound in harmony, first prudence, second fortitude, third temperance. And in this union and order is justice.[31]

St. Augustine did not choose to carry this treatise on Genesis in such a purely allegorical manner further than the end of the third chapter and the moment of the expulsion of Adam from Eden. That also is the limiting event in that much longer treatise written later, the *De Genesi ad Litteram*, where we may find him concerned to defend the literal, historical sense of the holy book, a sense which he would seem to have felt was threatened or undermined by such exclusively allegorical interpretations as those of Philo and Ambrose — perhaps indeed by such as his own treatise against the Manicheans had been. Even so, as we have noted already, Augustine is not disposed to deny or rule out the spiritual sense, in spite of this later intention to read Genesis according to the letter. What he proposes to do is to see both meanings, the literal and the spiritual, the historical and the allegorical. And, in passing, it can be noted that Augustine's focus on allegory in this instance is precisely Dante's in the *Divine Comedy*. We might therefore take special note of it. Thus, when Augustine comes again, in this later treatise, to the description of Eden, we may remark the general question of method which he raises before he ventures to interpret that chapter of Genesis.

> *Et plantavit Deus paradisum in Eden ad orientem et posuit ibi hominem quem finxit*. I am not without knowing that many persons have said many things about the Paradise. However there are three ways in general of understanding this matter. One of these would have it that the Paradise is to be understood only in a corporeal sense; another of these would take it only in a spiritual sense. And the third of these would understand the Paradise in both ways, now in the corporeal sense and now in the spiritual. I may be brief and confess that the third way is the one which pleases me. It is in this way that I have undertaken now to speak of the Paradise.[32]

Augustine goes on to recognize here that when he had written his treatise on Genesis against the Manicheans he had not yet understood how one could defend the literal sense of some of the events and things narrated in that Book of Scripture, and had therefore had more then to say about the spiritual sense. But even then he had seen that the true goal for the exegete is to understand the whole narration of Scriptures in a literal and not a figurative sense, even though this may remain a goal not everywhere attainable, there being many passages in Scripture that must be explained as *figures* and not as historical truths.

We had already taken note, moreover, of an excellent example of Augustine's method in interpreting an event recounted in Genesis, that, namely, of the placing of Adam "opposite" Paradise when he was expelled from the Garden. Augustine had found that this was done "for the sake of signifying" but added, "yet it *was* done." The whole method is apparent in those words and there is, I repeat, no better focus for the reading of Dante's *Comedy* in its full range of meaning, literal and allegorical.

Thus, as he notes in this treatise *ad litteram*, when he comes to those verses which speak of the Tree of Life that was planted in

the midst of the Paradise and the Tree of the Knowledge of Good
and Evil, Augustine is quite prepared to see both senses, literal
and allegorical, but is especially concerned to defend the literal:

> Clearly what then follows "and the tree of life in the midst of para-
> dise and the tree of the knowledge of good and evil" is to be exam-
> ined most diligently lest it be read merely as allegory, as though these
> were not trees but something else was signified by the term "tree."
> It has been said, indeed, in speaking of Wisdom [Sapientia]: "She
> is a tree of life to them that lay hold upon her." For even as there
> is an eternal Jerusalem in Heaven, even so there is a city built on
> this earth by which that city is signified; and Sara and Agar, though
> they signify the two Testaments, still were two certain women; and
> if Christ on the Cross of His passion sprinkled us with a spiritual
> water, he was nonetheless also the stone from which, under the rod,
> sprang the water to the thirsty people, of which it is said: "And that
> rock was Christ" (I Cor. 10.4). All these things signified things other
> than themselves, and still they had actual corporeal existence. And
> when these things were commemorated by the narrator, his manner
> of speaking. was not figurative but was the specific narration of
> those things which figured what was to be. There was, therefore,
> a tree of life even as there was a stone which was Christ. And God
> did not will that man should live in the Paradise without the mystery
> of spiritual things being represented by corporeal things.[33]

When Augustine comes, then, in this later treatise on Genesis,
to the mention of the four rivers of Eden, he is more concerned to
defend the literal sense of these streams than he had been when
he wrote against the doctrines of the Manicheans. His suggestion
that the four were real rivers, flowing underground to come up
at their apparently separate sources, has been noted. Yet this in
no way denies what he had said of the four streams in the earlier
treatise. Moreover, from what he has ruled in defense of the two
meanings for the Tree of Life, one readily sees the method of reading Scripture by which the rivers of the Garden can be both real
rivers and the four cardinal virtues. For God willed, even as
Augustine noted, that the corporeal things of the Garden should
point beyond themselves, to spiritual mysteries.

It holds no surprise that, following three such authorities as
Philo, Ambrose and Augustine, the allegory of the four rivers of
Eden as the four cardinal virtues became firmly established in

what, by Dante's time, was a very long tradition of exegesis. St. Gregory, for instance, in his widely read *Morals on the Book of Job*, may not be commenting on Genesis, but when he reaches the verse in Job which tells of a great wind that came down from the mountains and smote the four corners of Job's house, he recalls at once the four rivers of Eden in the context of such an event, when he goes on to explain the moral sense which such a happening must have:

> As we have before said, "the wilderness" is the deserted multitude of impure spirits, which, when it forsook the felicity of its Creator, lost, as it were, the hand of the cultivator. And from the same there *came a strong wind*, and overthrew the house; thus strong tempta-tion seizes us from the unclean spirits, and overturns the conscience from its settled frame of tranquility. But this house stands by four corners for this reason, that the firm fabric of our mind is upheld by Prudence, Temperance, Fortitude, Justice. This house is grounded on four corners, in that the whole structure of good practice is raised in these four virtues. And hence do four rivers of Paradise water the earth. For while the heart is watered with these four virtues, it is cooled from all the heat of carnal desire.[34]

In the centuries after Gregory (d. 604) it is an easy matter to follow the line of a tradition which never forgot that the four rivers of Eden represent the four cardinal virtues. Bede notes this meaning with no departures whatever from the established view;[35] and the *Glossa Ordinaria*[36] quotes the very passage in Gregory which we have just read. The four rivers as the four virtues ornament the capital of a pillar in the abbey church of Cluny.[37] It is a standard article in Hexaemeron literature, and passes abundantly into a literature more profane.[38]

Dante, as we began by recalling, does not make the allegory of the four rivers of Eden any part of his conception. The streams in his Eden are two, and they do not represent any pair of virtues. But we are prepared now to see what Dante has done: he has simply devised a "star allegory" to replace a "river allegory." Instead of four rivers in Eden signifying the four cardinal virtues, we have now four stars shining down on Eden signifying those same virtues.

The whole point of such an excursion into the allegory of the four rivers of Eden is thus evident: we are brought to face the fact that Dante has simply changed those rivers of Genesis into stars. Nor is the mere fact of this metamorphosis the important thing to note. It is rather this: once we have found, in the allegory of four rivers in Eden, the key to Dante's allegory of the four stars, we find ourselves in a position to see answers to troubling questions respecting the allegory of the poem. Why, for instance, should a lament center, as it clearly does, on the loss of four stars or four virtues, and not on the loss of seven stars and all seven of the virtues? Or why not rather on the three theological virtues, which are also there as stars over Eden, rather than on the four? The answer comes clear when we see the model for Dante's allegory at this point. It is an answer which has led us straight to Genesis. The rivers of Eden were four, not seven: such, simply, is what is given by the sacred text, and any allegory must begin with that literal statement of fact. Therefore it did begin there and the four rivers were recognized to be those four virtues that are grouped together as the cardinal virtues. No one denied that the theological virtues would have been present also in Eden. Indeed, if ever the question were raised as to whether Adam had all seven of the virtues, the answer must be that he did. But in the allegorical interpretation of Eden, one began with *four* rivers, not seven. Therefore there was an inevitable stress on the fact that the four cardinal virtues were specific to Eden and to man's condition there before sin. The four are peculiar to that place, because four rivers are peculiar to it.

To be driven from Eden, to lose Eden, would mean of course to lose all the delights of the Garden of which the rivers, in their allegorical sense, were a significant part. Those rivers, i.e., those virtues, belong to the Garden in a quite special way. Thus, granted the transposition from four rivers to four stars which Dante has made, we may say that loss of Eden now means, for one thing, the loss of four stars, if Adam and Eve are placed opposite Eden when they are driven therefrom and may no longer see those stars even as they could no longer see the rivers. And if the loss is irreparable, if there may never be a return to Eden, then the four stars will never be seen again by mankind, for man has been placed "opposite" Eden and in misery, in due punishment for his first sin.

There remain unanswered questions, of course. But this much would seem to be the particular background out of which arises Dante's allegory of the four stars as something pertaining to Eden and man's condition there. And yet it must be confessed that Dante's transmutation of rivers into stars can seem entirely arbitrary unless we consider that there was, in quite another tradition than that stemming from Genesis, a strong pointer in the very direction which the poet chose to follow: namely, a classical myth about a "prima gente" and man's original condition in a first time of history. The myth concerns "justice" and how Justice itself became a constellation in the sky. And since this myth is one of justice and not one of *four* virtues, it is well to recall, as we turn from the allegory of the four rivers, that the fourth river, even as Philo had observed, was justice, which is "the harmony of the three parts of the soul." Ambrose, then, in turn, had sought a reason why Genesis does not tell where the fourth river ran, and had thought that the answer lay in the accepted fact that justice, signified by that river, is not particular but general, not a part but a whole: justice is the harmony of the other virtues, justice is "quasi mater omnium." This being the case, perhaps we shall not find it so hard to accept the fact that when four stars replace four rivers, in an allegory which is that of the four cardinal virtues, then these four stars, even though they are separately those virtues, are to be seen as a constellation of justice: the justice which a "first people" had in Eden; because justice, it is agreed, is the harmonizing principle of the other virtues and is a whole, is "mother of all."

Notes

1. *Purgatorio* XXIX–XXXIII.
2. The right-hand side is already a "better" side than the left as early as Pythagoras, as Thomas Aquinas noted in his *Summa contra Gentiles*, III, 8. This notion is present in the *Comedy* in the contrast in the direction of turning through Hell and through Purgatory: in Hell, Virgil and Dante

descend turning always to the left, whereas in climbing Purgatory Mountain they turn to the right. Moreover, that the right side of the chariot is the "higher" position is confirmed by the fact that the group of three maidens on the right is later said (*Purgatorio* XXXI, 130) to be of a "higher order" than the four on the left.

3. *Purgatorio* XXIX, 121–126:

> Tre donne in giro dalla destra rota
> venian danzando: l'una tanto rossa
> ch'a pena fora dentro al foco nota;
> l'altr'era come se le carni e l'ossa
> fossero state di smeraldo fatte;
> la terza parea neve testè mossa.

It is evident that Hope is rated as the least of the three theological virtues, for we are told that now Faith leads the dance of the three and now Charity. This is in keeping with established doctrine (see Aquinas, *Summa Theol.* II–II, q. 17, a. 7 and 8). However, the other two take their tempo from Charity's song (*Purgatorio* XXIX, 127–129):

> e or parean dalla bianca tratte,
> or dalla rossa; e dal canto di questa
> l'altre toglien l'andare e tarde e ratte.

On the supremacy of charity among all the virtues, a point on which all the theologians agree with St. Paul, see Aquinas, *Summa Theol.* II–II, q. 23, a. 6, resp.: "Et ideo caritas est excellentior fide et spe; et per consequens omnibus aliis virtutibus. Sicut etiam prudentia, quae attingit rationem secundum se, est excellentior quam aliae virtutes morales, quae attingunt rationem secundum quod ex ea medium constituitur in operationibus vel passionibus humanis."

4. *Purgatorio* XXIX, 130–132:

> Dalla sinistra quattro facean festa,
> in porpora vestite, dietro al modo
> d'una di lor ch'avea tre occhi in testa.

5. A bibliography of the writings of the theologians on the virtues, even in Dante's century, would be voluminous. Among the most important recent studies of the theology of the twelfth and thirteenth centuries on this subject are those of Dom O. Lottin, *Psychologie et morale au XIIe et XIIIe siècles* (Paris, 1949), III, 99 ff., "Les premières définitions et classifications des vertus au moyen age"; pp. 459 ff., "Les vertus morales infuses pendant la seconde moitié du XIIIe siècle"; and *passim* in the several volumes of this work. For an extensive discussion and bibliography in general, see *Dictionnaire de theologie catholique*, ed. Vacant, Mangenot, et al. (Paris, 1930), s.v. "Vertu" and separately for the different virtues. The distinction between the acquired virtues and the infused virtues becomes an especially acute problem in Christian theology following the revival of Aristotle in the 13th century. See the studies of Dom Lottin. St. Augustine had marked the distinction, of course, long before this time (*De Civitate Dei* V, 12; *Contra Julianum Pelagianum* IV, 26, *PL* 44.751) nor was it ever lost sight of following him, although, as compared with Augustine's dim view of them, the pagan virtues had undergone a considerable rehabilitation by Dante's time.

See Thomas Aquinas, especially his *Quaestio disputata,* "De Virtutibus in Communi," a. 8–10; and following this, in most editions of the *Quaestiones Disputatae,* the article "*De Caritate.*" Also *Summa Theol.* I–II, q. 65, a. 2.

Students of Dante will recall his discussion on the virtues according to Aristotle's doctrine, in *Convivio* IV, xvii, 1 ff.

6. Cato (*Purgatorio* I) and Rifeo the Trojan (*Paradiso* XX) are the exceptions noted in the poem.

7. To put it so is to recall the phrase of the poem (*Paradiso* XXXII, 82) on this point: "Ma poi che'l *tempo della grazia* venne . . ." (q.v.).

8. For Dante, the color of charity is not merely red, but is almost always indicated as the color of fire or flame. His *Paradiso* is full of such symbolism, and Beatrice, as early as her first appearance in the *Vita Nuova* is dressed in "sanguigno," as every reader knows. No doubt the notion of the flame color of charity is precisely the notion that establishes red as charity's color. In this connection we may remark a note by Augustine on the symbolism of the *coccinum* or scarlet-oak berry (*Quaestionum in Heptateuchum* IV, 34, *PL* 34.734): "Coccinum charitas est, quod fervorem spiritus igneo colore testatur."

9. On the point that charity is the form of the virtues, see Aquinas, *Summa Theol.,* II–II, q. 23, a. 8: "Utrum caritas sit forma virtutum."

10. *Purgatorio* XXXI, 103–105:

> Indi mi tolse, e bagnato m'offerse
>   dentro alla danza delle quattro belle;
>   e ciascuna del braccio mi coperse.

11. *Purgatorio* VII, 34–36:

> quivi sto io con quei che le tre sante
>   virtù non si vestiro, e sanza vizio
>   conobber l'altre e seguir tutte quante.

Virgil is clearly not given to subtle distinctions between the acquired and the infused cardinal virtues. In Christian terms, he must mean the *acquired,* even though he may not be aware of this.

12. The point here concerns what was known as the "connection" of the virtues, by way of which one who had one of the cardinal virtues had them all. (See Aquinas, *Summa Theol.* I–II, q. 65, a. 1; also I–II, q. 65, a. 3, "Utrum caritas possit esse sine aliis virtutibus moralibus," resp., "Cum caritate simul infunduntur omnes virtutes morales.") For a study of this, see O. Lottin, *Psychologie et morale,* III, 197 ff.

13. *Purgatorio* VIII, 85–93:

> Li occhi miei ghiotti andavan pur al cielo,
>   pur là dove le stelle son più tarde,
>   sì come rota più presso allo stelo.
> E'l duca mio: "Figliuol, che là su guarde?"
>   E io a lui: "A quelle tre facelle
>   di che'l polo di qua tutto quanto arde."
> Ond'elli a me: "Le quattro chiare stelle
>   che vedevi staman son di là basse,
>   e queste son salite ov'eran quelle."

14. *Purgatorio* XXXI, 130–138.

15. *Purgatorio* XXVIII, 121–126.

16. *Eunoè* is devised from the Greek εὔνοια to signify "well-minded."

17. That this is Matelda's habitual function is clear from Beatrice's words to her in *Purgatorio* XXXIII, 127–129:

> Ma vedi Eunoè che là deriva:
> menalo ad esso, *e come tu se' usa*,
> la tramortita sua virtù ravviva.

18. Tigris and Euphrates are remembered in *Purgatorio* XXXIII, 112.

19. Philo, *De Opificio Mundi*, in *Philo*, with an English translation by F. A. Colson and G. H. Whitaker, Loeb Classical Library (New York, 1929), I, 6 ff.

20. *Ibid.*, pp. 187 ff.

21. *S. Ambrosii Opera* in *CSEL*, XXXII, ed. C. Schenkl, Part 1, pp. 265 ff. Also in *PL* 14.291 ff. I quote from the edition of Schenkl, but refer also to *PL*.

22. *Ibid.*, p. 272 (*PL* 14.296): "erat fons qui inrigaret paradisum. qui fons nisi Dominus Iesus Christus, fons vitae aeternae sicut pater?"

23. *Ibid.*, p. 272 (*PL* 14.297): "hic fons, qui inrigat paradisum, hoc est virtutes animae eminentissimo merito pullulantes."

24. *Ibid.*, p. 275 (*PL* 14.297).

25. *Ibid.*, pp. 276–77 (*PL* 14.298–99): "quartus est fluuius Euphrates, qui latine fecunditas atque abundantia fructuum nuncupatur praeferens quoddam insigne iustitiae, quae omnem pascit animam. nulla enim abundantiores videtur fructus habere virtus quam aequitas atque iustitia, quae magis aliis quam sibi prodest et utilitates suas neglegit communia emolumenta praeponens. plerique Euphratem ἀπὸ τοῦ εὐφραίνεσθαι dictum putant, hoc est a laetando, eo quod hominum genus nullo magis quam iustitia et aequitate laetetur. causam autem cur ceteri qua commeant fluuii describantur, regiones locorum qua Euphrates commeat non describantur, illam accipimus, quia aqua eius uitalis adseritur et quae foueat atque augeat, unde Auxen eum Hebraeorum et Assyriorum prudentes dixerunt, contra autem fertur esse aqua aliorum fluminum, deinde quia ubi prudentia ibi et malitia, ubi fortitudo ibi iracundia, ubi temperantia ibi intemperantia plerumque est et alia vitia, ubi autem iustitia ibi concordia virtutum est ceterarum, ideo non ex locis qua fluit, hoc est non ex parte cognoscitur; non enim pars est iustitia, sed quasi mater est omnium."

26. *Confessions* V, 13–14.

27. *De Genesi Contra Manichaeos*, *PL* 34.173 ff.

28. *Ibid.*, col. 173: "Solent ergo Manichaei Scripturas Veteris Testamenti, quas non noverunt, vituperare."

29. *Ibid.*, col. 197.

30. *Ibid.*, col. 202–203.

31. *Ibid.*, col. 203–204: "13. Flumen autem quod procedebat ex Eden, id est ex deliciis et voluptate et epulis, quod flumen a Propheta significatur in Psalmis (Psal. xxxv, 9), cum dicit, Torrente voluptatis tuae potabis eos; hoc est enim Eden, quod latine voluptas dicitur: dividitur in quatuor partes, et quatuor virtutes significat, prudentiam, fortitudinem, temperantiam, justitiam. Dicitur autem Phison ipse esse Ganges, Geon autem Nilus, quod etiam in Jeremia propheta animadverti potest: nunc aliis nominibus appellantur. Sicut nunc Tiberis dicitur fluvius, qui prius Albula dicebatur. Tigris vero

et Euphrates etiam nunc eadem nomina tenent: quibus tamen nominibus virtutes, ut dixi spirituales significantur, quod etiam ipsorum nominum interpretatio docet, si quis hebraeam linguam vel syram consideret. Sicut Jerusalem quamvis sit visibilis et terrenus locus, significat tamen civitatem pacis spiritualiter: et Sion quamvis sit mons in terra, speculationem tamen significat; et hoc nomen in Scripturarum allegoriis ad spiritualia intelligenda saepe transfertur: et ille qui descendebat ab Jerusalem in Jericho, sicut Dominus dicit (Luc. x, 30), et in via vulneratus, saucius et semivivus relictus est a latronibus, utique locos istos terrarum, quamvis secundum historiam in terra inveniantur, spiritualiter cogit intelligi.

Prudentia ergo, quae significat ipsam contemplationem veritatis, ab omni ore humano alienam, quia est ineffabilis, quam si eloqui velis, parturis eam potius quam paris, quia ibi audivit et Apostolus ineffabilia verba, quae non licet homini loqui (II Cor. xii, 4). Haec ergo prudentia terram circumit, quae habet aurum, et carbunculum, et lapidem prasinum, id est disciplinam vivendi, quae ab omnibus terrenis sordibus, quasi decocta nitescit, sicut aurum optimum; et veritatem, quam nulla falsitas vincit, sicut carbunculi fulgor nocte non vincitur; et vitam aeternam, quae viriditate lapidis prasini significatur, propter vigorem qui non arescit. Fluvius autem ille qui circuit terram Aethiopiam multum calidam atque ferventem, significat fortitudinem calore actionis alacrem atque impigram. Tertius autem Tigris vadit contra Assyrios, et significat temperantiam, quae resistit libidini, multum adversantis consiliis prudentiae, unde plerumque in Scripturis Assyrii adversariorum loco ponuntur. Quartus fluvius non dictum est contra quid vadat, aut quam terram circumeat; justitia enim ad omnes partes animae pertinet, quia ipsa ordo et aequitas animae est, qua sibi ista tria concorditer copulantur, prima prudentia, secunda fortitudo, tertia temperantia; et in ista tota copulatione atque ordinatione justitia."

32. *De Genesi ad Litteram*, *PL* 34.371: "Non ignoro de paradiso multos multa dixisse; tres tamen de hac re quasi generales sunt sententiae. Una eorum qui tantummodo corporaliter paradisum intelligi volunt: alia eorum qui spiritualiter tantum; tertia eorum qui utroque modo paradisum accipiunt; alias corporaliter, alias autem spiritualiter. Breviter ergo ut dicam, tertiam mihi fateor placere sententiam. Secundum hanc suscepi nunc loqui de paradiso."

33. *Ibid.*, col. 375: "Illud plane quod sequitur, 'Et lignum vitae in medio paradisi, et lignum scientiae dignoscendi bonum et malum,' diligentius considerandum est, ne cogat in allegoriam ut non ista ligna fuerint, sed alius aliquid nomine ligni significent. Dictum est enim de sapientia: 'Lignum vitae est omnibus amplectentibus eam' (Prov. iii, 18). Verumtamen cum sit Jerusalem aeterna in coelis, etiam in terra civitas qua illa significaretur, condita est; et Sara et Agar quamvis duo Testamenta significarent (Gal. iv, 24), erant tamen quaedam etiam mulieres duae; et cum Christus per ligni Passionem fluento spiritali nos irriget, erat tamen et petra, quae aquam sitienti populo ligno percussa manavit, de qua diceretur: Petra autem erat Christus (I Cor. x, 4). Aliud quam illa omnia significaverunt, sed tamen etiam ipsa corporaliter fuerunt. Et quando a narrante commemorata sunt, non erat illa figurata locutio, sed earum rerum expressa narratio, quarum erat figurata praecessio. Erat ergo et lignum vitae, quemadmodum petra Christus; nec

sine mysteriis rerum spiritalium corporaliter praesentatis voluit hominem Deus in paradiso vivere."

34. I have quoted the translation of St. Gregory the Great, *Morals on the Book of Job*, Library of Fathers of the Holy Catholic Church (Oxford, 1844), I, 118. Latin text in *PL* 75.509 ff.; this particular passage: col. 592.

35. *In Pentateuchum Commentari: Genesis, PL* 91.206.

36. Walafrid Strabo, *Glossa Ordinaria, PL* 113.87.

37. Reproduced in *Speculum*, VII (1932), facing p. 27.

38. For a thorough discussion of the whole subject and its copious literature in Dante's time and beyond, see H. Patch, *The Other World* (Cambridge, Mass., 1950), pp. 142 ff.

Chapter XI

Virgo or Justice

In turning once more to those puzzling verses about four stars seen only by a "prima gente" and then seen no more by anyone, we must admit that the term "first people" seems somewhat strange, if, that is, we are to understand that two persons only, Adam and Eve, are intended by those words. Certainly "gente" would ordinarily not be used if considerably more than two individuals were not meant. To be sure, in that first time those two were in themselves the whole of the human race. Still, the term is somewhat odd if they alone are intended.

Moreover, if we do understand "prima gente" to mean Adam and Eve, there is another point to be considered: the very brief time that Adam and Eve remained in the Garden, on Dante's view. It was a question which had received no little attention from the theologians, and a number of differing estimates as to the length of that time had been made. The one chosen by Dante is one which others had advanced; and it is the one which grants to our first parents the briefest time in Eden, something over six hours, a mere morning in the Garden, before their expulsion. In the *Comedy*, it is no less an authority on the matter than Adam himself who assures us of this.[1]

Even so, it is not the brevity of the sojourn in the Paradise that leaves us with any special problem. No doubt the first innocence and then the Fall, viewed in that light, are to be seen as a persuasive instance of the familiar adage, *corruptio optimi pessima*. For God had made Adam right,[2] that is, perfect, even as He had made the angels perfect in their nature, and that nature higher than man's. But precisely those angels who fell from that first perfection would seem to confirm the truth of what that formula in Latin affirms, for we know, again on Dante's view, that it took an even briefer time for the angels to fall: "in less time than it takes to count to twenty," as the poem has it.[3] The corruption of the best is not only the worst, it is quicker in coming about!

Indeed, it is simply those two words "first people" as a term denoting two persons only that gives us pause. But we may remark that the sense of difficulty here is an old one. Some of the early commentators who were near contemporaries of Dante note it. Benvenuto da Imola,[4] for one, holds that those who understand that Adam and Eve alone are intended by such words are guilty of taking them in too narrow a sense. It is interesting too that Benvenuto advances, as one objection to such a narrow reading, precisely the point about the very brief time which Adam and Eve had spent in Eden. Benvenuto recognizes at once, of course, that the stars are the virtues, recalling that there are three stars farther along in Canto VIII of *Purgatorio* which must be considered along with the four in Canto I:

Thus, according to the letter; the poet says: *io mi volsi a man destra*, that is, toward the south, *e posi mente*, that is, I looked with the eye of my mind, *a l'altro polo*, that is, the southern, which was high there as it is low to us, *e vidi quattro stelle*, that is, the four cardinal virtues, as the author himself glosses and expounds in the next to the last chapter [i.e. Canto XXXII] of *Purgatorio*, which virtues are properly called stars because they are bright and incorruptible like stars. And note that around this other pole there are three very bright stars opposite these four, as will be told later on, in Canto VIII, which allegorically are the three theological virtues; and he says, *non viste mai*, that is, not seen now for many centuries by

vice-ridden men, but the ancients cultivated them egregiously, hence
he says: *fuor che a la prima gente*. And note this, that there are some
who expound this to mean "except by Adam and Eve." But this is
too strict an interpretation, because our first parents remained but
a brief time in the state of innocence and cultivated these virtues too
little. And moreover he [the poet] at once makes clear that Cato
was illuminated by these. Others interpret "except by the first people," that is, by men of the first age, which is said to have been
golden, which did not know vice and cultivated the virtues in innocence: and yet I do not find what the time of this age was. Yet I
believe that the poet means that miserable modern men have lost the
sight of these four stars, which our ancients beheld well and by the
light of which they lived and moved (to which virtues are reduced
the other moral virtues), as did the ancient Romans. Wherefore
Augustine in the fifteenth of the *City of God*: "In the most opulent
rule of the Romans God shows what the worth of the civil virtues
is even without true religion"; and great philosophers and poets,
Greek as well as Latin [affirm this]. And this is seen to be the true
intent of the author, which he himself makes clear later, in Canto
VIII, where Virgil says that he dwells with those who knew these
four virtues entirely, etc.[5]

Benvenuto is the most thoughtful and thorough of the early
commentators, and here as elsewhere his gloss on a specific point
is extensive enough to reflect the difficulties which a reader in
Dante's own time could have with the two tercets concerning the
four stars. Curiously enough, just that particular question, singled
out by Benvenuto as one debated in his time, has continued to result in those same two opposing interpretations reported by him.
Do the words "prima gente" refer to Adam and Eve, or do they
mean mankind living in a first age which was golden? And, as
against the first reading, Benvenuto advances the objection we
have already noted: Adam and Eve lived a very short time in the
Garden and could have cultivated those four virtues very little.
It may be observed in passing that if Benvenuto means that our
first parents were in some way lacking in those virtues, in their
first state of perfection (however brief that may have been), he
shows himself curiously ignorant of orthodox theological opinion
on this matter in his own time.[6]

Along this same line, we should note likewise Benvenuto's
entire disregard of the question whether these cardinal virtues,

signified by the four stars, might be the acquired virtues known
to the ancient Romans, or the infused virtues not known to them:
a disregard making for difficulties that have continued to come
up in commentaries on the *Comedy* into our own day.[7] Since Benvenuto would have it that "the ancient Romans" are meant by the
words "first people," he is overlooking that very distinction, of
course, and he is quick to cite Virgil in support of this. But that
view leads him to read the whole verse "not seen except by the
first people" in a modified way, as not meaning strictly what it
says, but rather "not seen *now for many centuries* by vice-ridden
men." Yet he must know that this is a loose interpretation and
that the words "mai fuor che" actually mean what his Latin equivalent expresses: "praeterquam."

For all the several problems raised by Benvenuto's reading of
the verses, for the moment it is of interest to note his understanding that "first people" means "mankind in the golden age," even
though he frankly admits that he cannot discover when that age
was. Others in his time hold this view, apparently agreeing with
him that to understand simply "Adam and Eve" is to limit the
meaning too much. But this is at least to admit that "Adam and
Eve" might be part of the intended meaning. And we may be
certain that such is the case. For it is surely what Genesis tells us
of man's first innocence and of the Fall from Paradise that gives
rise to the lament which is uttered in these same verses. What
Genesis tells us, in this case, is the literal historical fact, and this
lament must have reference to such fact. And yet, even as Benvenuto and others testify, it is most natural that such an appellation
as "prima gente" should call to mind that myth of the golden
age sung by the poets, of a time when mankind lived in innocence
and virtue. This would mean, to be sure, not the ancient Romans
in the usual sense, but that first people who had lived in an age
long before, a time which Roman poets and philosophers had celebrated. Are we right, then, in sensing the presence of that familiar
myth of the Golden Age in these verses in *Purgatorio* which speak
of four stars?

It seems well to look to the end of the *Purgatorio* for guidance
to a possible answer. We should attend to words spoken by the

maiden Matelda, words which refer precisely to that myth. Matelda appears to go somewhat out of her way to speak them. She calls these words of hers a "corollary" to all that she has already declared about Eden. And when she has spoken this corollary, Virgil and Statius, the two ancient poets who stand there to hear her, smile. We know this smile of theirs to be a smile both of recognition and of satisfaction in the words she speaks, for those words affirm that there is a connection after all between that first time of innocence in Eden and the poets' dreamed-of golden age of Saturn.

To the three poets who stand before her Matelda has been concerned to explain at some length that the place before their eyes now is Eden, the Paradise which was created for man, and how man through his sin lived "but a brief time here," exchanging the joy and pleasure of this place for tears and hardship.[8] And thereupon this maiden, who continues apparently to live in the Paradise from which man was driven forth to misery, advances the words which, as she says, go quite beyond what was promised in the way of explaining Eden; and what she says causes the ancient poets to smile:

> "E avvegna ch'assai possa esser sazia
>   la sete tua perch'io più non ti scopra,
> darotti un corollario ancor per grazia;
>   nè credo che'l mio dir ti sia men caro,
>   se oltre promission teco si spazia.
> Quelli ch'anticamente poetaro
>   l'età dell'oro e suo stato felice,
>   forse in Parnaso esto loco sognaro.
> Qui fu innocente l'umana radice;
>   qui primavera sempre ed ogni frutto;
>   nettare è questo di che ciascun dice."
> Io mi rivolsi' n dietro allora tutto
>   a' miei poeti, e vidi che con riso
>   udito avean l'ultimo costrutto;
> poi alla bella donna torna'il viso.

Purgatorio XXVIII, 134–148.

"And although your thirst might be quite satisfied even if I disclosed no more to you, I will make you the further gift of a corollary; nor do I think that my words will be less dear to you if they go beyond what was promised. Those ancients who

wrote in poetry of the golden age and its happy state, perhaps
dreamed in Parnassus of this place. Here the first human stock
was innocent; here there was perpetual spring and every fruit;
this is the nectar of which all speak." I then turned me quite
around to my poets, and noted that they had heard these last
words with a smile. Then I turned to face the beautiful maiden.

We too may smile in our own sense of recognition as we listen
to Matelda's "corollary," for her words do indeed affirm a relation,
a kind of correspondence, between the account of a "first time"
in Eden, as given by Genesis (which speaks the truth), and the
"dream" of a golden age on the part of those "who anciently wrote
poetry." We should not overlook the little word "forse" used by
Matelda: "*perhaps* the ancient poets dreamed of this place when
they wrote of the golden age." The suggestion is tentative, and
the more suggestive in being so.

The affirmation of a certain correspondence between what is
"dreamed by the poets," on the one hand, and what is the Biblical
truth, on the other, is a familiar feature of Dante's poem, certainly
by the time the reader has reached the last cantos of the *Purgatorio*. The principle on which such a correspondence rests has
already been variously manifested through the *Inferno*. Capaneus,
the pagan of whom Statius himself had written, blasphemes Jove,
the god of the pagans; and yet the mighty figure stretched on the
burning sand exemplifies pride and blasphemy, nonetheless, as
judged within a biblical frame.[9] And those giants who loom as
towers around the innermost circle of Hell are, as the ancient
poets had taught, those giants who had tried to scale Olympus;
and now, in this "Christian" place, they anticipate and pre-figure
Satan himself who aspired in pride to soar so high.[10] So throughout the *Inferno*. For, as Dante makes clear in another work, there
is always the "scripture of the pagans" to turn to for concordance
and confirmation of the truth.[11]

In the *Purgatorio*, such a concordance of the "two scriptures"
is even more to the fore and more emphatically declared — in the
examples of the virtues and the opposing vices, for instance, on
each of the seven terraces, where a constant alternation of the
biblical and the pagan example is the more strictly observed,

affirming this same principle. Thus, as an instance of this, Matelda's corollary comes simply as something quite familiar, though now with a special insistence, in being declared a "corollary."

As we watch her move so gracefully about this place at the summit of the mountain and listen to her explanation, we learn from her that this is indeed the paradise that was given to man as a token and anticipation of the life of peace in eternity to come.[12] Meanwhile, two ancient poets are standing by, one Christian, the other pagan. To them Matelda speaks the words that "go beyond the promise," and at once a bridge is thrown out, connecting their ancient dream of a golden age of innocence with the biblical reality and truth which is now before their eyes. Their dream, they may know, was a "true" dream, because it was strangely close to the truth. Matelda is saying that between their dream of a golden age and the reality which they are now privileged to behold, there is a striking correspondence — and it is one which makes them smile, when they see it.

Yet it can occur to us to wonder, in this respect, if we, as readers of the poem, have actually seen the whole of that correspondence, even though it is so explicitly pointed out to us in this canto. Have we not generally forgotten one central feature of that "poet's dream" about an age of innocence and the first time of man? I mean the myth of a maiden named Astraea (whose other name was Justice), who, as a goddess, had lived among the first men before they fell into corruption. Astraea was also known as Virgo and could bear both names because she became that constellation of stars in the sky. She was therefore "star-maiden." Certainly, the figure of Virgo is one which, as readers of the *Comedy*, we are not apt to forget, because the memory of her is forever engraved in that Fourth Eclogue of Virgil which counts for so much in the structure of the poem. The famous prophetic verses of the Eclogue become, in fact, verses in *terza rima* in the *Purgatorio* itself, at the point when Statius has joined the two wayfarers and tells them how it happened that he became a Christian. He had read these verses of the Eclogue, he here declares to Virgil, and had seen that their true message was a prophecy of Christ's Advent:

"quando dicesti: 'secol si rinova,
  torna giustizia e primo tempo umano
  e progenie scende da ciel nova.' "

Purgatorio XXII, 70–72.

"when you said, 'the age is renewed, justice returns and the first
age of man, and a new progeny descends from heaven.' "

It is evident that the words "justice returns" translate the "iam
redit et Virgo" of the eclogue. Elsewhere, in the *De Monarchia*,
Dante has affirmed this same identity, having occasion there to
refer to Virgil's prophecy and its significance in history: "Virgo
was called Justice whom they also called Astraea." [13]

If we have in fact tended to overlook the myth of Virgo as
part of that whole "poets' dream" of a golden age, we shall do
well to recall it here at the summit of Purgatory; for it may be
that Matelda's corollary is meant to bring to mind even that feature
of the ancient myth. And if this should be so, we may come to
see that Matelda herself, as part of the "biblical reality" of this
place where she dwells, is precisely the figure which corresponds
to the figure of Astraea in the poets' dream, that star-maiden
whose other name was Justice.

*   *   *

"This is that nectar of which all speak," says Matelda, meaning
the poets who write of a golden age; and in the moment she says
this, it must be that she points to the stream that flows between her
and the three poets whom she addresses. For a verse in Ovid will
come to mind at those words, one of a number near the beginning
of the *Metamorphoses* where an account is given of the first age
of man: "flumina iam lactis, iam flumina nectaris ibant"; which
can serve to remind us that among those ancients who had "poet-
ized of the golden age" Ovid ought perhaps to be thought of first:

Golden was that first age, which, with no one to compel, without
a law, of its own will kept faith and did the right. There was no
fear of punishment, no threatening words were to be read on brazen
tablets: no suppliant throng gazed fearfully upon its judge's face;
but without judges lived secure. Not yet had the pine-tree, felled
on its native mountains, descended thence into the watery plain to
visit other lands; men knew no shores except their own. Not yet

were cities begirt with steep moats; there were no trumpets of straight, no horns of curving brass, no swords or helmets. There was no need at all of armed men, for nations, secure from war's alarms, passed the years in gentle ease. The earth herself, without compulsion, untouched by hoe or plowshare, of herself gave all things needful. And men, content with food which came with no one's seeking, gathered the arbute fruit, strawberries from the mountain-sides, cornel-cherries, berries hanging thick upon the prickly bramble, and acorns fallen from the spreading tree of Jove. Then spring was everlasting, and gentle zephyrs with warm breath played with the flowers that sprang unplanted. Anon, the earth, untilled, brought forth her stores of grain, and the fields, though unfallowed, grew white with the heavy bearded wheat. Streams of milk and streams of sweet nectar flowed, and yellow honey was distilled from the verdant oak." [14]

Then, as Ovid goes on to relate, Saturn was banished from his rule and the world came under the sway of Jove. A silver race came, "lower in the scale than gold," and, with this change, the familiar story tells of the gradual decline and fall of man, from age to age and from corruption to greater corruption, silver age, then bronze and at last, hard iron. And with this last age "all evil burst forth":

> "The age of hard iron came last. Straightway all evil burst forth into this age of baser vein. . . . Piety lay vanquished, and the maiden [*virgo*] Astraea, last of the immortals, abandoned the blood-soaked earth." [15]

In the familiar passage, Ovid makes only this final fleeting mention of the virgin Astraea. Evidently he presumed in his readers the knowledge that this "last of the immortals" had lived with men and walked about among them in that first golden age. For just so had poets in Greek, and long before Ovid, told the tale: notably Aratus, among them. Aratus had written a poem on the Constellations, the *Phaenomena*,[16] wherein, as he came to Bootes the Waggoner driving the Wain of the Bear, and then, in due order, to the constellation of Virgo, he recorded a story wherein that immortal maid is given a more prominent role than Ovid allowed her:

> After Helice, Arctophylax, very like a waggoner, is borne along,

commonly known by the name of Bootes, because he appears to
drive the Wain of the Bear, and appears conspicuously bright. Beneath his girdle rolls Arcturus, the most brilliant of stars. Below
both feet of the waggoner the Virgin appears, who holds in her
hand the splendid star Spica. Whether she be the offspring of
Astraeus, the reputed father of primeval stars, or of some other,
matters not. There is another story current among men that she was
at one time well acquainted with earth; nor did she shun the society
of old men, or women, but mingled freely with them, although she
herself was immortal; moreover, they call her Justice. Associating
with old men at one time, in the market place, and at another in the
open air, she, by her wisdom, demonstrated the laws of State.

As yet they were ignorant of pernicious strife, contentious wran-
gling, and sedition, but lived a quiet life, and ignorant of the danger
of the sea, for as yet no ships brought them food from foreign lands,
but oxen and the plough; the lady herself, Justice, the upholder of
right, supplied all the wants of the people. Then also was the time
when earth nourished the golden race. Rarely and with somewhat
less interest did she visit the silver race, being solicitous for the
welfare of the ancient people; nevertheless, she had not forsaken
the silver race; but would come to them alone, at eventide, from
the high mountains, never returning, however, in good humour with
any. When she had filled the great cities with crowds of men she
ever and anon assumed a threatening attitude, rebuking them for
their wickedness.

"Never more," she said, "will I take any notice of your entreaties.
'Tis wonderful how the golden fathers left so degenerate a race,
but you will leave behind you a race still more degenerate. Then
bloody wars and many feuds will be in store for your posterity
and grievous pain will be attendant upon the distress." Having
spoken these words she would return to the mountains, taken away
from the people with whom she was, who with straining eyes
watched her departure.

As soon as many of this race were dead, others were born — a
brazen age — in which the then race of men were more wicked than
their ancestors; they were the first to bring into use the evil-bearing
sword; who first, also, established the practice of eating oxen. Then
Justice, hating this race of men, betook herself to heaven and firmly
established herself therein, where by night may be perceived the
Virgin shining conspicuously some distance from Bootes.[17]

It seems quite probable that Ovid was familiar with Aratus'
version of the myth of Virgo. Cicero translated a portion of the
Greek poem,[18] as did the poet Germanicus Caesar. The latter

made almost a literal translation of the *Phaenomena*,[19] and therein gave full attention to Astraea's role. Through him and Ovid, and yet others, the figure of Astraea or Virgo becomes firmly established in the meaning "Justice," a justice which was known to men in the first age of mankind. And when, in Christian times, no less a champion of the faith than Lactantius composes a treatise on the subject of Justice, it is Germanicus' translation of Aratus that he recalls and cites (among others) when he has occasion to refer to the myth of the Virgin.

In the fifth book of his *Divine Institutes*, Lactantius maintains to the Emperor Constantine the Great that justice is either by itself the greatest virtue or is by itself the fountain of virtue, sought after not only by philosophers but also by poets who "were esteemed as wise before the origin of the name of philosophy." These ancient poets therefore understood, in their wisdom, that justice, being offended with men in their wickedness, departed from the earth and withdrew to heaven; and in order to teach what it means to live justly, these poets cited examples of justice in the time of Saturn, which they called the golden time, and they told of the condition of human life while justice still remained on earth. Lactantius, in fact, reminds the Emperor of Ovid's verse which speaks of the rivers of nectar that flowed in that time. He mentions Cicero's translation of Aratus. And he quotes from the translation by Germanicus the verse, "Deseruit propere terras justissima virgo," "The most just maid left the earth at once." [20]

The presence of the maiden Astraea among men, in a first and golden age of man, tended to make the whole myth of that age a myth of Justice: of an original justice which once had prevailed and which then was lost, when mankind fell into sad corruption.

Among those who "dreamed" of such things as these, there came one who chose to prophesy as poets sometimes do, and in prophecy to acclaim, in a famous eclogue, the return of the Golden Age. In doing this, he conceived, of course, that the maiden Astraea, whose other name is Virgo, would also return with that returning age of Saturn. What indeed made that age "golden" if not the very presence of Justice living among men? And Virgil wrote:

Magnus ab integro saeclorum nascitur ordo;
iam redit et Virgo, redeunt Saturnia regna,
iam nova progenies caelo demittitur alto.

Eclogue IV, 5-7.

The great order of ages begins anew; now the Virgin returns,
now the rule of Saturn, now a new progeny descends from
heaven on high.

One can feel little wonder indeed that, in the Christian centuries
following, these verses should have been seen as prophetic.[21] Statius
the Christian, who rises from his terrace in Purgatory to walk
along with Virgil, had found them to be so. For surely Virgil had
foretold the advent of the Saviour who is Christ, and the coming
of a new time for mankind. This would be the return of an age,
a golden age. Pagans might thus think of the myth of Virgo, but
Christians knew from their Genesis, too, what such a golden age
must really be, if they were perceptive enough to note the evident
points of correspondence between the dreams of poets and the
truth of Scripture and of history, and if they would only bear in
mind much that they had heard of the advent of a second Adam.

The wonder is rather, since the words "nova progenies" were
understood to refer to Christ, that "Virgo" of the preceding verse
was not taken to mean the Virgin Mary. This in fact did happen,
and we find the Emperor Constantine himself so understanding
the prophecy.[22] But the Emperor's reading remained quite the
minority opinion in this matter, if we may believe the records
we have. Instead, those scholiasts who came to be such great
authorities for the interpreting of Virgil's works held firmly
to the understanding that Virgo meant Justice. Servius so ruled;
and Philargyrius repeats him: "Virgo, id est Justitia." [23] And
Dante, as we noted, putting the very verses into Statius' mouth,
translated it "giustizia": "torna giustizia e primo tempo umano."

In this way the myth of Virgo, of Justice living among men
once in an age of innocence, stood beside the account in Genesis
of a first, though briefer, time of innocence before sin, when man
dwelt in the abode of delights that God had fashioned for him.
In both accounts, a decline and fall into corruption and misery
had come about. Certainly, to hold them side by side, the two are

impressively alike in their essential features. And it is for us to note that this remains true even if we look to the particular feature in the poets' myth of the presence of the virgin Astraea, the presence, that is, of Justice. Genesis, to be sure, tells of no such maiden walking in the Garden among the first people. But of one thing all of Christian theology was certain: Adam and Eve, in their "golden age," had original justice. And when they sinned in disobedience to God, what they lost forthwith, as a just penalty for that first sin, was precisely that condition of justice in which they had been created and which is therefore known in theology as original justice. In fact, in the matter of the Fall and loss of Eden, nothing is more central in the theologian's interpretation of that event than this matter of the loss of original justice.

We come, in this way, to see that the two accounts of the condition of a "first people" and their fall are most strikingly in agreement on what is a primary feature in each: Justice, original Justice, and how that was lost. Even the author of that plodding work (composed in Dante's time), the *Ovide moralisé*,[24] is quick to seize upon this agreement and point it out to pious readers. Indeed, such concordance is of the essence of his method, and this allegorizer of a pagan poet can affirm as a general principle that

> La divine page et la fable
> Sont en ce, ce samble, acordable,

or, to turn it around as he does, with something less than a rhyme:

> La fable et la Divine page
> se vont, ce m'est vis, acordant.[25]

Then, when this poetaster comes to that verse in his Ovid which relates how Virgo quit the earth, we have this concordance of sacred page and fable expressed so:

> Or son li juge corrompu
> Et Justice a le col rompu.
> Justice est morte, ce m'est vis,
> Non est, ains est em paradis.[26]

*   *   *

Justice is not dead: rather, Justice is "em paradis." In this last

verse the moralizer of Ovid is clearly meeting the point that when
Astraea quit the company of men she retired, some said to Olympus, some said to the sky, to form there the constellation Virgo.
But translating this to the Christian truth, the best equivalent one
can find, of course, is "she retired to paradise." No doubt he means,
not that earthly paradise of delights that was Eden, but that
Heaven of eternal delight where God is. Nevertheless his own
turn of phrase, in such a deliberate search for equivalents, can
prompt us to take stock of the essential differences between the
two accounts of an age of innocence, of what happened to that
original justice which prevailed with man in that first time, in the
one version and the other. In the fable of the poets, it is the
maiden whose name is Justice who deserts the first people when
they fall away from the innocence of the golden age. And in the
"divine page" there is no such figure of a maiden. Even so, and
without personification, there was Justice in Eden. "God made
Adam right," which meant that Adam at his creation was given a
perfect inner justice or rectitude. Thus, if in the Fall, as Genesis
relates it, Justice personified cannot desert Adam in the same way
as in the fable, it may happen the other way round: Adam deserts
Justice. For Adam and his fair consort fell into sin and through
sin lost that original justice which was a most precious gift of God.
Adam and Eve were deprived of that justice, and it was never to
be regained by any of their posterity. They were deprived of
their original justice, which is to say that, when Adam and Eve
were driven from the Garden of delights, they were driven from
that Justice which was the chief of those delights. When they leave
Eden, they leave Justice behind them.

We might conceive, indeed, that a poet, far more profound in
his concordances of fable and divine page than was the allegorizer
of Ovid, would imagine (in the manner of poets) that a living
man, by an extraordinary dispensation of Grace, enters upon a
journey which leads him finally back to the Garden of Eden at
the summit of a mountain. And there, as he comes into this Garden
so long deserted, he meets a fair maiden who appears to dwell in
this place, and who declares to him that this is indeed Eden. She
speaks of man's brief sojourn here, in fact; then she goes on to

refer to the poets' dream of a golden age, pointing to the "truth" of that dream. That truth, she declares to the living man and to the ancient poets before her, is now before their eyes.

And indeed the truth of their myth is everywhere visible here: the delights of nature, eternal spring, a river of nectar: all is here — except one feature. If this be the true golden age, and if the poets' fable was a true fable, then where, in the "truth" now before us, is Astraea or Justice? We have toured the Garden and we have heard Matelda explain it all, but we have not met any counterpart of that star-maiden who, on the requirements of the poets' fable, should live and walk in this place.

Of course we see the answer, once the question is presented in this light. And when we see it, we have every right to smile even as Virgil and Statius do. For they too must see this. The "poets' dream" proves to be even truer than we have heretofore conceived. For, look, here before our eyes is the very "truth" of which Astraea was the "dream": the maiden before us whose mysterious name is Matelda *is* that truth. Astraea was Justice personified, Astraea was original justice. And so is Matelda, here in Eden. This is the further meaning of her corollary, undeclared except by her presence. But might a poet not think that presence to be declaration enough, since it is this maiden herself who goes "beyond what was promised," to speak of the truth of the ancient poets' dream?

There is much more to be noted by way of confirmation. Matelda acts out her significance as Justice when she comes here in Eden, and she herself declares what she is, more clearly than we have seen up to now. But if we view her for a moment yet as the counterpart of Virgo in the myth, we may find it worth noting how first we look upon Matelda through Dante's eyes and through a simile, as she comes toward the wayfarer who has called out to her. Matelda advances towards Dante in a kind of slow dance, almost in ritual, over the flowered meadow, "non altrimenti che vergine che gli occhi onesti avvalli," not otherwise than a virgin who lowers her modest eyes.[27]

Perhaps this touch would have been here, even if the presence of a virgin star-maiden were not there in the background of the simile to dictate it. Astraea, moreover, was a goddess; and, recalling this, may we not wonder if there is not that association also attaching to her figure here, when, again in simile, Matelda is seen first as Proserpine "when she lost the spring" and then as Venus when she was wounded by her own son's bow? Such strands of immortality do still cling to a Virgo transformed into a Matelda.[28] But Venus wounded gives us, of course, a Matelda in love — and with that touch this Christian poet is going quite beyond the dream of the ancient poets about Star-maiden.[29]

Here must be the place finally to return to the thought that this whole little excursion into the myth of Virgo had a beginning for us with the problem of four stars and a lament; and, more specifically, with the somewhat curious appellation of "first people" to designate two persons, Adam and Eve. We may now take stock of what has been gained by such ramblings.

First of all, it is evident that if we look back to the beginning of the *Purgatorio* from its end, and with full awareness of meanings that emerge at the end, we can see that Benvenuto da Imola, and all the other commentators after him who sensed in the words "prima gente" a reference to man in the golden age of the poets, were right, in some sense. We have simply to look at the whole purpose of Matelda's corollary, as we noted: the deliberate concordance of poets' dream and biblical truth. "First people" is indeed a curious way of speaking of two persons dwelling in Eden. Yet they are the persons intended, for they alone, in Christian truth, can be meant. And to put it so, to speak of them as "prima gente," is to do what Dante is so often concerned to do: to point to a concordance between the biblical truth and the dreams of the poets. Is there anything more strange about this than for a Christian to pray to "high Jove who wast crucified on earth for our sake?"[30]

Then there were those four stars over Eden which are the four cardinal virtues, representing a transformation of the four rivers of Eden which had that meaning. This still leaves the question, why *stars* for *virtues*? Why not, say, *plants* in the garden as virtues, even as Philo had construed them to be?

There are surely many sources of support for any poet of

Dante's time who would choose to conceive the virtues as stars; and any speculation as to what the background of Dante's particular conception was, could range widely through a varied symbolism which might have suggested it. Benvenuto commented that the virtues are properly called stars "because they are bright and incorruptible as stars." One may do better than that. We shall merely note in passing that already in the *Convivio* [31] Dante had glossed the word "star" as meaning "virtue," in one of the *canzoni* there included. But what we have noted of the manner in which Dante has brought into his poem (with a "corollary") the figure of Astraea, star-maiden, is in itself suggestive enough. And yet, if Astraea is thus transformed into a Matelda, Matelda does not become a constellation in the sky. But Matelda is Justice. And if we come to understand that these four stars in the sky over Eden are specifically *a constellation of justice*, we shall glimpse yet another aspect of Dante's concordance between fable and truth. Even the feature of nymphs (now in the plural to be sure) who are "also stars in the sky" has been kept. That these same four stars over Eden are to be seen as a constellation of "justice" must remain a mere working hypothesis for the moment, since we do not readily conceive how four stars which are the four cardinal virtues can stand for justice, when indeed we recall that justice is the name of *one* of these same four virtues. But as we look towards a further examination of the point, let this at least be remembered: the fourth river of Paradise was not said to flow to any particular part of the globe, as Philo and Ambrose and Augustine had noted, because justice, as the fourth of the cardinal virtues, was the very harmony of the other three, was not "ex parte" but was the virtue that contained the others as a whole, being "quasi mater omnium." That particular point takes on its importance, even as we can already see, and will enter into the conception of four stars as a constellation of that justice which was original in Eden. Thus if it proves possible to understand that such is their meaning, then we shall not only understand how there must be a lament for loss of them, that is, lament for loss of original justice, but we shall also see how these stars, by being the stars of justice, are Matelda's stars, belonging peculiarly to Eden, even as did the four rivers, even as does Matelda by dwelling there still. Justice, in any event, promises to come out as the controlling notion in this whole cluster of image, figure, and meaning. It therefore becomes more important than ever to understand what that first justice was which was given to the "first people" in their Paradise.

Notes

1. *Paradiso* XXVI, 139–142:
   > "Nel monte che si leva più da l'onda
   >   fu'io con vita pura e disonesta,
   >   da la prim'ora a quella che seconda,
   > come'l sol muta quadra, l'ora sesta."

2. From Augustine to Dante's day, two texts are constantly cited in support of Adam's original rectitude and perfection: Eccles. 7.30, first of all: "Solummodo hoc inveni, quod fecerit Deus hominem rectum"; and, of course, Gen. 1.27: "Et creavit Deus hominem ad imaginem suam." See *Purgatorio* XXVIII, 92: "fece l'uom buono e a bene"; *Paradiso* XIII, 83: "tutta l'animal perfezione," of Adam; *De Vulg. El.* I, v, 1.

3. *Paradiso* XXIX, 49–51:
   > "Nè giugneriesi, numerando al venti
   >   sì tosto, come de li angeli parte
   >   turbò il suggetto de' vostri elementi."

4. Benvenuto was born between 1336 and 1340. He lived until 1390. See P. Toynbee, "Benvenuto da Imola, etc.," in *An English Miscellany* (Oxford, 1901), pp. 436 ff.

5. *Comentum super Dantis Aldigherii Comoediam*, ed. Vernon (Florence, 1887), III, 15–16: "Ideo ad literam; dicit poeta: *io mi volsi a man destra*, scilicet versus meridiem, *e posi mente*, idest, respexi cum oculo mentis, *a l'altro polo*, scilicet australem, qui erat altus ibi sicut nobis est bassus, *e vidi quattro stelle*, idest, quatuor virtutes cardinales, ut autor se glosat, et exponit capitulo antepenultimo huius Purgatorii, quae merito appellantur stellae, quia sunt clarae et incorruptibiles, velut stellae. Et nota quod circa alium polum sunt tres lucidissimae stellae oppositae istis quatuor, ut dicetur infra capitulo VIII, quae allegorice sunt tres virtutes theologicae; et dicit, *non viste mai*, idest non visae jam per multa secula ab hominibus vitiosis, sed antiqui egregie coluerunt eas, ideo dicit: *fuor che a la prima gente*. Et hic nota quod aliqui exponunt hoc sic, idest, praeterquam ab Adam et Eva; sed ista est nimis stricta expo-

sitio, quia primi parentes parum stererunt in statu innocentiae, et nimis pauci fuissent cultores istarum virtutum; et tamen statim ostendet quod Cato fuit illustratus eis. Alii exponunt, praeterquam a prima gente, idest ab hominibus primae aetatis, quae dicitur fuisse aurea, quae ignoravit vitia et innocenter coluit virtutes: sed quando ista aetas fuerit non invenio. Sed credo quod poeta velit dicere, quod miseri moderni perdiderunt visionem istarum quatuor stellarum, quas antiqui nostri bene viderunt, et vixerunt ambulantes ad lucem earum, ad quas caeterae virtutes morales reducuntur, sicut antiqui romani. Unde Augustinus, XV *de Civitate Dei: ostendit Deus in opulentissimo regno romanorum quantum civiles virtutes valeant etiam sine vera religione:* et magni philosophi et poetae tam graeci quam latini. Et ista videtur vera intentio autoris, quod ipse clare manifestat infra capitulo VIII, ubi dicit Virgilius, quod stat cum illis qui plene noverunt quatuor virtutes, etc."

6. On the questions of the virtues given to Adam in his rectitude, see below pp. 210 ff.

7. Of course, to take "prima gente" to mean the Romans is to choose to ignore the fundamental distinction between the acquired cardinal virtues which the Romans as pagans could know and the infused cardinal virtues which they could not know. And there is a tendency among the humanists to overlook any such distinction. Thus Petrarch in two of his letters among the *Variae* (I have to thank my colleague E. H. Wilkins for pointing these letters out to me) sets forth an allegory of the virtues which is quite in line with what Benvenuto says here, assigning the cardinal virtues to a first time which is that of the ancients, not of Adam and Eve (*Epist, De Rebus Familiaribus et Variae*, ed. Fracassetti, Florence, 1863, epistles 50 and 61 among the *Variae*). Benvenuto and Petrarch were friends. See also below, pp. 261 ff.

8. *Purgatorio* XXVIII, 76 ff.

9. *Inferno* XIV, 46–72.

10. *Inferno* XXXI.

11. *Epist. ad Can. Gran.*, 63: "Quod etiam scriptura paganorum contestatur; unde Lucanus in nono: 'Jupiter est quodcunque vides, quocunque moveris.'"

12. On which point see below, p. 274.

13. *De Mon.* I, xi, 1: "Preterea, mundus optime dispositus est cum iustitia in eo potissima est. Unde Virgilius commendare volens illud seculum quod suo tempore surgere videbatur, in suis Bucolicis cantabat. 'Iam redit et Virgo, redeunt Saturnia regna.' 'Virgo' namque vocabatur Iustitia, quam etiam Astream vocabant. 'Saturnia regna' dicebant optima tempora, que etiam 'aurea' nuncupabant."

14. *Metamorphoses* I, 89–112. I have quoted the translation of F. J. Miller, Loeb Library, I, 9.

15. *Ibid.*, I, 113–150.

16. Aratus died in 239 B.C.

17. I have used the translation of C. L. Prince, *A Literal Translation of the Astronomy and Meteorology of Aratus* (Lewes, 1895), pp. 20–21.

18. Cicero, "Arateorum Fragmenta," in Vol. III of Aratus, *Phaenomena*, ed. J. T. Buhle (Leipzig, 1801), pp. 3 ff.

19. Germanicus Caesar, *Reliquiae*, ed. Giles (London, 1838), pp. 3–4.

20. Lactantius (in *CSEL*, Vol. XIX): *Divinae Institutiones*, ed. S. Brandt (Vienna, Prague, 1890), pp. 412 ff. An English translation is found in Vol. VII of the *Ante-Nicene Fathers* (Grand Rapids, Mich., 1951), pp. 135 ff.

21. For abundant evidence of general familiarity with the myth of Astraea in later time, and for many useful references, see Frances A. Yates, "Queen Elizabeth as Astraea," in *Journal of the Warburg and Courtauld Institutes*, X (1947), 27 ff.

22. Constantine, *Oratio ad Sanctorum Coetum* XIX (*PL*, 8.456).

23. *Servii Grammatici*, ed. Thilo and Hagen (Leipzig, 1902), Vol. III, Appendix Serviana; and, pp. 73 ff., the commentary of Philargyrius. The other interpretation, *Maria*, is recognized here as possible.

24. *Ovide Moralisé*, ed. C. DeBoer (Amsterdam, 1915), Vol. I.

25. *Ibid.*, vv. 2139–40; v. 1462.

26. *Ibid.*, vv. 1029–1033.

27. *Purgatorio* XXVIII, 56–57.

28. *Purgatorio* XXVIII, 49–66.

29. See below, pp. 207 ff.

30. *Purgatorio* VI, 118–119.

31. *Convivio* IV, xix, 5: "*Dice adunque: Sì com'è'l cielo dovunqu'è la stella*, e non è vero questo *e converso*, cioè rivolto, che dovunque è cielo sia la stella, così è nobilitade dovunque è vertude e non vertude dovunque nobilitade: e con bello e convenevole essemplo, chè veramente è cielo ne lo quale molte e diverse stelle rilucono. Riluce in essa le intellettuali e le morali virtudi."

Chapter XII

Matelda

At the end of *De Monarchia* Dante writes of the two goals which Divine Providence established for mankind, one earthly and the other heavenly, one of this life and the other of the life to come; and, in making this point, he refers to the earthly paradise (Eden) as "figuring" the goal of happiness in this life.[1] Important as this matter is, and ultimately relevant to present considerations, this is not the place for an inquiry into the particular notion of man's two goals. What is useful here is precisely the conception expressed by Dante's verb "to figure," as used in such a context. The terrestrial paradise, he says, "figures" the goal of happiness in this life. And his meaning is clear: Eden, as that place must be conceived through scriptural authority and established doctrine, is the visible embodiment, the true image, of perfect happiness on this earth.

"Figure," in this sense, is the notion we require in order to see Matelda in proper focus and understand her role and meaning in the episode at the summit of the mountain. "Figure" is to be taken in the sense of Augustine's "gratia significandi," that is, things in

Eden are "for the sake of signifying." Matelda figures man's first condition before sin, while he dwelt, as she still does, in the earthly Paradise. Matelda has this meaning simply by "imaging" that condition. We see her there, moving about in the Garden in her normal way of life, for, in that first moment, she appears unaware that anyone else is there to see her. What she does in that moment is therefore all the more evidently what she habitually does, the true picture of her life here, of "life" here: Matelda is thus seen to "act out" the way of life and happiness of the "first people" in the Paradise. Furthermore, it is important to note that her manner of life here exemplifies both the active and the contemplative life. Matelda, going about her daily occupation, gathers flowers and makes of them a garland. And this, as we know already from a certain dream which came to Dante near the dawn of this very day,[2] is the activity of Leah who stands for the active life, even as her sister Rachel represents the contemplative. But Matelda's life here in the Garden is not confined to the active. Matelda contemplates, a point which she herself appears concerned to stress, perhaps because it might not so readily meet the eye.

Matelda is singing as she gathers flowers for her garland, and when she turns her eyes toward Dante, it is at once apparent to him that Matelda is in love. It is that exceeding joy of hers that first strikes the attention of the onlooker. Matelda expects this to be so, and it is her first assumption that the three who stand gazing at her from beyond the stream of Lethe will wonder at that joy. And, if they should, then she would refer them to a certain psalm which, she says, might shed light on the matter and drive ignorance from their minds:

> "Voi siete nuovi, e forse perch'io rido,"
>   cominciò ella, "in questo luogo eletto
>   a l'umana natura per suo nido,
> maravigliando tienvi alcun sospetto;
>   ma luce rende il salmo *Delectasti*
>   che puote disnebbiar vostro intelletto."
> > > *Purgatorio* XXVIII, 76–81.

"You are new here, and perhaps because I rejoice," she began, "in this place chosen for mankind as its nest, some doubt holds

you in wonder: but the psalm *Delectasti* gives light which can
dispel the mists of your minds."

The psalm referred to is the ninety-first of the Vulgate Bible,
as perhaps Virgil, at least, could not be expected to know. But we,
as readers, are also new to this place and we too, it is assumed, will
wonder at Matelda's joy; and thus, upon her suggestion, we recall
this particular psalm for the light it can bring. If we turn to the
psalm we see that certain specific verses are intended to be called
to mind, for "delectasti" is not the first word of the psalm, nor is
the verse containing that word the first verse. The point of the
reference is thereby the more evident; and the verses intended
must be these:

> Quia delectasti me, Domine, in factura tua;
> et in operibus manuum tuarum exsultabo.
> Quam magnificata sunt opera tua, Domine.

> Because Thou didst delight me, Lord, in Thy work;
> and in the works of Thy hands I will rejoice.
> How praiseworthy are Thy works, O Lord.

It may be of more than mere erudite interest to note that over
a century before Dante wrote this canto of his poem, Peter Abelard had found that this particular psalm, and indeed the same
verses referred to by Matelda, were relevant to the matter of the
original condition of man in Eden. In his treatise on the work of
the Creation, *Hexaemeron*, when he enters into the "moral" interpretation of the events in Genesis, Abelard writes a commentary
on those delights which man, even now in his fallen condition,
may experience in the created universe, in all the creatures which
have been made for him:

> The things and creatures of the universe can hold out a varied pleas-
> ure to man, according to the diversity of man's senses: as with song
> they caress his ear, or with the beauty of their form they delight
> his eye, or with sweet odor refresh his sense of smell; or by what-
> soever manner through their divers natures studiously known by
> man they may otherwise inspire in us love and praise of the Creator,
> even as the Psalmist says, addressing Him: "Delectasti me, Domine,
> in factura tua et in operibus manuum tuarum exsultabo." [3]

The meaning of Matelda's reference to the psalm would be evident, even without testimony of this kind from Abelard. But his mention of the verses in precisely this context is of special interest, since he singles out the same verses as Matelda does to explain her own joy. Moreover, by what Abelard here observes respecting the delights which man may have from God's work now, after the Fall, we are prompted to think how much greater those delights must have been in Eden. Abelard specifically refers to the beauties of nature that meet our eyes, to the songs of birds and the fragrance of flowers in particular. And we may note that as Dante first enters the divine forest at the summit of the mountain, these are severally the specific delights which he experiences.[4] Still more important, in guiding us to the whole meaning of the reference to this particular psalm, is Abelard's qualification of it as a song in praise and love of the Creator. This, too, must be the essential point of Matelda's alluding to it, this must be the light which, as she says, should derive from it. We are not to understand merely that Matelda feels delight and joy in these wonders of God's handiwork, even as Adam must have felt them here. Matelda, by her allusion to the psalm, is telling us that the joy she experiences is the joy of love, and that her song (the words of which we do not hear) is a love song in praise of the Lord who made these things. Thus it is evident at once to Dante, at his first glimpse of this maiden, that Matelda is in love. It is presumed that we should wonder: in love how? What is the cause and object of her love, alone as she is in Eden? Now, it is in answer to this question that the psalm *Delectasti* should "uncloud our minds": Matelda rejoices, even as the Psalmist, in the works of God, and her song is a song in praise of Him.

We should also see, in this way, that Matelda, being the living embodiment of man's original condition here, exemplifies, on this particular score, a point of established doctrine regarding that condition. For we should know that man, in his first state of rectitude, loved God above all else, and referred his love of all else to God. St. Augustine had put a special insistence on this aspect of man's first righteousness and the love by which man before sin *adhered* to God. Because of this original gift to man of righteous

love, there was peace in man's spirit, the peace that comes whenever right order prevails therein. As God had made him, man was
right in the sight of God. Man had a perfect love, a love which is
properly named charity. It is through charity, and charity alone,
that man adheres to God and lives in due subjection to His will.

> In Paradise, then, man lived as he desired, so long as he desired what
> God had commanded. He lived in the enjoyment of God, and was
> good by God's goodness; he lived without any want, and had it in
> his power to live so eternally. He had food that he might not hun-
> ger, drink that he might not thirst, the tree of life that old age
> might not waste him. There was in his body no corruption, nor
> seed of corruption, which could produce in him any unpleasant
> sensation. He feared no inward disease, no outward accident. Sound-
> est health blessed his body, absolute tranquility his soul. As in Para-
> dise there was no excessive heat or cold, so its inhabitant was exempt
> from the vicissitudes of fear and desire. No sadness of any kind was
> there, nor any foolish joy; true gladness ceaselessly flowed from the
> presence of God, who was loved out of a pure heart, and a good
> conscience, and faith unfeigned.[5]

Love is an operation in the human soul. Charity is right love,
right order in the will with respect to the end, and God is that end
for man. Right order before God is due subjection to God; and
due subjection must mean that man refers all things to God as to
his last end. Thus Thomas Aquinas, in speaking of man's first condition of innocence, says: "Because man's will was subject to God,
man referred all things to God as to his last end, and in this consisted man's justice and innocence." [6] And we may note that
Thomas goes on directly to give to this first condition of man,
so viewed, the accepted name that most concerns us: *original
justice*. "And this so orderly condition in man is called original
justice." [7]

We may recall, moreover, that Dante himself, outside the
Comedy, had held it unthinkable that the first man would not
have praised the Creator by uttering His name as the first word
he spoke:

> Now I have no doubt that it is obvious to a man of sound mind
> that the first thing the voice of the first speaker uttered was the
> equivalent of God, namely *El*, whether in the way of a question

or in the way of an answer. It seems absurd and repugnant to reason that anything should have been named by man before God, since man had been made by Him and for Him. For, as since the transgression of the human race, every one begins his first attempt at speech with a cry of woe, it is reasonable that he who existed before the transgression should begin with joy; and since there is no joy without God, but all joy is in God and God himself is wholly joy, it follows that the first speaker said first and before anything else "God." [8]

Looked at through such fundamental notions as these, Matelda's love, which is at once so evident, finds its proper name. Her love is the love of charity, which is love of God above all else; and in this she is representing man's original state in what was its most important constituent element. In this way, the full import of her allusion to the psalm stands clear. Even as Abelard had recalled, the *Delectasti* is a song of love and praise for the Creator as He may be seen and loved, in and through the work of His creation. To know Him so, not in direct vision but in the mirror of His works, is an act of contemplation as well as of love, an act of intellect as well as of the will.[9]

We see that both ways of life, the active and the contemplative, are figured by Matelda. In her we are expected to see Adam's condition and first manner of life. But not Adam's alone. Matelda speaks of this "nest" of Eden as a place chosen for "human nature." And so it is: Matelda exemplifies human nature as it was before sin and as it would have been had there been no sin. The point is of importance, as we proceed, and we may take brief note of what Thomas Aquinas says on this:

> . . . which condition was given to the first man, not as to some particular individual person, but as to the first beginning of human nature, in order that thus through him it might be passed on to posterity.[10]

One is reminded of other words spoken by Matelda: "Qui fu innocente l'umana radice." [11]

But Adam was driven from the Garden long ago. And now, as this man returns to Eden, he beholds there the living and radiant image of man's happiness and perfection, as that had originally

been established by God. "God made man right," that is, He
made human nature right.

And because man was made right by God, there can be little
question as to the virtues which man must have had before sin.
For if Adam had charity, as is most evident, then it follows that
he had the other virtues as well. Philo had seen the virtues everywhere present in Eden.[12] St. John Damascene had held that "Adam
was adorned with every kind of virtue." [13] And when Peter Lombard advances the same opinion in his *Sentences*, one recognizes
that he is giving expression to a point of doctrine long since
firmly established, as he shows in his own citations from Augustine and Ambrose as authorities, concluding his question "whether
man would have had the virtues before the Fall": "It is not to be
doubted that man before sin did shine with the virtues; but through
sin he was stripped of them." [14]

More specifically, and in strict theology, it must follow that if
before sin Adam had charity, greatest of the infused virtues, then
Adam must also have had the other two, faith and hope. Moreover, since Adam had charity, it must be that Adam had also the
infused cardinal virtues. Indeed, such a truth is in no way con-
tested in theology. As usual it receives its clear formulation from
Thomas Aquinas:

> In the state of innocence, man in a certain sense possessed all the
> virtues; and this can be proved from what precedes. For it was
> shown above that such was the rectitude of the primitive state, that
> reason was subject to God, and the lower powers to reason. Now
> the virtues are nothing but those perfections whereby reason is
> directed to God, and the inferior powers regulated according to
> the dictate of reason, as will be explained in the Treatise on the
> Virtues. Wherefore the rectitude of the primitive state required
> that man should in a sense possess every virtue.
>
> It must, however, be noted that some virtues of their very nature
> do not involve imperfection, such as charity and justice; and these
> virtues did exist in the primitive state absolutely, both in habit and
> in act. But other virtues there are of such a nature as to imply im-
> perfection, either in their act or on the part of matter. If such im-
> perfection be consistent with the perfection of the primitive state,
> such virtues necessarily existed in that state; as faith, which is of
> things not seen, and hope which is of things not yet possessed. For

the perfection of that state did not extend to the vision of the Divine Essence and the possession of God with enjoyment of final beatitude. Hence faith and hope could exist in the primitive state, both as to habit and as to act.[15]

Before sin, therefore, Adam had all the virtues, even as man, had he not sinned, would have continued to have them all. Adam had charity to perfection. From this it must follow that Adam had sanctifying grace as well; for where such grace is not found, charity may not be.[16]

Thus Matelda figures the condition of man as it was, and was to have been, in Eden. As she moves about there, beyond the stream of Lethe, we see her living that life of happiness on earth which man forfeited by sin. But Dante, a living man who by special dispensation has now returned to the Eden which Adam lost, to find this maiden dwelling here (remembering Astraea we shall say *still* dwelling here), not only notes at once that she is a maiden very much in love, but for his own part, as he looks upon her, he feels a most intense love himself. The love he feels is desire of the maiden. He would possess Matelda. This comes with some surprise. It is, indeed, a feature of this whole episode that is well worth our close attention, for it must be noted that in this the poet has provided for a cardinal point in theological doctrine. Thus a review of Dante's encounter with Matelda, as given in the concrete detail of this canto, is very much in order.

*   *   *

Dismissed by Virgil and told by him "to sit or go" as he pleases, Dante chooses to go. It is early morning in the beautiful forest at the summit of the mountain and he is eager to explore the delights of this most remarkable place. As he moves forward (to see and feel him do this for the first time without a guide and on his own, is in itself a new experience for the reader), he comes upon a clear stream cutting across his path; and as he looks to the far side he sees suddenly appear there a most beautiful maiden who goes about gathering flowers along her way and singing as she goes. Somehow a first impression is that this must be a place familiar to her, and that she is doing now what she habitually does.

In the first words Dante speaks to her across the stream, asking
her to come nearer to him, it is also clear that this maiden is in
love. This Dante had seen at once:

> "Deh, bella donna, che a' raggi d'amore
> ti scaldi, s'i' vo' credere a' sembianti
> che soglion esser testimon del core,
> vegnati in voglia di trarreti avanti,"
> diss'io a lei, "verso questa rivera
> tanto ch'io possa intender che tu canti."
>
> *Purgatorio* XXVIII, 43–48.

"Pray, fair lady, who warm yourself by love's rays, if I am to
believe looks that are wont to be witnesses of the heart, may it
please you," I said to her, "to come forward to this stream so
near that I may hear what you are singing."

To this request the maiden responds, turning in a manner resembling a dance and coming toward the man who has called out
to her, "like a virgin who chastely lowers her eyes," so that the
sweet music of her song and the words of it can now be heard. As
she comes to stand directly across the stream from Dante and
raises her eyes to meet his, what was already somehow clear at
a distance is now most evident. This maiden is indeed in love:
Venus herself was not more so, when once her son Cupid had
shot his own mother with his arrow:

> Tosto che fu là dove l'erbe sono
> bagnate già dall'onde del bel fiume,
> di levar li occhi suoi mi fece dono:
> non credo che splendesse tanto lume
> sotto le ciglia a Venere, trafitta
> dal figlio fuor di tutto suo costume.
> Ella ridea dall'altra riva dritta,
> trattando più color con le sue mani,
> che l'alta terra sanza seme gitta.
> Tre passi ci facea il fiume lontani;
> ma Ellesponto, là 've passò Serse,
> ancora freno a tutti orgogli umani,
> più odio da Leandro non sofferse,
> per mareggiare intra Sesto ed Abido,
> che quel da me perch'allor non s'aperse.
>
> *Purgatorio* XXVIII, 61–75.

As soon as she was where the grass was just bathed by the waves of the beautiful river, she made me the gift of raising her eyes: I do not believe that such light shone from beneath Venus' eyelids when she was pierced by her son quite out of custom. She stood smiling on the opposite bank, arranging in her hands the many colors which this high land produces without seed. The river kept us three paces apart; but Hellespont where Xerxes crossed — still a curb to human pride — was not more hated by Leander for its high waves between Sestos and Abydos than was that water by me because it did not open then.

Soon it is not only Matelda who is in love; the sight of her there, in her beauty and innocence, has inspired love in the man gazing at her across the water. The image of a Leander desiring to be with his Hero and hating the waters that divide him from her is affirming this plainly enough. And it is also an image performing a certain definite function for the alert reader who is keeping in mind the broader context of this event. This love, which the sight of Matelda has at once inspired in Dante, as the simile is saying, is as Leander's was for his beloved. But was Leander's not a most sensual love? [17] And is not the comparison saying that Dante hates the separating waters and but for them would be with Matelda, as her lover, if he could? But how can such love, how can any such desire, be now in Dante? It was but yesterday that he passed through the last of the terraces of purgation on this mountain, through the fire that burns all carnal lust away. It was only a moment ago, indeed, that Virgil told him that his will was free, straight, and whole again, and that it would be a mistake not to follow where it leads. Surely here he may not be feeling any such desire as a Leander had felt. But the poem, in recalling that famous pair of lovers, appears to suggest precisely this.

If the name of Leander here is prompting such reflections in the reader's mind, it may be doing its calculated work, which is to bring the reader to a special awareness: namely, that what seems to be, cannot be; that is, that since the literal import of the simile cannot hold, he must look beyond the literal for the meaning. This is nothing but a familar focus for one kind of allegory and the well-known sign of it, as found, for instance, in that Book which is this poet's model for allegory.[18]

It seems worth our while at this point to note how confirmation of this particular matter of a certain focus for allegory can come from yet another tradition which the poet felt could be called to his reader's mind. This, too, is a matter of love and of two lovers, but in a situation and setting that are far less familiar to us than the Hellespont and that other pair just recalled. It concerns a certain literary form, current in Dante's day and known as the *pastorella*.[19]

The *pastorella* was a genre of lyric poetry taking its special name more from its content than from its form. For, though lyrical, this kind of poem was also and primarily a little narrative wherein the poet, speaking always in the lyric first person, related an adventure, an encounter with a *pastorella* or shepherdess, whence the name of the genre itself.

Now it is of the greatest interest to note that the whole encounter with Matelda falls exactly into the traditional pattern of that little genre which we have nearly forgotten. It is not often that we meet with such deliberate transpositions in the *Comedy* out of other genres of poetry.[20] Moreover, it is this very awareness of the particular transposition which Dante has made in this instance which performs the function of focusing for allegory.

In the traditional *pastorella* the poet tells how he had wandered alone one day into the countryside, how he had there come upon a rustic maid, a shepherdess, in love, as was evident at once. Birds were singing, it was spring and the time for love; and love was what the poet had himself felt at once: a strong desire to be with this maiden and to possess her. To be sure, the final outcome of such an encounter could vary from one account to the other. As Dante's "first friend," the poet Guido Cavalcanti, had conceived it in his *Pastorella*, the ending could be most happy indeed, in *gioia*; and we may take Guido's poem in its entirety to represent the type:

> In un boschetto trova' pasturella
> più che la stella — bella al mi' parere.
> Cavelli avea biondetti e ricciutelli

e gli occhi pien d'amor, cera rosata;
con sua verghetta pasturav' agnelli,
e, scalza, di rugiada era bagnata;
cantava come fosse 'nnamorata;
er'adornata — di tutto piacere.

D'amor la salutai mantenente
e domandai s'avesse compagnia,
ed ella mi rispuose dolcemente
che sola sola per lo bosco gïa
e disse: — Sacci, quando l'augel pia
allor disia — 'l me' cor drudo avere —.

Po' che mi disse di sua condizione,
e per lo bosco augelli audio cantare,
fra me stesso diss'i': — Or è stagione
di questa pasturella gio' pigliare. —
Merzè le chiesi sol che di baciare
e d'abracciare — le fosse 'n volere.

Per man mi prese, d'amorosa voglia,
e disse che donato m'avea 'l core:
menommi sott'una freschetta foglia
là dov'i' vidi fior d'ogni colore;
e tanto vi sentio gioia e dolzore
che dio d'amore — parvemi vedere.[21]

In the woods I found a shepherdess, more beautiful than any star, it seemed to me.

She had blond hair in tiny curls, eyes full of love and a rosy face: with her staff she was tending lambs and, barefoot, she was bathed with dew; she was singing as though in love; she was adorned with all pleasure.

I gave her greeting of love at once and asked her if she had companions; and she answered me sweetly that she was going about the woods quite alone, and said: "Know that when the birds sing, then does my heart desire to have a lover."

When she had told me of her condition, and I heard birds sing throughout the woods, I said to myself: "Now is the season to take my pleasure with this shepherdess." I begged her only that she should let me kiss and embrace her.

She took me by the hand, in amorous desire, and told me she had given me her heart; she led me beneath the new leaves, there where I saw flowers of every color; and so much did I feel joy and sweetness there, that I seemed to see the very god of love.

There is no need whatever to argue the points of resemblance which this little scene bears to the scene in Purgatory. It is quite enough to read Guido's poem keeping in mind all the while the encounter with Matelda in the *boschetto* atop the mountain. But what is perhaps one of the most revealing points of this correspondence in close detail is not at once apparent and should be noted: in the *pastorella* encounter, not only in Guido's but typically, the maiden is not named. Nor is Matelda yet named, in Canto XXVIII.

That, however, is but a further confirming detail, not the main point of Dante's deliberate transposition. That point is this: Dante, in staging his meeting with Matelda, has meant to call to mind a familiar little genre of poetry with its traditional encounter of two lovers, the woman as one enamored and the man conceiving a desire to possess her — and then, as does *not* happen in the *pastorella*, to stop his encounter at that. Which is, precisely, to bring into this context thus, by association, a kind of simile not unlike that suggested by the name of Leander. The purpose is the same, to place the reader in the familiar focus for a certain kind of allegory: what seems to be suggested cannot be, Dante's desire for this maiden cannot be that kind of desire which Guido had felt for his, and for the same reason that it may not be literally as Leander's for his beloved. And since the literal may not be, we look beyond, for the other meaning.

It is evident, therefore, that in the encounter with Matelda, it contributes no little to the desired focus that she remains unnamed, even as the shepherdess always was. The question which arises here must be *what* she is, not *who* she is; or at least, not yet *who* she is, not as long as in this Canto XXVIII she is framed to mean just what she "figures."

Yet it seems necessary to recognize a further question that must inevitably arise here. If what Dante is seen to desire is that innocence and rectitude which Adam once had here in Eden, that is most understandable, for what condition on this earth could be more desirable than that? That is indeed as attractive as Matelda herself and the happiness she plainly enjoys. That he should want to possess that condition as such is natural enough. The question is: Why may he not do so? The stream, we are distinctly told, is only three steps wide. Yet Dante may not cross it to possess the object of his desire. Or rather, he may not cross over yet, not until Beatrice comes. But when Beatrice has come, his eyes will be all for her. Matelda, to be sure, will remain on the scene, will indeed be the one who leads him through the water up to the handmaids of Beatrice on the far side, who in their turn lead him to Beatrice.[22] But that is no longer in Canto XXVIII, and Matelda is then no longer at the center of the focus as that which is desired. And we never in fact see that Dante "possesses" Matelda, for the simple reason that we do not see him wish to do so, once he has crossed the stream. It must be that Matelda, beyond Canto XXVIII, no longer figures what she does when she acts and speaks as in that canto. Indeed, it is significant that it is not until we are well beyond that canto that we even know her name to be Matelda.

All of which seems to be saying clearly enough that Dante, on beholding the condition of original justice, desires to have it; but, for all his desire, he would seem never to come into possession of that justice. Can this be an aspect of meaning intended by the poet here? What sense does it make? Can Paradise, or our first condition there, not be regained?

We see at once that such questions arising out of the encounter with Matelda in Eden cry their connection with those prompted by the four stars over Eden and a lament about their loss. To note this connection, indeed, is to begin to see that the two things are parts of one thing. Not only does this prove to be true; but, in seeing this, we come into position to remark another of those symmetries which make the structure of the *Comedy* so remarkable. For so it is: at the beginning of the *Purgatorio*, at the foot of the mountain, four stars are seen over Eden and, at the sight of them, lament is heard that the living can no longer behold them; at the end of the same canticle, at the summit of the mountain, a fair maiden (unnamed) is seen dwelling still in Eden and a living man desires to possess her but may not do so. The meaning must be that the maiden is "lost" to the living even as are the four stars which were "never seen except by the first people." And this maiden represents the very condition of that first people. Seeing the connection in this light, we catch a shadowy glimpse of a

figure, now familiar, in the background: Astraea, "star-maiden."
Could those four stars be, in some sense, "Matelda's stars"? This
might mean that, in the background, we should sense the presence
of a constellation known as Virgo — and Virgo is justice.

Thus Matelda, figuring as she does that perfection of human
nature which man enjoyed in Eden before his fall, is presented by
the poet as figuring a perfection of nature not to be enjoyed again
by any living man; even as four beautiful stars shining in that
southern sky can be enjoyed by the living no more. Two things
that we have tended to consider as unconnected, in our reading
of the poem, prove now to be connected, parts of one thing. And
that one thing of which they are parts is evident in the very question which holds them together: can Paradise be regained? The
answer, it would seem, is no. Or perhaps the answer is both yes
and no. Indeed it was St. Augustine himself who had given just
such a double answer, and the tradition in theology beyond him
had proceeded to scrutinize this question with the greatest interest:

> In what manner therefore are we said to be renewed, if we do not
> regain what the first man lost in whom we all die? Clearly we do
> regain what he lost in one sense, and we do not regain what he lost
> in another sense.[23]

Notes

1. *De Mon.* III, 16.
2. *Purgatorio* XXVII, 94–108. For a more thorough discussion of the
dream see above, pp. 108 ff.
3. Peter Abelard, *Expositio in Hexaemeron*, PL 178.762: "Possent et
delectationem nonullam homini afferre secundum sensuum diversitatem,
cum ex cantu auditum mulcerent vel ex pulchritudine formae visum oblec-
tarent, vel odoris suavitate olfactum reficerent vel quibuscunque modis di-
versae ipsorum naturae diligenter cognitae in amorem et laudem Creatoris
nos amplius excitarent, juxta quod eum Psalmista dicit: *Delectasti me,
Domine, in factura tua, et in operibus manuum tuarum exsultabo.*"
4. *Purgatorio* XXVIII, 1–22.

5. *De Civitate Dei* XIV, 26 (*PL* 41.434): "Vivebat itaque homo in paradiso sicut volebat, quamdiu hoc volebat quod Deus jusserat: *vivebat fruens Deo*, ex quo bono erat bonus: vivebat sine ulla egestate, ita semper vivere habens in potestate. Cibus aderat, ne esuriret; potus, ne sitiret; lignum vitae, ne illum senecta dissolveret. Nihil corruptionis in corpore vel ex corpore ullas molestias ullis ejus sensibus ingerebat. Nullus intrinsecus morbus, nullus ictus metuebatur extrinsecus. Summa in carne sanitas, in anima tota tranquillitas. Sicut in paradiso nullus aestus aut frigus, ita in ejus habitatore nulla ex cupiditate vel timore accedebat bonae voluntatis offensio. Nihil omnino triste, nihil erat inaniter laetum: *guadium verum perpetuabatur ex Deo, in quem flagrabat charitas de corde puro et conscientia bona et fide non ficta* (I Tim. i, 5)." (Italics mine.)

I have cited the Dods translation of the passage.

6. *Compendium Theologiae ad Fratrem Reginaldum*, ch. 186: "Ex hoc vero quod voluntas hominis erat Deo subiecta, homo referebat omnia in Deum sicut in ultimum finem, in quo eius iustitia et innocentia consistebat." For further consideration of Thomas' views of man's first innocence, see below pp. 237 ff.

7. *Ibid.*, ch. 187: "Hic autem hominis tam ordinatus status, originalis iustitia nominatur. . ."

8. *De Vulgari Eloquentia* I, iv, 4: "Quid autem prius vox primi loquentis sonaverit, viro sane mentis in promptu esse non titubo ipsum fuisse quod Deus est, scilicet *El*, vel per modum interrogationis, vel per modum responsionis. Absurdum atque rationi videtur horrificum ante Deum ab homine quicquam nominatum fuisse, cum ab ipso et in ipsum factus fuisset homo. Nam sicut post prevaricationem humani generis quilibet exordium sue locutionis incipit ab 'heu,' rationabile est quod ante qui fuit inciperet a gaudio; et cum nullum gaudium sit extra Deum, sed totum in Deo, et ipse Deus totus sit gaudium, consequens est quod primus loquens primo et ante omnia dixisset 'Deus.' "

9. It is the condition of man after original sin as well as before that he knows or "sees" God by indirect vision, and this seeing is the act of contemplation at its highest summit. The standard text in support of which point is, over and over again, Rom. 1.20: "Invisibilia enim ipsius, a creatura mundi, per ea quae facta sunt intellecta, conspiciuntur." And it may be noted that Abelard himself typically recalls this text in the introductory chapter of the work referred to (*PL* 178.733), adding: "Quisquis enim de aliquo artifice an bonus vel solers in operando sit voluerit intelligere, non ipsum sed opera ejus considerare debet. Sic et Deus qui in seipso invisibilis et incomprehensibilis est, ex operum suorum magnitudine primam nobis de se scientiam confert."

10. *Compend. Theol.*, ch. 187: "Qui quidem status primo homini fuit concessus non ut cuidam personae singulari, sed ut primo humanae naturae principio, ita quod per ipsum simul cum natura humana traduceretur in posteros." On this point see below, pp. 230 ff.

11. *Purgatorio* XXVIII, 142.

12. See above, pp. 168 ff.

13. *De Fide Orthod.* II, 12 (*PG* 94.922).

14. *Liber II Sententiarum* d. xxix, ch. 2.

15. *Summa Theol.* I, q. 95, a. 3, resp.: "Homo in statu innocentiae ali-

qualiter habuit omnes virtutes. Et hoc dictis patet esse verum. Dictum est enim supra quod talis erat rectitudo primi status, quod ratio erat Deo subiecta, inferiores autem vires rationi. Virtutes autem nihil aliud sunt quam perfectiones quaedam, quibus ratio ordinatur in Deum, et inferiores vires disponuntur secundum regulam rationis ut magis patebit cum de virtutibus agetur. Unde rectitudo primi status exigebat ut homo aliqualiter omnes virtutes haberet.

"Sed considerandum est quod virtutum quaedam sunt, quae de sui ratione nullam imperfectionem important, ut caritas et iustitia. Et huiusmodi virtutes fuerunt in statu innocentiae simpliciter, et quantum ad habitum et quantum ad actum. Quaedam vero sunt, quae de sui ratione imperfectionem important, vel ex parte actus vel ex parte materiae. Et si huiusmodi imperfectio non repugnat perfectioni primi status, nihilominus huiusmodi virtutes poterant esse in primo statu; sicut fides, quae est eorum quae non videntur, et spes, quae est eorum quae non habentur. Perfectio enim primi status non se extendebat ad hoc quod videret Deum per essentiam, et ut habetur cum fruitione finalis beatitudinis; unde fides et spes esse poterant in primo statu et quantum ad habitum et quantum ad actum."

16. Neither charity nor any of the other infused virtues may be without sanctifying grace, which is as their root. See Aquinas, *Summa Theol.* I-II, q. 110, a. 3, resp.: "Manifestum est autem quod virtutes acquisitae per actus humanos . . . sunt dispositiones quibus homo convenienter disponitur in ordine ad naturam qua homo est. Virtutes autem infusae disponunt hominem altiori modo et ad altiorem finem; unde etiam oportet quod in ordine ad aliquam altiorem naturam. . . . Sicut igitur lumen naturalis rationis est aliquid praeter virtutes acquisitas, quae dicuntur in ordine ad ipsum lumen naturale: ita etiam ipsum lumen gratiae, quod est participatio divinae naturae, est aliquid praeter virtutes infusas, *quae a lumine illo derivantur*, et ad illud lumen ordinantur" (my italics).

The point is too clearly established everywhere in theology to require documentation.

17. The very clear answer can be found in the version of the story doubtless known to Dante: Ovid, *Heroidum Epistula* XVIII.

18. The point that this is allegory "of a kind" is worth stressing, for it differs notably from the kind we have, for instance, in the figures of a Virgil and a Beatrice, wherein the literal-historical meaning is given first as a foundation for the other. With Matelda, instead, while the literal-historical is not denied, neither is it affirmed in this canto. We are simply guided to the allegorical meaning. For the Bible as Dante's model for allegory, see *Dante Studies 1*, pp. 13 ff. However, the kind of allegory represented by Matelda was only encountered in Scripture wherever it did not seem possible to accept the literal sense as such, as, for example, in the case of the love dialogue of the Song of Solomon. This instance is, indeed, quite close to that of Matelda in Canto XXVIII, as to type.

19. For the *pastorella* see A. Jeanroy, *La poésie lyrique des troubadours* (Toulouse, 1934), II, 282 ff.; E. Faral in *Romania*, XLIX (1923), 204 ff.; Th. Gérold, *La musique au moyen âge* (Paris, 1932), pp. 127 ff. More than one hundred examples of the genre in French and Provençal are known.

20. One other striking instance is to be noted at the end of *Inferno*,

where Dante transposed the wintry scene of Cocito, and the combined stylistic effect, out of his own poems for the "donna Petra."

21. *Rimatori del dolce stil nuovo*, ed. L. Di Benedetto (Bari, 1939), p. 55.

22. *Purgatorio* XXXI, 91–105.

23. *De Gen. ad Litt.* VI 24 (*PL* 34.353): "Quomodo ergo, inquiunt, renovari dicimur, si non hoc recipimus quod perdidit primus homo, in quo omnes moriuntur? Hoc plane recipimus secundum quemdam modum, et non recipimus secundum quemdam modum."

Chapter XIII

Natural Justice

If a Christian poet should conceive a journey to God which, in one of its stages, would be a "return to Eden," he might very well feel bound to respect the ambiguity of such an answer as Augustine had given to the question of that "return," especially if that answer had become the accepted one in the theological doctrine of the poet's day. A *return* to Eden: can Paradise be regained? The answer is "yes" and it is also "no." And on the hypothesis that such is indeed the double answer that Dante chose to stage in his poem, it becomes necessary to obtain a more particular understanding of the nature of this ambiguity. We know of course that the poet is neither formulating nor teaching doctrine. In so far as the poet is dealing with doctrine at all, he is staging it, representing it in the outline of an event, a journey. This is his responsibility to established truth. And more often than not the way in which he will make such truth a part of his poem is in shaping the line of literal event in such manner and detail as to call to our mind the specific doctrine on which that line rests, in order to convey it, in allegory. Only, we must be able to see that the poet is doing this, and when and where he does it. Clearly we must know the specific line of doctrine which he would call to our mind.

What we come to see is this: Dante has indeed staged the accepted answer to the question "Is Paradise regained?" with a deep concern for the ambiguity which that answer must show, if it is to be the true answer. The question must necessarily focus on what the first man or the "first people" had before sin, then on what Adam lost through sin, then on what we who descend from Adam may regain of that which he lost. And since original justice is the accepted name for what the first man had before sin, the question becomes precisely a question of justice lost and of justice regained.

Justice, in such a sense, might also be called a "dignity," if we but think of the perfection in which God must surely have created the first man. Moreover, God must have given this justice to human nature as a condition which was to have continued to be if man had not sinned and been expelled from Eden. "Dignity" is in fact the term which Dante chose to use when the time came in his poem [1] to enter into full discussion of man's first sin and God's mercy in atoning for that sin. Man's possible "return to Eden" inevitably becomes, of course, a part of such a question. Return to Eden is simply the question of returning to the lost dignity.

"Dignity" and "nobility" are both proper and usable terms in such a context. Man was created with certain original gifts or endowments to his nature. These taken together constituted his original dignity, in such a way that if he should lose any one of these gifts, he must perforce fall from such "nobility." This first condition can also be thought of as a "freedom." Now sin is precisely what causes man to fall from this God-given dignity which has made him like God. Through sin man falls away from the divine likeness in which he was created. Nor may man ever regain such likeness unless there be atonement for the sin by which he lost it.

When Adam sinned, it was human nature itself that sinned in its very seed. The sin was total, involving all of human nature; [2] so total, indeed, that no way remained open for atonement except

that God himself should move to bring this about. The necessity
of this may be stated in other terms: the first sin was essentially a
sin of pride, and atonement for such a sin must be through what
opposes pride, humility. It was in pride that the first man aspired
to rise up beyond limits set by God's command, eating of the Tree
of Knowledge of Good and Evil to become, as he thought, like
God. Such is the essence of man's first sin. Thus, if due atonement
is ever to be made by man for such a sin, it is required that man,
by his own powers, descend as low in humility as he had aspired to
rise in pride. But man by his human powers alone was quite in-
capable of descending so low. The very intended upsoaring by
which he had fallen had itself exceeded man's limits, and it must
therefore follow that the required and compensating descent to
lowliness lay also beyond man's powers. Only God Himself had
the power to descend so low in humility and to perform the great
act of atonement for man's sin. Thus did Christ die in the humilia-
tion and ignominy of the Cross and the tomb. Then Christ had
risen from such lowliness and had ascended that man might re-
ascend; Christ opened the way for man's return to dignity, which
is, as it were, a "return" to Eden.

It is necessary to recall the whole of Beatrice's exposition of the
Fall and the Atonement (in *Paradiso* VII) in these terms if we are
to come into the proper view of the particular and concrete shape
which Dante gave to the journey as "return to Eden." It may be
noted, for one thing, that at the point where Beatrice expounds
this point of doctrine so, the summit of the mountain where Eden
is has already been left far behind; yet Eden comes into her words
in the context of such a matter in precisely the metaphorical sense
in which we should conceive Eden as the image of man's first
dignity. As Beatrice puts it, man's very fall from "dignity" was
his loss of Eden, and her simile comes so naturally in the line of
her argument that it can escape our notice.

> Vostra natura, quando peccò tota
>   nel seme suo, da questa dignitadi,
>   come di paradiso, fu remota;
> nè ricovrar potiensi, se tu badi. . . .
>
> *Paradiso* VII, 85–88.

> Your nature, when it sinned completely in its seed, was removed
> from these dignities as from paradise; nor could they be recov-
> ered, if you will consider. . . .

Loss of Eden and return to Eden are notions clearly present in
the background of Beatrice's words. Loss of the dignities must
mean loss of paradise, to recover them must mean to recover
paradise.

If we will but keep the entire frame of this conception in mind
when the journey has reached the foot of that mountain which
bears Eden at its summit, we shall be able to see the whole cluster
of meanings which the poet would summon to his reader's mind
at such a point. Here now is a journey which is to be truly a return to Eden, a regaining of what man had lost in his fall from
that lofty place. The wayfarer's descent through Hell, by which
he has attained to this point, had begun at the very time of Christ's
atonement on the Cross, the evening of Good Friday. The descent
through Hell, in fact, and the whole stretch of the journey to this
point has required, as to time, precisely the days and nights that
Christ was in the tomb, for this now is Easter Sunday morning
when Dante comes forth from Satan's sorry tomb [3] to see the stars
again. How right it is that the wayfarer should be told now to go
to the lowest shores of this mountain island to gird on the rush,
girdle of humility, for now this man is ready and able (as he was
not able before) to climb towards freedom,[4] to return to dignity,
at the summit.

On close scrutiny, the cluster of meaning at this juncture of
the journey is so rich that the reader, once he is aware of the
essential nature of it, seems never to have done exploring its detail and noting how the many strands of meaning converge here.
And the sense of this richness continues beyond the first canto
of the *Purgatorio*. In the second canto, souls are seen to come
over the ocean waters in a boat propelled and steered by an
angel. The souls are many, but sing together in unison. Their
song is a psalm that recalls the Exodus and thus casts them for us
at once in the figure of a chosen people crossing over the Red
Sea and leaving Egypt behind. But how is thought of the Exodus
relevant at such a point in Dante's journey? This is Easter Sunday

morning now. Is it fitting that we should have such an Old Testament event brought to mind?

In the matter of such questions of relevance (and how often they must occur to us, especially with this poem!), we shall do well sometimes to check and test possible answers by turning to that commemoration of events which is the liturgy of the Church. Like the poem, the liturgy holds things together along the line of man's history and the drama of his salvation which we might sometimes think were not connected. Fortunately, because of the great help it can bring at times to our study of the *Comedy*, we are able to turn to what is perhaps the most exhaustive treatment of the symbolism of Christian liturgy of any time, one compiled in the very time of Dante: the *Rationale of Divine Offices* of Durandus, Bishop of Mende. We have only to put to that remarkable book our question of relevance to get even more light than we might have expected. We turn of course to the service for Easter, since this moment at the foot of the mountain is Easter Sunday morning. But rather than reading Durandus directly it may prove easier to follow the digest which E. Mâle made of the relevant passage, since Mâle has conveniently singled out and summarized the capital points which Durandus makes through all of several chapters:

> The second part of the ceremony [Easter Eve] is devoted to the baptism of the neophytes, which the Church ordained should take place on that day because, says Durandus, she saw mystic affinities between the death of Jesus and the symbolic death of the new Christian who in baptism dies to the world to rise again with the Saviour. But before being led to the baptismal fonts, the catechumens listen to twelve passages from the Bible dealing with the sacrament which they are about to receive. These are, to give examples, the story of the Deluge whose water purified the world, the passage of the Red Sea by the children of Israel (a figure of baptism) and the verse in Isaiah which speaks of those who thirst for the water of life.
>
> The reading ended, the bishop blesses the water. He first makes the sign of the cross above it, then dividing it into four he sprinkles it towards the four cardinal points in memory of the four rivers of the terrestrial Paradise. He next dips the paschal candle, type of Christ, into the water to remind them that Jesus was baptized in Jordan, and by His baptism sanctified all the waters of the world.

He dips the candle into the font three times in remembrance of the Redeemer in the tomb. The baptism then begins, and the neophytes in their turn are dipped three times into the font that they may know that with Christ they die to the world, with Him are buried, and with Him rise to life eternal.

It is evident that in such a ceremony no detail is without symbolic value.[5]

That baptism should be thought pertinent to the service of Easter holds no surprise. But through Durandus we may see how many other moments can enter into commemoration of the feast of Easter: atonement and the descent to the tomb as the great act of humility, the Exodus, the Resurrection, descent before ascent becomes possible — all these things in this service are bound together in commemoration and symbolic affinity. But are we not especially struck by one detail: after the reading and the blessing of the water with the sign of the cross, the bishop by such a sign divides the water into four and sprinkles it toward the four cardinal points *in memory of the four rivers of the earthly paradise?* Thus in the context of this whole cluster of associations at the Easter moment, thought of the four rivers is also relevant. And turning back to Dante's staging of that moment in the poem, we remember of course that he too has provided for this, turning to four stars instead of four rivers. And we know now on what principle Dante had transformed rivers into stars, keeping the meaning that had long before been established for the rivers, the four cardinal virtues.

There is thus much light to be had from Durandus to support our sense of the relevance of things and of allusions in such a paschal moment. Indeed, in the line of present considerations, we are prompted by Durandus' mention of the four rivers to return to the point where we began, with four stars and a lament over their loss. We come back to confront the fact that, for all our excursions into the theological doctrine which informs Dante's poem, we have not yet entirely understood how what is said in that lament may properly be said: that such stars were seen only by the "first people," by them and never again since the Fall. We understood the literal sense, of course. But what can this

mean, if these stars are the four cardinal virtues? It is not Durandus who will solve that problem for us. But it may be that in
facing the ambiguity of the question "Is Paradise Regained?" we
have come into a focus in which solution can be had. Durandus
can only show us that thought of Paradise and its four rivers is
something expected when it is Easter time in the poem. That is
already much.

*   *   *

The accepted answer to the question in terms of both "yes and
no" must mean that man can indeed regain the dignity he had in
Eden, but only in a certain sense. This, as we come to understand
it, is precisely the case. For man may regain only part of the
whole of his original nobility and only part of those gifts which
went to make it up. The truth is that some of those original gifts
of God are never regained. But the more striking truth in this
respect is that those gifts are never repossessed in the way in
which they were originally possessed before sin. We have in this
to understand that man's original dignity was indeed a gift from
God, but that it was a gift to *human nature*, not to persons as
such. We have noted Dante's way of putting this in the verses
where Beatrice speaks of the sin by which the dignity was lost:
"Your nature sinned completely in its seed," says Beatrice. Human
nature sinned when Adam sinned, and what was lost by Adam's
sin was a dignity given to human nature itself. And just before
this, at the beginning of her argument, Beatrice has said that human nature was "united to God" in its original condition.

Now man never regains that original gift made to his nature.
That gift was a rectitude, a justice, in which human nature was
united with God. Or if such a truth appears to derogate from
the atonement made by Christ, we should rather say that at the
end of time human nature will again be so united.[6] But what of
now, as man returns to lost dignity through Christ, how is a return to Eden to be conceived in this life? The answer is that now,
in this life, man may indeed attain to a dignity, a justice, through
Christ; man may be said to regain justice; but justice so regained

is always *personal* justice, never the justice that was given to *human nature* in Adam.

Such in brief is the import of the ambiguous answer. One notes that there is actually a latent metaphor in that very ambiguity. In terms of two justices, natural and personal, such an answer to the question must mean not simply that man regains only in part the justice that he lost, but that even such "regaining" is meta-phorical. For, to speak out of metaphor, the justice regained is never the same as the justice lost, because justice repossessed through Christ is never the same kind of justice as that which was first possessed. Justice regained is *like* the justice lost, or as we shall see, is in part like the justice lost. And here, in such likeness and difference, lies the possibility of metaphor which a poet could cast into the shape of an event, an actual and literal return to Eden. Indeed, as we shall see, Dante has been at special pains to make evident the fact that he did build this metaphor into the broad outline of his poem and into (as he hoped) the awareness of his reader.

Much of the evidence that supports this fact, we have already witnessed. Matelda is a figure central to the whole shape of it: Matelda figuring man's original dignity in the Garden, dwelling there still, desired but not possessed by one who returns there. Matelda desired in vain. Does man regain the lost dignity? Matelda is a poet's answer, and it is "no." Matelda is not had again, in Eden. But then this man, who does literally return to that place, is seen to attain to Beatrice across the stream that had separated him from Matelda, and (if we are prepared to read the allegory and the symbols) Beatrice is a "justice." Beatrice comes to Eden to meet the man returned, and with her are all seven of the virtues. Since she comes so, there is no mistaking her meaning. Beatrice comes as sanctifying grace, and those virtues are indeed the virtues which unite or, as here, reunite with God. But is not such a reuniting with God precisely the *reattainment* of the dignity of original justice? The answer must be metaphorical, for the answer, to be true, must bear ambiguity. The poet has staged the answer: Matelda on the one hand who is not attained, and Beatrice on the other who is. A sinner is justified through Christ's grace. Is Eden regained in this? Yes, for this is Eden where Beatrice comes. But is the justice which man once had in Eden regained? The answer is no, for Matelda is there still, desired in vain. Matelda is the justice which was forever lost.

With Beatrice come all seven of the virtues, as her handmaids, but there is no such group of virtues attending Matelda. And yet we know that the virtues must somehow be understood to attend her too, for in that original condition of which she is the figure, man had all the virtues, all seven of the infused virtues together with sanctifying grace. But if Matelda is not seen to have any such escort of maidens as the virtues, it is possible that certain stars which are also virtues must be understood to be *her* stars. We have not forgotten the background presence of Astraea or Virgo, and now we note the evident relevance of that figure. When the four maidens coming with Beatrice declare that they are nymphs here and "in the sky they are stars," they leave us to seek an understanding, without further guidance from them. Some difference there must be between existence in the sky as stars and existence as handmaids to Beatrice. May we not seek light on the meaning here from what we have learned through these excursions in theology? Can the affirmed difference between existence as stars and existence as Beatrice's handmaids be pointing to the fact that the cardinal virtues as stars over Eden belong to a different order or kind of justice from that of the cardinal virtues that come with Beatrice?

This may prove to be so, but it is certainly not a matter which we may take for granted. In fact, we may take it only as a working hypothesis, through which to grope for a glimpse of the possible meaning here; and such groping calls for yet another venture into a doctrine of established theology concerning two kinds of justice.

*   *   *

The justice which God first gave to man was not natural as distinct from supernatural. In fact, that justice was actually a supernatural gift, as we have noticed St. Thomas concerned to point out, bestowed upon man as something quite above and beyond the limits of his own nature and his own powers. Original justice was natural justice in that it was a gift to human *nature*, not to persons; a gift not to Adam the person, that is, but to human nature in Adam. Original justice is therefore natural, not as distinct from what is above nature (for its source is above nature) but as distinguished from personal justice, which is given to persons, to this or that individual merely, and not to human nature.

One readily conceives that such a notion of original justice as a gift to human nature had been developed and elaborated in theology in close relation to the notion of original sin. For it is most certainly true that original sin was a sin of human nature (we have noted the verse in the *Comedy* pointing to the fact) and this in the sense, therefore, of a sin *in the nature*, i.e., not personal. This fact is evident, if we consider the consequences of original sin. Again it is certain that original sin, as regards its "stains" and its effects in human nature generally, is passed down through the generations of mankind from Adam and by Adam to all who descend from his seed. We were all in Adam when Adam sinned, we all sinned when Adam sinned. Human nature, that is, sinned when Adam sinned, and it is because of this that his sin, with all its woeful consequences, abides in and is transmitted through human nature. The fallen condition of man which resulted from that first sin has replaced original justice which was our condition before sin. Surely, since original sin now passes *naturally* from Adam down the whole line of his progeny, so was original justice to have passed on. There are grave problems here. Original sin is by man and of man, as original justice is not. Original justice is of God, a gift from God. It was a supernatural gift. How it could have been supernatural and yet have been transmitted through the nature, i.e., naturally, is a question on which one may find no dearth indeed of theological speculation. It involves points that will concern us later. For the moment it is important only to note the unanimous agreement that had followed St. Anselm's definitions to the effect that original justice was a gift to the nature, and was therefore *natural* justice. Characteristically, Anselm looks at the matter of original justice through the notion of original sin as a sin of the nature, this as evidenced by its transmission:

> Adam's sin was in man, that is in nature, and it was in him who is named ADAM, that is in the person; there is the sin that everyone bears with nature in his very origin, and there is the sin that he does not bear with nature, but he himself commits that sin after he is already a person distinct from other persons. That sin therefore which is born out of one's very origin is called "original," which can also be called "natural," not because it is of the essence of the nature, but because through nature's corruption it is had in having nature. But the sin which one may commit after he is a person can be called "personal," because it will be through personal vice. Thus one may speak of original and of personal justice. Even as Adam and Eve "originally," that is, in their very beginning, were just in the very moment that they existed as human beings. And justice may be called "personal" whenever one who is unjust receives justice, which he did not have through his origin.[7]

Such in barest outline is the conception we must bear in mind of that justice which was first had by man and the justice which he may now have. The latter is "personal" and is gained when a sinner attains to complete justification. The former is "natural," as is evident from the fact that the sin or injustice which replaces it is natural, that is, of the nature. We do not note the actual term "iustitia naturalis" here in Anselm; but that his conception of "iustitia originalis" (and he was long remembered for being the first to use that term in the long line of speculation) can easily bear that other adjective as well, is at once evident to us on this statement by him as it was to theologians nearer to Dante's time. Thus we find Alexander of Hales (d. 1245) using all three of the established terms interchangeably: "original innocence," "original justice," and "natural justice"; and this he does in a context wherein he cites precisely the treatise by Anselm quoted above:

> According to what Anselm says in his De Conceptu Virginali there was in Adam, before sin, natural justice, by which all who descended from him would have been just in their origin, if he had remained in that justice. . . .
>
> . . . And thus it is evident that, according to what Anselm says, original sin is the absence or privation of due justice, that is, of that natural justice or innocence through which all men would have been just if our first parents had kept it.[8]

And Albertus Magnus, commenting on the *Sentences* of Peter Lombard, had also found the term "iustitia naturalis" to be the proper one for the justice which was given to our nature in Adam.[9]

We may understand the full import of such definitions when we think of the remedy that came for loss of original justice, the way which was opened up by Christ that we might rise out of our sinful nature and be restored to our dignity, to justice. And one meets with common agreement here in theological doctrine: the justice that we gain through Christ is, like original justice, a gift of God; but unlike the justice first given to man, this justice through Christ is never natural, is never a gift to human nature, at least not *now in* this life. It is always a gift to persons only. Only *persons* are justified in Christ.

That inner event and process by which an individual rises out of his sinful nature to attain to the summit of justice through Christ is known in Christian doctrine by the familiar name of "justification of the ungodly": *iustificatio impii*. Christian doctrine has much to say about such an inner event in the soul, and much indeed that a poet could represent in the pattern of a "return to Eden," as we have already seen. The very outline of that hoped-for inner event is the outline of personal redemption. Many persons have moved along that way, and many do so move, towards a goal of righteousness through Christ. But on a further point regarding this there are no dissenting voices: the end goal of justification through Christ is always a justice attained by this or that person, never is it a justice in human nature as such. Indeed, one would hardly conceive of a justice given to human nature if, looking back through the known consequences of original sin, we did not see that the justice that was man's first dignity and was to have remained such if there had been no sin, was a natural justice, given to human nature to be passed on *through the nature.*

We understand more clearly in this way the essential terms in which Dante has staged this "equation" between what was lost and what is regained. For if Beatrice's advent in Eden bears a striking resemblance to Christ's advent, that is not without reason.

Nor is it merely accidental or arbitrary that Dante, the wayfarer who stands in judgment before Beatrice, should finally be known, at that point only in the poem, by his personal name.[10] Beatrice's advent is the advent of grace through Christ, the grace that re-unites an individual to God, and her coming to the wayfarer completes a return to Eden as a return to justice. To come to Beatrice here in Eden means to regain all that this or that person can regain in the way of justice lost. And is this little? May we not think that, through Christ, grace now abounds and that more is gained through Him than was lost through Adam? This must indeed be so, and we exclaim "O felix culpa!" [11] Nonetheless, the melancholy fact remains that the justice so gained through Christ is ever a personal justice and that the justice that man first had was a natural justice; and that there are woeful consequences in our loss of natural justice.

One may grasp this point even more clearly, perhaps, by considering the matter in Adam himself, taken as a sort of test case. Adam was justified after sin, though due allowance must be made for the differences between Adam's justification and the justification of persons in A.D. time. It was given to Adam only to believe in the advent of his Redeemer in an implicit and not an explicit way. Still Adam did believe in Him and was eventually saved through Christ, after centuries of waiting for His coming to Limbo. Adam was thus saved through Christ's grace. We shall therefore do no violence to this particular point of doctrine if we try to imagine that Adam "returns to Eden" even as we see Dante do in the poem. Adam, that is, regains *eventually* just that measure of lost dignity that we see Dante regain in Eden, no more nor less. And if the poet had chosen to represent such a return in the figure of Adam rather than in himself, he must still have shown us Adam meeting with Matelda here in Eden (where he had left her — and coming upon her no doubt with a quite special sense of recognition!). Adam, like Dante, would have desired to possess Matelda, to repossess her — but in vain. Adam lost Matelda forever when he lost Eden. Adam, after sin, may possess only a justice which is personal.

All of which serves to lead us back to the urgent question: what are we to understand to be the essential difference between the condition of original justice and that of personal justice? What exactly is the measure of that difference in terms of man's condition? What precisely would Adam *not* regain of the original gifts? Desire for Matelda there is, at the summit; but there is no lament that she is not possessed. And when Beatrice comes, Matelda is no longer in the focus of desire. But, if there is no lament voiced for Matelda lost, there is lament at the foot of the mountain for four stars lost, not to be seen or "had" again after the Fall. Once more it is a question we have faced time and again, but always, it seemed, with an insufficient awareness of the precise issues involved. Now it is time, finally, to lay hold of such terms and, as between *natural* justice on the one hand and *personal* justice on the other, to weigh in the balance the exact measure of the irreparable loss that could have prompted that lament at the beginning of *Purgatorio*.

*   *   *

Justice as originally given to man was a threefold gift. Such a conception is in part already latent in St. Augustine's thought even if not sharply defined there. Augustine had tended to stress the aspect of concupiscence as the primary evil consequence of Adam's sin, a radical disorder in man in that the lower part of him falls into a persistent rebellion against the higher part, the flesh against the spirit. In this sense, then, original rectitude was seen by Augustine as the very order which had prevailed before such a disorder as concupiscence replaced it, a justice by which reason sat in perfect dominion over the lower powers of appetite.[12] As for death, this was certainly the consequence of Adam's sin, even as the Apostle had affirmed. But as to the question in particular how immortality of the body had been given to Adam, Augustine had understood this in a somewhat material or natural way. It was, he thought, by the fruit of the Tree of Life that Adam's body had been preserved from death. Thus when our first parents were driven from Eden and from all possibility of access to that Tree, then the body could no longer be kept from falling away into death.[13]

St. Anselm's writings on original justice established him quite firmly as the next great authority along this line. Anselm gave a different emphasis to such considerations. For him justice was primarily a matter of rectitude in the will *propter se servata* and a matter of the rule of the will over the lower powers. The affinity with Augustine's view is at once evident. There is only a change in emphasis. Anselm's stringent logic and his almost exclusive insistence on the will as the seat of justice were such that in later doctrine it is his definition of original justice that is most quoted: *iustitia est rectitudo propter se servata*.[14]

Theological speculation in the fertile century of Dante's birth and Aristotle's rebirth carried the definition a significant step further, or higher, one might say.[15] It seems clear that the revival of Aristotle counted for much in this. St. Thomas, among the many others, is quick to cite even the Philosopher's *Physics* in support of the guiding principle of the step taken, namely, the proposition that things which are for an end are established by reason of that end.[16] For St. Thomas will not insist on defining original justice as right love, or as the absence of concupiscence or bad love, as Augustine had done; nor will he primarily insist with Anselm that original justice is of the will exclusively and *propter se servata*. Thomas maintains that original justice must be defined with respect to the end for which it was established. God had given that justice to man in view of the end to which He had appointed him. That end is beatitude with God, eternal beatitude in the direct vision of God in His essence. Thus, for St. Thomas, if original sin is the act by which man loses original justice, that loss must be defined as loss of the vision of God: *carentia divinae visionis*. Concupiscence and disorder in the will are also consequences, but they are the *material* result. The *formal* consequence of original sin is loss of the sight of God, loss of the end for the sake of which that justice had been given to man.[17]

Such an extension of the definition of original justice to include this end as the determining feature brought with it a complete definition of that gift from God in terms of a due ordering of man with respect to this appointed end. Due order in this sense is due subjection to God, and original or natural justice is conceived in terms of a total subjection, made up, first, of subjection to God at the highest level, and, second, of two lower subjections determined by that highest one. The gift of original justice is thus a matter of three gifts, or of a threefold gift, for the sake of the end; a matter of three subjections, these to be distinguished in order from highest to lowest, so:

1. The highest part of man, his intellective soul (consisting of the two faculties, intellect and will) was perfectly subjected to God in original justice, was "ordered to" God as to that beatitude for which man was created.

2. The lower part of man, his sensitive nature with its powers and passions, was in turn perfectly subjected to the higher part, the intellect and will (or, as sometimes stated, the reason).

3. Man's body was perfectly subjected to the soul and completely obedient to it.

Thomas' definitions of original justice in these three parts are so concise that several examples may be given in the briefest space. It will be well to take note of these, in order to conceive clearly the terms in which this threefold subjection of original justice was formulated:

A.

The first sin alone brought the defect that pertains to nature: for that sin cut off man's adherence to God. Because man did then continuously adhere to God, to him was given the power that the lower powers should continuously be subject to the rule of reason, and that the body should be subject to the rule of the soul, by virtue of the fact that man's reason was continuously subject to what is above it. But when that first obedience was broken off, in that the first man's reason turned away from God in sin, there resulted a disruption in the order of the lower powers to the reason, and of the body to the soul.[18]

B.

Human nature was so established when it was first brought into being that the lower powers were perfectly subject to the soul, the reason to God, and the body to the soul, God supplying by grace

that which nature lacked for the purpose. Now this boon, which
some call original justice, was bestowed on the first man in such
wise that he was to transmit it together with human nature to his
posterity. But when the first man sinned, his reason rebelled against
God, and the consequence was that his lower powers ceased to be
perfectly subject to reason, and his body to his soul. And this, not
only in the first man that sinned, but also the same defect passed,
as a result, to his posterity, to whom was to have passed the aforesaid original justice. Hence the sin of the first man, from whom all
others are descended, according to the teaching of faith, was not
only a personal sin, in so far as it deprived the first man himself of
his own good, but also a sin of nature, inasmuch as the result of that
sin was that both he and his posterity were deprived of a gift bestowed on the entire nature.[19]

C.

The nature of man may be considered in another way, according as
divine providence provided for man by way of original justice.
This justice was a certain rectitude by which man's mind would be
under God, and the lower powers would be under the mind, and
the body under the soul, and all exterior things under man: in such
wise that as long as man's mind should be subject to God, the lower
powers would be subject to reason, and the body subject to the
soul, receiving infallibly life from the soul; and external things subject to man that all might serve him and that he should feel no harm
from them. Divine providence, moreover, established this because of
the dignity of the rational soul, which, since it is by nature incorruptible, was owed an incorruptible body.[20]

D.

But the very rectitude of the primitive state, wherewith man was
endowed by God, seems to require that, as others say, he was created
in grace, according to Eccles. vii, 30, *God made man right*. For this
rectitude consisted in his reason being subject to God, the lower
powers to reason, and the body to the soul: and the first subjection
was the cause of both the second and the third; since while reason
was subject to God, the lower powers remained subject to reason,
as Augustine says. Now it is clear that such a subjection of the body
to the soul and of the lower powers to reason, was not from nature;
otherwise it would have remained after sin. . . . Hence it is clear
that also the primitive subjection by virtue of which reason was
subject to God was not merely a natural gift, but a supernatural
endowment of grace; for it is not possible that the effect should be
of greater efficiency than the cause.[21]

E.

Original sin is opposed to original justice, by which the higher part
of the soul was conjoined to God and commanded the lower powers
and could even preserve the body from corruption.[22]

The definition of original justice in terms of a threefold subjection in man is the most comprehensive definition of such justice
known to Christian theology. One may safely assume that it was
indeed recognized as such in Dante's own day. It proves likewise
to be the only definition by which an adequate measure may be
taken of the essential difference between original justice and personal justice — which is, at the present, our chief concern with it.
Keeping in mind therefore the primary fact that a difference is
recognized, we may proceed to take stock of it in terms of this
comprehensive conception of that first justice which man lost
through sin. An obvious procedure is to move from the highest
to the lowest of the three subjections, and, as it were, in the figure
of a fall down through such a scale of dignity, to take precise
account of the consequences of original sin at each level of subjection, asking what was lost and what might be possibly regained
at each of the levels.

We easily note at once that the highest subjection means union
with God, adherence to God. Matelda figures that union and that
adherence in her abounding love and song of praise. In Eden man
referred all to God, himself first of all. Such union with God is
by way of sanctifying grace and charity. The infused virtues
must be present in it.

Now, as we think of "return to Eden" and Beatrice's advent
there, we must conceive that man does, in personal justice, attain
to due subjection to God through Christ's grace. The final goal
in the justification of a sinner is union with God and a righteous
subjection to God. Is this not the highest subjection of original
justice? Through Christ's grace man is restored to due order with
respect to God, and this would seem to be the essence of the highest level of the first justice as given to Adam. Thus, if we are
attempting to take the measure of a difference between the one
justice which is lost and the other which is gained, there would

not appear to be any significant or lamentable loss at this highest
level of subjection.

Always in descending order, we may pass to the next lower or
middle subjection of the three. Here that part of man which is
lower than the intellective part, man's sensitive nature with its
powers and passions, was duly ordered in its turn to the higher
part of man, was perfectly subject to that part. In short, the lower
powers obeyed the rule of reason in the higher part. No movement of appetite was contrary to reason's commands, and if reason was in turn in perfect subjection to God, one understands
why due rectitude and justice must prevail in the lower part.
We recognize in this conception of the second subjection, in fact,
that very notion of original justice which Augustine had so much
emphasized. The concupiscence which resulted from original sin
is precisely the disorder which takes place in this area. Man's
appetites and passions refused the rule of reason, in consequence
of man's sin. Rebellion in the lower parts followed upon rebellion
in the higher.

It is well for us to recall that this is also that area of man's inner
life wherein Plato had conceived the perfect rule of justice to
prevail. Nor had theology in Dante's century forgotten that such
was Plato's definition, as Albertus Magnus may serve to witness:

> It must be said without any doubt, according to Anselm, that parents
> were to have transmitted original justice to their children: but such
> justice is nothing if not the due order of the natural parts among
> themselves, in which the body is ordered to the soul and the soul
> to the reason, as Plato says, according to ruling justice [*secundum
> dominalem iustitiam*].[23]

Of course, in Albert's day, one might rather expect the theologian to turn to Aristotle if he should choose to cite the authority of "philosophy" in such matters, even as Albert and Thomas
and many another did in fact, observing that Aristotle in the
Nicomachean Ethics, by now so popular, had given a definition
of justice in this sense, which we have noted before:

> Metaphorically and in virtue of a certain resemblance there is a
> justice, not indeed between a man and himself, but between certain

parts of him; yet not every kind of justice but that of master and servant or that of husband and wife. For these are the ratios in which the part of the soul that has a rational principle stands to the irrational part; and it is with a view to these parts that people think a man can be unjust to himself, viz. because these parts are liable to suffer something contrary to their respective desires; there is therefore thought to be a mutual justice between them as between ruler and ruled.[24]

We might reflect that justice in this middle area of man's inner disposition is in fact a matter which could also be formulated in terms of the four cardinal virtues:[25] a point which may prove to be not without due significance for us, as we remember the allegory of the four rivers of Eden. We recall that justice, in that allegory, was seen to be the harmony of the other virtues, the "mother of them all." Justice is the covering, integrating, virtue among the four, and in Philo and in Ambrose the derivation in this from Plato was evident.

Justice in this middle area was lost when the whole of original justice was lost; and we have noted in the several definitions by St. Thomas how the reason for this stands clear. The highest subjection is the cause of the next lower one. The powers of man's sensitive soul could remain duly subject to the rule of reason only so long as the reason is duly subject to God. Loss of due subjection at the highest level will bring loss of the same at this next lower level.

But what if we turn back now to thought of justice regained, of return to Eden as to *personal* justice through Christ? We have just noted that in the gaining of personal justice the highest subjection of natural justice appears to be regained. Does this not therefore bring about a due subjection at the next lower level? It would seem that this ought to follow. Yet such, strangely enough, is not the case. And it is just at this level (in descending order) that we begin to take stock of the remarkable difference existing between the two kinds of justice.

That a due order restored at the lower level (second subjection) does not result from the highest subjection of grace and charity through Christ may be witnessed by two spokesmen well qualified to speak to this very point, and who indeed do speak eloquently about it: St. Paul and St. Augustine. For surely we must think that the Apostle, when he wrote his Epistles, had attained to the fullness of Christ's grace, to sanctifying grace and to that charity which unites man to God, of which he spoke with such authority. And yet we know that Paul continued to speak of a law of the flesh that wars against the spirit, and to point to that war as continuing first of all in himself.[26] Such a war is the very disorder of original sin at the second level. It must be that grace and charity in Paul did not restore such order in the lower powers. We know also that Augustine echoed time and again Paul's words on this point, and that he meant to speak of himself as an example of man's fallen nature at this level.[27] But surely we must think that Augustine had attained to sanctifying grace and charity, which is the highest subjection of personal justice.

Such witnesses should suffice. Even without them it must be evident that the justice that is regained through Christ does not cause perfect order to be restored in man's lower powers, that the rebellion of the flesh against reason continues in the most saintly. Whereupon we take note, at the second level of the three subjections, of a considerable gap between the gift of natural justice and the gift of personal justice. Although, in the latter, order and due subjection may be gained, or we may say *regained*, in the highest part of man, the effects of that high subjection do not in turn extend to the next lower level, as in the case of natural justice. If, then, we are remaining ever alert to note a sufficient reason why a lament might come over loss of Eden, it is evident that we begin here to touch upon the possible existence of just such a reason. This fact is most illuminating for us, as we recall that this area wherein order and subjection are *not* restored is precisely the domain of the cardinal virtues. Indeed this is so much the area proper to those virtues that they might be taken to represent it. In this way, and in terms now far more precise than might have been before, we come to understand why a lament for loss of Eden should focus in particular upon four stars over Eden and not upon seven.

Before turning to the third and lowest subjection, it is useful to remember once more the precise moment in the poem when the

four stars are seen and the lament is heard. This is that moment
when the wayfarer has but now come to stand under the skies
over Eden and at the foot of a mountain which he is now to
ascend. Eden lies at the summit; and if he is to "return" to Eden,
a long hard climb lies ahead for him. To return to Eden is to
come back to the lost "nobility." And indeed, when the climb is
over, we do see the wayfarer Dante attain at last to what is clearly
justice at the highest level, justice as due subjection to God and
reunion with God. This is given him through sanctifying grace
and the infused virtues. But there, we may not forget, not only
do the three higher virtues come with Beatrice, but the four lower
virtues as well, and they are tinged with charity. They are the
infused cardinal virtues. The question thus arises: if these four virtues are attained here, the four infused cardinal virtues, how is it
that we may not think that original justice is entirely regained
at the second level which is their level? Can it be that the infused
cardinal virtues which are had in *personal* justice do not bring
that same order at the second level which had prevailed in *original* justice?

   This in fact appears to be the truth of the matter. We may not
doubt Paul's testimony, or Augustine's, of the continuing disorder
in man's sensitive appetites. The fact remains that although a man
may regain justice through Christ, and in such justice attain to
all the infused virtues, he does not regain the due subjection of
the second level which had attended the cardinal virtues as given
in natural justice. Thus, as between natural justice and personal
justice, we take the exact measure of a significant difference at
precisely this second level, and in the area of the cardinal virtues.
Must we not conceive this as a difference between the infused
cardinal virtues of original justice and the infused cardinal virtues
of personal justice? In the one case, in natural justice, the order
and subjection in their area is perfect; and in the other case, in
personal justice, we have it on good authority that order and
subjection in their area is far from perfect, when gained: so far
from perfect, indeed, that we have good cause to lament a great
loss on this particular score.

   Of course, if we take thought of the point in the journey at

which the lament arises, it must be noted that it is not at the foot
of the mountain that the cardinal virtues would have been attained in any case, but only at the summit. At the moment when
the lament is heard a difficult climb lies ahead. And yet it is not
the hard fact of the climb ahead that is regretted. The lament
focuses upon four stars *never seen except by the first people*, upon
four virtues lost by man when Eden was lost, upon four virtues
never regained.

Finally we understand. Lament is focused upon exactly that
part of original justice which is the area of the cardinal virtues,
for it is there, in their area, that significant loss as between the
two kinds of justice exists to be lamented. The four stars over
Eden are the four infused cardinal virtues as given to natural
justice. They were to have remained an essential part of that justice at the second level of the threefold subjection, and were, as
such, a part to be transmitted *in the nature* to all of Adam's de-
scendants. But at this level that original justice is never regained
(except in metaphor). The infused cardinal virtues are given in
the justice "regained" (herein the metaphor). But they are somehow not equal to the infused cardinal virtues that were once given
in natural justice, if we take the measure of the difference by the
subjection or lack of subjection resulting at this level. And the
poet has built that "somehow" into his poem.

Finally we understand. Only now can we see what the four
maidens mean when they declare that they are nymphs, as they
come with Beatrice, and that in the sky they are stars. Coming
as the handmaids of Beatrice, they come as the infused cardinal
virtues given in personal justice through Christ. But such virtues
were once given to the first people not as a part of *personal* justice, but as a part of *natural* justice, when in their area, in natural
justice, there was a perfect subjection of man's lower powers to
his reason. Perfect order prevailed at their level, in original justice. That perfect order was lost forever. This being the case,
what continuing existence could be more appropriate for these
lost virtues than their existence as stars in the skies over Eden, so
far to the south that they are no longer seen by man dwelling
opposite Eden and in misery? Indeed these four stars are as a con-

stellation of justice in those skies, a reminder of the justice that was forever lost. Even as Matelda is also a reminder of that same justice lost. These are *her* stars, in this sense.

There is, in short, a difference (shall we say "somehow"?) between nymphs and stars. And we might of course recall that the three theological virtues could also have declared what the four do affirm, that they too are nymphs here, as they come with Beatrice, and that in the heaven they too are stars. For this is the fact. But it is noteworthy that the three do not affirm this. The three theological virtues point up no difference, that is, between their part in personal justice, as it is now given to persons, and their part in natural justice as it was once given to human nature. And the reason for this is also now clear. We have taken stock of the difference between the subjection of original and personal justice at the highest level of the three. Subjection at that level is not strikingly different, not *lamentably* different, in the two justices. But, unlike the three, the four maidens who are the cardinal virtues have reason to make a special point of the difference existing in their area, at their lower or second level. They make it through a deliberate reference to the moment when they were seen as stars, at the foot of the mountain. Moreover, as for the lament heard there, it is not heard again, we recall, when later the three stars are seen to have replaced the four. Again we understand: the event at the summit matches the event at the foot of the mountain even in this sequence and manner.

* * *

The lament we hear there is for the great loss in the lower area of original justice. But we must not forget that the area of the cardinal virtues is only the second of three subjections, taken in descending order. There was yet a third and lowest gift making up the total order of original justice, as is evident from the several definitions of Thomas Aquinas wherein we have seen him always at pains to include it as a third subjection. In the justice first given to man, there was justice also with respect to the body: that is, the soul had such perfect rule over the body that the body could in no way disobey it and might not therefore fall into the disorder of death. Such is the full meaning of subjection at the third and lowest level: through it man was given immortality of the body. Adam was not to die the death if he had not sinned. In his *Compendium of Theology*, Thomas Aquinas gives an especially concise formulation of the principle upon which the third gift, immortality of the body, rested:

> The rational soul, beyond the manner of other forms, exceeds the capacity of all bodily matter, as is shown by the intellectual operation which it has without the body. In order therefore that bodily matter be suitably adapted to the soul, it was necessary that some disposition be added to the body, through which it might become suitable matter for such a form. As this form comes into being from God alone through creation, so also that disposition exceeding the nature of a body was given by God alone to the human body, a disposition which would preserve the body itself incorrupt, so that thus it might match the unbroken existence of the soul. This disposition remained in man's body as long as man's soul clung to God; but when the soul of man turned from God by sin, fittingly also the human body lost that supernatural disposition through which it was immovably subject to the soul, and so man incurred the necessity of death. If therefore one regard the nature of the body, death is natural; but if one consider the nature of the soul and the disposition which on the soul's account was in the beginning added supernaturally to the human body, death is *per accidens* and against nature, since it is natural for the soul to be united to the body.[28]

"By one man sin entered into the world, and death by sin: and so death passed upon all men": we have only to grasp this sad fact in the light of the threefold subjection of original justice to conceive in the fullest measure the difference between the justice that was to have been and the justice that can now be in persons. If we are thinking in terms of justice recovered, then we realize that we may perhaps speak of some partial recovery of a subjection in the second or middle area. But we confront the sad fact that in the area of the lowest or third subjection nothing is recovered. The loss is total. Thus Adam, even though he was saved through Christ, did not escape death; even though he was reunited to God through the highest subjection of grace and charity, that subjection did not bring with it the subjection of body to soul through which the body was saved from death. And all of Adam's progeny is mortal as to the flesh. Death is the absolutely irreparable consequence of original sin.

To be sure, at this point our thoughts might also turn to that beatitude which through Christ we are to have at the end of time, when the body (glorified) will again be united with the soul and will be in even more perfect subjection, completely spiritual, having no need of material food or drink to sustain it.[29] That happy time, that beatitude, is guaranteed us by His Resurrection, and once more we might exclaim "O felix culpa." And yet if we remember that Adam was not to have died the death if he had not sinned, nor were any of us to die; if we remember that the gift of the body's immortality was one of the gifts included in natural justice, then we shall lament the Fall and loss of such a dignity with loss of Eden — unless death seems a happy event to us and not a grievous one.

Again we see that there is cause for lament at precisely the point in the poem where lament comes. Here, as so often in this work, beauty is the beauty of relevance. If through the sin of the first man death entered into the world, it is also through the death and resurrection of the Saviour that the great victory over death prevails. Now the moment of the lament in the poem is Easter Sunday morning, just before dawn, the very moment of the Resurrection. Should not the Easter hour cause our thoughts to turn to our sore loss of immortality through sin, loss of Eden and the Fall, that had made the Resurrection necessary? We look up at four stars and we think such thoughts.

For it should be noted that there are no virtues properly assigned to the area of the third, lowest subjection of natural justice. It was not through any set of three or of four virtues that perfect subjection of the body to the soul prevailed therein. There are no virtues to represent the third subjection. Yet the lament over the four which pertain to the second lower level must be felt to extend to the concomitant loss in the area of the lowest subjection as well. For this climb up the mountain will prove to be a return to Eden. Ahead, we perceive (however dimly), will lie the areas of a justice restored first at the second and then at highest level of the virtues; and when we reach the summit this proves to be so. But restoration in the area of the third subjection is not ever to be had. Death still prevails. A lament for loss of Eden and loss of justice cannot fail to include the melancholy thought that in the natural justice which the "first people" had, and lost, death was no part of our lot.

Notes

On the entire concept of original justice I have found two works especially enlightening, and have made use of them in this chapter: 1) J. B. Kors, *La justice primitive et le péché originel d'après S. Thomas*, Kain, Belgium, 1922; and 2) W. A. Van Roo, *Grace and Original Justice According to St. Thomas* (Rome, 1955), *Analecta Gregoriana*, vol. 75, Series Facultatis Theologicae, Sectio A, no. 13. The two works differ significantly, in their views of original justice, on the question whether that justice must be thought to lie entirely within the domain of nature, on which point I have found the position of Van Roo the more convincing. I may also add that I have followed the translations of the latter in several of the passages quoted from Aquinas.

1. In the summary statement here it will be evident that I am paraphrasing the argument in *Paradiso* VII, 64-120.

2. Augustine, *Contra Duas Epist. Pelag.* IV, 4: "Restat ut in illo primo homini peccasse omnes intelligantur, quia in illo fuerunt omnes quando ille peccavit: unde peccatum trahitur." *De Nupt. et Concup.* II, 5: "Per unius illius voluntatem malam omnes in eo peccaverunt, quando omnes ille unus fuerunt, de quo propterea singuli peccatum originale traxerunt."

Anselm, *De Conc. Virg.*, ch. 2: "Et quia tota humana natura in illis erat et extra ipsos de illa nihil erat, tota infirmata et corrupta est."

Honorius d'Autun, *Elucidarium* II, no. 11 (cited by Kors, p. 41, n. 8): "Deus iustitiam ab omni homine exigit, quam primo dedit. Omnis autem homo *in natura* est Adam, *in persona* filius Adae."

3. The word *tomba* comes, most significantly, as Dante begins his climb out of Hell: *Inferno* XXXIV, 128.

4. *Purgatorio* I, 71: "libertà va cercando ch' è si cara." For "liberty" as synonymous with justice at the summit, see St. Anselm, *De Conc. Virg.*, ch. 12: "Siquidem Adam factus est iustus et liber a peccato et debito saepefato et a poena peccati, et beatus et potens semper servare acceptam iustitiam, et per iustitiam eam quam dixi libertatem et beatitudinem."

5. E. Mâle, *Religious Art in France in the Thirteenth Century*, trans. Dora Nussey (New York, 1913), p. 13 (quoted by permission of the pub-

lisher, E. P. Dutton & Co.). The passage summarized thus by Mâle is to be found in Durandus, *Rationale Divinorum Officiorum* VI, chs. 80–82.

6. In this sense, of course, the reparation of human nature through Christ was to be complete at the end of time, when through Him we shall have our resurrected body and perfect justice. But this is not now, in this life.

7. *De Conceptu Virginali et de Originali Peccato*, ch. 1, *PL* 158.433; *Opera Omnia* (Rome, 1940), II, 140: "Est tamen peccatum quod quisque trahit cum natura in ipsa sui origine, et est peccatum quod non trahit cum ipsa natura, sed ipse facit illud postquam iam est persona discreta ab aliis personis. Illud quidem quod trahitur in ipsa origine dicatur 'originale,' quod potest etiam dici 'naturale,' non quod sit ex essentia naturae, sed quoniam propter eius corruptionem cum illa assumitur. Peccatum autem quod quisque facit postquam persona est, 'personale' potest nominari, quia vitio personae fit. Simili ratione dici potest originalis et personalis iustitia. Siquidem ADAM et EVA 'Originaliter,' hoc est in ipso sui initia mox ut homines extiterunt, sine intervallo simul iusti fuerunt. 'Personalis' autem dici potest iustitia, cum iniustus accipit iustitiam, quam ab origine non habuit."

One should note, of course, that the distinction between original justice and personal justice along these lines was already evident in Augustine, though without Anselm's terminology and with Augustine's characteristic accent on concupiscence and libido: "Pudet igitur huius libidinis humanam sine ulla dubitatione naturam, et merito pudet. In ejus quippe inobedientia, quae genitalia corporis membra solis suis motibus subdidit, et potestati voluntatis eripuit, satis ostenditur quid sit hominis illi primae inobedientiae retributum: quod in ea maxime parte oportuit apparere, qua generatur ipsa natura, quae illo primo et magno in deterius est mutata peccato: a cujus nexu nullus eruitur, nisi id quod, cum omnes in uno essent, in *communem* perniciem perpetratum est, et Dei justitia vindicatum, Dei gratia *in singulis* expietur." (Italics mine.) *De Civ. Dei* XIV, 20 (*PL* 41.428).

8. *Questiones disputatae* in the text established by D. Lottin and given in his *Psychologie et morale aux xii⁰ et xiii⁰ siècles*, IV, 197–198: "Secundo quod dicit Anselmus in libro de conceptu virginali, in Adam ante peccatum erat iustitia naturalis qua omnes procedentes ab ipso essent originaliter iusti, si stetisset. . . . Et ex hoc etiam patet quod secundum quod dicit Anselmus quod peccatum originale est carentia vel nuditas debite iustitie, id est iustitie naturalis vel innocentie qua essent omnes homines originaliter iusti, si primi parentes stetissent."

9. *In II Sent* d. xvi, a. 5, sol.: "Iustitia autem naturalis dicitur ordo rectus virium inferiorum ad superiores, et superioris ad Deum, et corporis ad animam et mundi ad corpus. Et in hoc ordine creatus est homo."

The term may also be noted in Honorius d'Autun, the *Elucidarium* II, no. 11, col. 1142 (See Kors, p. 41, n. 3): "Infans recens animatus vel natus tribus de causis reus existit. Prima, quia naturalem iustitiam non habet quam Deus primo homini contulit. . . . Igitur quia naturalis iustitia in infante non invenitur, a iustitia Dei iuste repellitur."

10. *Purgatorio* XXX, 62–63: "quando mi volsi al suon del nome mio, che di necessità qui si registra."

11. The notion of "felix culpa" derives primarily from the familiar passage in Rom. 5.15: "si enim unius delicto multi mortui sunt, multo magis

gratia Dei et donum in gratia unius hominis Jesu Christi in plures abundavit."
In commenting on this point Aquinas (*Summa Theol.* I–II, q. 109, a. 10,
ad 3) cites St. Augustine's statement on the same in his *De Natura et Gratia*,
wherein one sees the essential resolution of the matter which was then generally adopted in Christian theology: "Sicut Augustinus dicit in libro *De
Nat. et Gratia*: 'Homo in primu statu accepit donum per quod perseverare
posset, non autem ut perseveraret. Nunc autem per gratiam Christi multi
accipiunt et donum gratiae quo perseverare possunt, et ulterius eis datur
quod perseverent.' Et sic donum Christi est maius quam delictum Adae. Et
tamen facilius homo per gratiae donum perseverare poterat in statu innocentiae, in quo nulla erat rebellio carnis ad spiritum, quam nunc possimus
quando reparatio gratiae Christi, etsi sit inchoata quantum ad mentem, non-
dum tamen est consummata quantum ad carnem."

It is to be noted, moreover, that the "O felix culpa!" is part of the blessing of the Paschal candle (Aquinas, *Summa Theol.* III, q. 1, a. 3, ad 3).

12. Of the many passages from Augustine's works which might be cited
on this point, perhaps the following may serve as typical in its emphasis,
De Civ. Dei XIII, 13 (PL 41.386): "Nam posteaquam praecepti facta trans-
gressio est, confestim gratia deserente divina, de corporum suorum nuditate
confusi sunt. Unde etiam foliis ficulneis, quae forte a perturbatis prima
comperta sunt, pudenda texerunt. . . . Senserunt ergo novum motum in-
obedientis carnis suae, tanquam reciprocam poenam inobedientiae suae. Jam
quippe anima libertate in perversum propria delectata, et Deo dedignata
servire, pristino corporis servitio destituebatur: et quia superiorem Dominum suo arbitrio deseruerat, inferiorem famulum ad suum arbitrium non
tenebat: nec omni modo habebat subitam carnem, sicut semper habere po-
tuisset, si Deo subdita ipsa mansisset."

For Augustine's particular views on original sin and justice as seen in
the frame of the whole tradition, see Kors, *La justice primitive*, pp. 3 ff.

13. *De Gen. ad Litt.* XI, ch. 32: "Haec mors ea die accidit, qua factum
est quod Deus vetuit. Amisso quippe statu mirabili, corpus ipsum cui status
etiam de ligno vitae virtute mystica praebebatur, per quem nec morbo ten-
tari, nec mutari aetate potuissent, ut hoc in eorum carne, quamvis adhuc
animali et in melius postea commutanda, jam tamen significaretur per escam
ligni vitae."

14. On the decisive influence which St. Anselm had on the development
of the concept of original justice and on the attribution to him of the term
"originalis iustitia," see Kors, *La justice primitive*, pp. 23 ff.

Anselm gave his definition of original justice as "rectitudo voluntatis
propter se servata" in his *De Veritate*, ch. 12. He refers to it later and
argues on the basis of it in his *De Conceptu Virg.*, ch. 3 and *passim*. Hugh
of St. Victor and Albertus Magnus, among others, acknowledge this definition (see Kors, p. 44).

15. On the development of the concept of original sin from Augustine
to St. Thomas, see Kors, *La justice primitive*; from St. Anselm to St. Thomas,
see in particular Lottin, *Psychologie et morale*, IV, 11 ff. (which gives a
complete and recent bibliography of the subject as well).

16. As one example merely of such a reference to Aristotle in this connection: *In II Sent.* d. xxx, q. 1, a. 1, sol.: "Ea quae sunt ad finem, disponun-

tur secundum necessitatem finis, ut ex 2 Phys. (text 78) patet. Finis autem ad quem homo ordinatus est, est ultra facultatem naturae creatae, scilicet beatitudo, quae in visione Dei consistit." And with this beginning Aquinas goes on to define original justice in terms of the three subjections.

17. One may note that a number of theologians (Alexander of Hales, Albertus Magnus, St. Bonaventura and others) sought a reconciliation of Augustine's emphasis on concupiscence and Anselm's on justice in the will; thus they hold that concupiscence is the material element and that privation of justice in the will is the formal element (see Kors, p. 67).

When the third step is taken and original justice is viewed as involving *three* levels, St. Thomas in turn would reconcile Augustine's emphasis with this. Thus concupiscence becomes the material element and *carentia divinae visionis* the formal. See especially Aquinas, *De Malo* q. 5, a. 1: "Utrum poena originalis peccati sit carentia divinae visionis."

18. *In II Sent.* d. xxxiii, q. 1, a. 1, sol.: "Defectum autem ad naturam pertinentem solum primum peccatum induxit: ipsum enim discontinuavit adhaesionem hominis ad Deum. Ex hoc autem quod continue homo Deo adhaerebat, haec virtus illi indita erat ut sub obedientia rationis continue subderentur inferiores vires, et sub obedientia animae corpus, propter hoc scilicet quod ratio suo superiori continue subdita fuerat. Intercisa autem prima obedientia per hoc quod ratio primi hominis a Deo aversa est per peccatum, consecuta est disturbatio ordinis in inferioribus viribus ad rationem, et corporis ad animam."

19. *Summa c. G.* IV, 52: "Sic natura humana fuit instituta in sui primordio quod inferiores vires perfecte rationi subiicerentur, ratio Deo, et animae corpus, Deo per gratiam supplente id quod ad hoc deerat per naturam. Huiusmodi autem beneficium, quod a quibusdam *originalis iustitia* dicitur, sic primo homini collatum fuit ut ab eo simul cum natura humana propagaretur in posteros. Ratione autem per peccatum primi hominis se subtrahente a subiectione divina, subsecutum est quod nec inferiores vires perfecte rationi subiiciantur, nec animae corpus: et hoc non tantum in primo peccante, sed idem defectus consequens pervenit ad posteros, ad quos etiam dicta originalis iustitia perventura erat. Sic igitur peccatum primi hominis, a quo omnes alii secundum doctrina fidei sunt derivati, et personale fuit, inquantum ipsum primum hominem proprio bono privavit; et naturale, inquantum abstulit sibi et suis posteris consequenter beneficium collatum toti humanae naturae."

20. *In Epistolam ad Rom.* V, lect. 3: "Alio modo potest considerari natura hominis secundum quod per divinam providentiam fuit ei per iustitiam originalem provisum. Quae quidem iustitia erat quaedam rectitudo, ut mens hominis esset sub Deo, et inferiores vires essent sub mente, et corpus sub anima, et omnia exteriora sub homine: ita scilicet quod quamdiu mens hominis Deo subderetur, vires inferiores subderentur rationi, et corpus animae, indeficienter ab ea vitam recipiens, et exteriora homini, ut scilicet omnia servirent, et nullum ex eis nocumentum sentiret. Hoc autem providentia divina disposuit propter dignitatem animae rationalis, quae cum naturaliter sit incorruptibilis, debebatur sibi incorruptibile corpus."

21 *Summa Theol.* I, q. 95, a. 1, resp.

22. *De Malo* q. 4, a. 6, ad 4. "Peccatum originale opponitur iustitiae

originali, per quam superior pars animae et Deo coniungebatur, et inferioribus viribus imperabat, et etiam corpus absque corruptiones poterat con-
servare."

23. *Summa Theol.* II, tr. xiv, q. 85 (ed. Borgnet, XXXIII, 138): "Dicendum quod sine dubio secundum Anselmum, originalem justitiam transfudis-
sent parentes in parvulos: sed illa nihil aliud est, nisi debitus ordo naturalium
inter se, quo corpus ordinatur ad animam, et anima ad rationem, ut dicit
Plato, secundum dominalem justitiam."

It may be noted that Albertus is here distinguishing sharply an order of
nature from an order of grace, so that his definition does not cover the
whole order of original justice, but only the lower order, in the domain of
the cardinal virtues.

24. *Ethics* V, ch. 11 (Ross trans.).

25. That the area of the second subjection is the area of the moral or
cardinal virtues is not a point that requires much documentation, being
so obvious. Any doubt or question about this may be met by referring to
the discussion of this matter by Thomas Aquinas, *Summa Theol.* I–II, q. 59,
a. 4; q. 60, a. 1, in the responses: "Moral virtue perfects the appetitive part
of the soul by directing it to good as defined by reason"; "the moral virtues
are habits of the appetitive faculty"; "in moral matters the reason holds the
place of commander and mover, while the appetitive power is commanded
and moved." See also here his solutions to q. 61 where the cardinal virtues
are assigned to specific areas within this area of the passions and powers of
the sensitive soul.

26. Rom. 7.14–25.

27. Among the many eloquent passages in Augustine on this score, none
is better than the pages of his *Confessions*, Book X, ch. 30 ff. witnessing
his condition *after conversion*.

One meets this point in theological formulation in the following representative forms:

Augustine (as quoted by Thomas Aquinas in note 11 above): "Et sic
donum Christi est maius quam delictum Adae. Et tamen facilius homo per
gratiae donum perseverare poterat in statu innocentiae, in quo nulla erat
rebellio carnis ad spiritum, quam nunc possimus quando reparatio Christi,
etsi *sit inchoata quantum ad mentem, nundum tamen est consummata quantum ad carnem*" (my italics).

Aquinas (*De Malo* q. 4, a. 6, ad 4): ". . . unde manet post baptismum
et necessitas moriendi et concupiscentia quae est materiale in originali
peccato. Et sic quantum ad superiorem partem animae participat novitatem
Christi; sed quantum ad inferiores animae vires, et etiam ipsum corpus,
remanet adhuc vetustas quae est ex Adam."

28. *Compendium Theologiae ad Fratrem Reginaldum*, ch. 152: "Anima
rationalis praeter modum aliarum formarum excedit totius corporalis materiae facultatem, quod eius operatio intellectualis demonstrat, quam sine
corpore habet. Ad hoc igitur quod materia corporalis convenienter ei aptata
fuerit, necesse fuit quod aliqua dispositio corpori superadderetur, per quam
fieret conveniens materia talis formae. Et sicut haec forma a solo Deo exit
in esse per creationem, ita illa dispositio naturam corpoream excedens, a solo
Deo corpori humano attributa fuit, quae videlicet ipsum corpus incorrup-

tum conservaret, ut sic perpetuitati animae conveniret. Et haec quidem dispositio in corpore hominis mansit, quamdiu anima hominis Deo adhaesit. Aversa autem anima hominis per peccatum a Deo, convenienter et corpus humanum illam supernaturalem dispositionem perdidit per quam immobiliter animae subdebatur, et sic homo necessitatem moriendi incurrit. Si igitur ad naturam corporis respiciatur, mors naturalis est; si vero ad naturam animae, et ad dispositionem quae propter animam supernaturaliter humano corpori a principio indita fuit, est per accidens et contra naturam, cum naturale sit animae corpori esse unitam."

I have given the translation of Van Roo, *Grace and Original Justice*, pp. 50–51, where his particular discussion of this subjection may be found, along with further references. See also Aquinas, *Summa Theol.* I–II, q. 85, a. 5, resp.; II–II, q. 164, a. 1, resp.

29. Thus, one thinks of I Cor. 15.22: "Sicut in Adam omnes moriuntur, ita et in Christo omnes vivificabuntur."

For Aquinas on the immortality which Adam had, compared with that which we shall have through Christ in eternity, see *In II Sent.* d. xix, q. 1, a. 5, sol.

Chapter XIV

Crossing Over into Eden

By way of such considerations, precise measure may be taken of the proportion which the poet built into that outline of an event which is a "return to Eden," a proportion resting upon two terms of a great simile: on the one hand, original justice lost, and on the other, personal justice regained. It is the first term of that proportion, the total range and order of original justice with its three subjections, which provides the possibility of this measure, since that first justice extended further and included more than does the order of personal justice. Original justice, established by reason of that end for which God had created man, may be viewed as a kind of three-sectioned ladder raised towards Him, a means given to man by which he could "ascend" to the appointed goal so far above and beyond his own natural powers of attainment. But the first man turned from God in disobedience and fell in sin; the whole ladder collapsed.[1] Nor was it possible for man to rebuild that ladder for himself, any more than he might have built it by himself in the first instance. Only God could rebuild as God had built. And God did rebuild a ladder (though not that same first ladder), giving His only Son: a ladder of personal justice

through Christ's grace. Between the two ladders there is the correlation of a "proportion," a resemblance in difference, with which
a poet can work, as with a metaphor.

We may hold these two "ladders" side by side, and take stock
of the similitude and the disparity which they exhibit, by looking
across from the original ladder, at each of its three levels or sections, to ask what the rebuilt ladder offers that corresponds. Thus,
beginning at the bottom and proceeding upward, we note the
sorest loss at the first, lowest level. The most lamentable difference
is encountered there, for there we find no restoration whatever
of that subjection through which the body was so ruled by the
soul that it was not subject to death. And in the "return," at the
point where the climb proper is to begin, we hear lament over
this. What has replaced that lowest subjection of original justice
is now another kind of subjection to which we may attain through
Christ and through conformity with Him: the subjection of
humility. The rush is girded on. But it is right that there should
be thought here of what was lost, of what only a first people had.

Lament at this point, where the climb begins, concerns the four
cardinal virtues, represented by four stars seen only by the first
people. What is said of those stars is a clear invitation to the reader
to conceive of the two ladders of justice in terms of the virtues.
The second or middle section of the ladder is the area proper of
these four virtues, whereby, in original justice, the lower powers
were in perfect subjection to the rule of reason. But, in the matter
of personal justice and on this particular score, we have learned
that our eye must look to the summit of the ladder, for it is there
and there only that the four cardinal virtues of that justice are
given. They come as handmaids to Beatrice, and they are not
attained until the highest level of personal justice is attained, when
she is reached. When Beatrice comes with the three theological
virtues (and dressed in their colors) it is evident that the third
and highest level of personal justice is had with her, and not merely the second or middle level. And yet the four virtues of the
middle subjection are with Beatrice, at this highest point, and are
not given before she comes. It is at just this point that the correspondence between the two ladders of justice is made explicit by

the four maidens, in their reference to the four stars in the sky as to that part of original justice to which their present place as maidens corresponds in the scale of personal justice.

Which is to say that, in personal justice, the four cardinal virtues are not given until sanctifying grace and charity are given. The four are tinged with the red of charity. They are, therefore, the infused cardinal virtues. And if we are keeping in mind the correspondence of the two ladders of justice, we know that this is as it should be, because the cardinal virtues of original justice were likewise the infused cardinal virtues, given when sanctifying grace and charity were given. Even so, though they were first given then, as now, at this highest point, the fact remains that the area proper of the cardinal virtues is that middle area of the powers of the soul. Their domain is there, and it is because of this that there is special significance in what the four maidens so explicitly declare as they come to lead to Beatrice: "Here we are nymphs, and in the sky we are stars." There *is* a difference, and we must understand it at the second or lower level which is their area: there, at that level in personal justice, subjection is not perfect, even though those virtues be tinged with charity. Again the difference represents a loss that may be lamented, and in the poem it is lamented, when the four stars are seen.

At the highest level of subjection on the ladders of justice, that is, a perfect subjection of man to God, which is the level proper to the theological virtues and to sanctifying grace, there is also a difference to be noted. But there is hardly occasion for lament in this. Indeed, according to the Apostle, grace through Christ's justice does more abound now than in the justice given to Adam.

Through such a summary review of the main points of this doctrine, it is evident that the proportion noted comes finally to focus our attention sharply on the middle area of the second subjection: a fact made explicit by the poet himself with the clear lament over the four stars at the beginning of the upward climb, then by the words of the four maidens at the summit. At both the lowest rung of the ladder and at the topmost rung, we are invited to consider with special attention this middle region of the upward way.

But is not this middle area of the return precisely Virgil's area? Inevitably that question must arise. For we have seen that Virgil leads to what is surely a kind of rectitude, a justice. What else can the words mean which he addresses to Dante when they stand at last on the level of the summit? And if we look closely at the words there spoken by Virgil as he dismisses Dante from further guidance, the justice which he declares to have been attained with him is surely a justice in the middle area, a rule of the will and the reason. Such a rule must mean that reason and right will now govern the lower powers of the soul, for over what would reason rule if not over those powers? Reason's rule must mean due subjection of the lower powers to reason.

What, moreover, can it mean that Virgil should lead to this justice and then lead no further? In fact, as he himself declares, he "discerns no further." Now, as the poem is careful to make plain to us, Virgil guides as a kind of light. As we have come to understand, Virgil is the natural light of reason, Beatrice the light of grace. To attain to justice with Virgil must mean to come to a justice which is discernible by the natural light of reason and without benefit of the light of sanctifying grace; or shall we not say, discernible *before* the light of grace is had, for when Virgil dismisses Dante, Beatrice has not yet come, though she is expected. Here then is a problem calling for special scrutiny.

Virgil as guide, and as a kind of light, is not merely the natural light of reason as this is given to every man, but he is also that light as it was given to those philosophers and wise men who, like himself, came before Christ and were pagans. In allegory, he is the light which was given to them in that period of history, before the light of grace was come, which is Christ. Therefore, when Virgil declares that he "discerns no further" than that justice to which he brings his charge, we are not to overlook the extension of meaning evident in this historical sense. If Virgil discerns no further than this, it must be that "the philosophers," the *savi* who dwell as he does in Limbo, discerned no further, that this, and no more than this, was their conception of justice.[2] Virgil represents them and their limits of vision. We may single out the two most distinguished of all those who dwell now in Limbo, Plato, and

Aristotle *the* Philosopher, and put the question with respect to them. Did they discern such a justice as this, to which Virgil leads, this kind of inner rectitude by which reason rules over the lower powers of the soul, a justice corresponding to what we now recognize as the second subjection?

As we know already, the answer is that they did, of course, conceive of such a justice. But the problem then becomes this: Virgil leads to Beatrice and to attain to Beatrice must mean to win to the summit of personal justice as given through Christ. How then may a justice known to pagan philosophers be any part of the ladder by which we climb to a justice which is through Christ? Or we may put the problem even more sharply in terms of the virtues, and of precisely those virtues whose domain is the second subjection: do we not see the cardinal virtues come with Beatrice and come only with her? What place, then, can we find on the ladder of the upward way for a justice which is the right rule of reason over the lower powers and yet is attainable under Virgil's guidance *before* the cardinal virtues have come with Beatrice?

We may begin to seek an answer to such questions by recalling once more that the pagan philosophers had indeed discerned a kind of justice, an order in the inner man by virtue of which reason would sit in supreme and absolute dominion over the lower powers of the soul. Plato and the *Republic* especially come to mind, and we have noted that Albertus Magnus remembered Plato's conception of justice, calling it *dominalis iustitia*. Or, at other times, Albertus will give it another name: *iustitia generalis*; but whether it bears the one name or the other, the conception remains always essentially the same: "It is clear that the rectitude of the soul which is general justice consists in the due order of all the powers of the soul to their act." [3]

As for Aristotle, by Dante's time he would be thought of more often than Plato in this connection, because of his own formulation of such a conception of justice, given, as we have already noted, in the *Nicomachean Ethics*; and that this is a definition found in the Ethics must mean that it is one especially well known to all those philosophers and theologians of the thirteenth century who devotedly studied and wrote their commentaries on that great work. We may recall once more the Philosopher's words:

> Metaphorically, and in virtue of a certain resemblance, there is a justice, not indeed between a man and himself but between certain parts of him; yet not every kind of justice, but that of master and servant or that of husband and wife. For these are the ratios in which the part of the soul that has a rational principle stands to the irrational part; and it is with a view to these parts that people also think a man can be unjust to himself, viz. because these parts are liable to suffer something contrary to their respective desires; there is therefore thought to be a mutual justice between them as between ruler and ruled.[4]

One would of course expect St. Thomas Aquinas to make all possible use of such a definition by Aristotle. And indeed he did so, calling justice on such a definition *metaphorical*, a justice in the inner disposition of an individual man, to set it apart from *social* or distributive justice which is between men (the term "metaphorical" would in itself appear to recall Plato's *Republic*):

> Justice is so called inasmuch as it implies a certain rectitude of order in the interior disposition of man, in so far as what is highest in man is subject to God, and the inferior powers of the soul are subject to the superior, i.e., to the reason: and this disposition the Philosopher calls *justice metaphorically speaking* (Ethic. V, 11). Now this justice may be in man in two ways: First, by simple generation, which is from privation to form; and thus justification may belong even to such as are not in sin, when they receive this justice from God, as Adam is said to have received original justice. Secondly, this justice may be brought about in man by a movement from one contrary to the other, and thus justification implies a transmutation from the state of injustice to the aforesaid state of justice. And it is thus we are now speaking of the justification of the ungodly, according to the Apostle.[5]

Now, clearly, everything Thomas says here discloses its relevance to present considerations, for he explicitly brings Aristotle's conception of justice into the frame of the general idea of a "return to Eden." As already noted, the whole outline of such a notion is known in theology as "justification of the ungodly," even as Thomas here states. And we note his reference to that justice which was originally given to Adam "when not in sin."

Thomas, in fine, is thinking in terms of the very proportion with which Dante the poet is working. And in his first words we may even recognize the familiar distinction of two if not three of the subjections. This, on the whole, is a formulation of justice that we shall do well to examine with close attention.

Yet there is something about this definition that puzzles us. Does not Thomas appear to attribute to Aristotle the entire definition of original justice in terms of the two higher subjections? From such an impression there is no escape. Yet how can this be? Is it conceivable that the Philosopher, a pagan, could have had knowledge of that highest subjection of man to God which can only prevail through sanctifying grace and charity? Yet is it not most certain that Aristotle had no knowledge whatever of such grace or of such a virtue? Can any mention of either be found anywhere in his works? Thomas Aquinas, who knew those works so well, must surely admit to the negative. A pagan philosopher might not conceive of such a subjection as this highest one, because that can be known only through the revealed Christian truth and not by the natural light of reason.[6] Such a level of justice exceeds "philosophy" itself, as to knowledge; and such a justice is quite above the Philosopher's capacity, as to the possession of it. Aristotle could neither know nor possess such a subjection in personal justice; much less could he conceive of it as a part of original justice in Adam, of which likewise he must be thought to have been entirely ignorant. And this, we know, is why Aristotle and Plato must forever dwell in Limbo where Dante finds them on his journey to God.

It is of some interest to remark that the whole of the definition of justice which Thomas appears to assign to the Philosopher is in terms of only two of the subjections and not of the three. In the two named we recognize at once the familiar formulation of the two higher levels of subjection in original justice; but we find no mention here whatever of what we know to be a third or lowest subjection, that of the body to the soul, which preserved the body from death. Now, since this is a definition which Thomas means to attribute to the Philosopher, he does well to omit mention of that lowest level of Adam's condition. Aristotle, we may be sure, had never dreamt in his philosophy of such a gift to man, nor had any other of those pagans who sit with him in Limbo.

In fact, since it is necessary to deny to Aristotle any knowledge whatever of the highest subjection of original justice as well as any knowledge of the lowest, it must strike us as passing strange that Thomas would attribute to his Philosopher any definition whatever of *original justice*. We come up short in the face of this and are perplexed. Are we to think that Thomas Aquinas does not know the limits of Aristotle's philosophy, that he is not well aware of those boundaries beyond which the pagan "could not discern"? No one in the least familiar with the writings of Thomas can entertain any such doubt as this. Not only Thomas (especially Thomas!) but the whole of thirteenth-century theology was most keenly conscious of those limitations. The very revival of Aristotle and the incorporation of his thought into the Christian frame had made the boundary line of pagan philosophy a very bold and prominent line indeed.

The simple fact is that one has to learn to read Thomas Aquinas and his contemporaries with due caution on precisely this score. It is certain that they were ever mindful of the limits of an Aristotle, and yet the instance before us is typical. Thomas's definition of original justice is an excellent example of the manner in which such limitations may, on occasion, be disregarded.[7] Thomas knows full well that no pagan philosopher, not even *the* Philosopher, had any conception whatever of original justice as given to Adam. Or at best, we may say, the pagans had a myth of a golden age and a goddess Astraea. But nothing in that myth speaks of sanctifying grace and charity at the highest level of justice, which is man's subjection to God and union with God, nor of immortality of the body, which is the lowest level of Adam's justice. Indeed, Thomas, if pressed by such questions, would be obliged to admit that his Aristotle and pagan philosophy generally had known and spoken only of what, in the whole order of original justice, corresponds to the second or middle subjection. Such was Plato's conception of a rule of reason, and such was Aristotle's. Ancient wisdom had known justice only in this section of the three-sectioned ladder, this being precisely the area of the cardinal or

moral virtues, of Plato's four virtues: prudence, temperance, fortitude and justice.

Through such discriminations we are thus led back to a distinction respecting the four cardinal virtues which has already
proved to be most important in these considerations: a distinction
between the *acquired* cardinal virtues and the *infused* cardinal
virtues. The latter, tinged with the red of charity, were neither
known to the pagans nor given to them to possess. We may not
think that Plato or Aristotle or indeed Virgil could have had such
virtues, for we know that as pagans they did not have sanctifying
grace and charity. The acquired cardinal virtues, however, were
known to these pagans and we must think that virtuous pagans in
Limbo were virtuous in that they possessed these very virtues. In
fact, Plato was first to write of them, and these are his virtues and
Aristotle's virtues *par excellence*.

All of which amounts to reminding ourselves once more of a
quite simple fact: the pagan philosophers, and pagans generally
before Christ, were without grace and without charity. Prayer
itself was "disjoined" from God and, as Virgil declares in the
poem, was of no avail.[8] Man was disjoined from God. The time
was not a time of grace, not a time when men could discern by
the light of grace. To the pagans there was given only the natural
light of reason, and that hemisphere of light in which they are
seen in Limbo is the evident symbol of just such a light as they
had in this life.

It must follow, then, that having only the natural light, they
could have, among the virtues, only such as are ordered to that
natural light. We may hear Thomas Aquinas on this point:

> And thus, even as the natural light of reason is something besides
> the acquired virtues, which are ordered to this natural light, so also
> the light of grace which is a participation of the Divine Nature is
> something besides the infused virtues, which are derived from and
> are ordered to this light. . . . For as the acquired virtues enable a
> man to walk in accordance with the natural light of reason, so do
> the infused virtues enable a man to walk as befits the light of grace.[9]

The very term "ordered," as used here by Thomas, can bring
us back to the poem, as we remember that the four maidens who

attend Beatrice in Eden declare this of themselves. Beatrice comes as sanctifying grace and as the light of grace. To her are ordered the seven infused virtues, since we know that what the four maidens affirm of themselves is to be understood of the three of the higher *tribù* as well.

But we note what Thomas says here of the acquired virtues. These are ordered to the natural light of reason, whereupon we think inevitably of Virgil in the poem. Virgil is that natural light, being, in allegory, such a light as was given to "the philosophers" before Christ, a light not exceeding the proportion and limits of human nature; he is such a light, in short, as may be in man even without sanctifying grace. Why, then, are we not shown a Virgil attended by the virtues which are ordered to such a light as he thus represents? Would this not be appropriate? Virgil's escort would thus be those acquired virtues, the four cardinal virtues to which Plato had given a name, virtues constituting a kind of justice which ancient wisdom had conceived as prevailing whenever reason establishes its rule over the lower powers of the soul.

We are brought to put such questions the more urgently as we realize that Virgil as guide does indeed lead his charge to a "goal," and that this is precisely such a justice as Plato and Aristotle had defined: justice "metaphorically understood." We catch the sure sign of this in Virgil's last words to Dante, "I crown and mitre thee over thyself." Plato's metaphor of the *Republic* is unmistakably present in such words. This attainment to which Virgil leads is most evidently that rule of reason and right will over the lower faculties which Thomas notes in Aristotle's definition. To this Virgil guides, and beyond this Virgil may not guide, for Virgil discerns no further, even as Aristotle and Plato had discerned no further. At this point in the journey, when Virgil dismisses Dante, the completion of justification in its highest subjection is not yet. That completion lies beyond Virgil, is had with Beatrice and the infused virtues; it lies on the farther side of a stream in Eden, over which Virgil may not cross. Virgil thus leads Dante to justice as ancient wisdom had conceived it — so far and no further. And that justice, if we measure it against the pattern of the three subjections of original justice, is precisely the subjection which corresponds to the second or middle one; the rule of reason over the lower powers. We may note, of course, that Virgil, in declaring the attainment, does not actually speak of such powers. He seems at first to speak only of the will and of attainment in terms of the will: "Your will is free, straight and sound again." But as Virgil speaks yet another verse we know that this is more than a matter of the will alone: "fallo fora non fare a suo senno." It is a matter of reason as well as of will, for the *senno* of the will must be the reason. Reason and right will, therefore, rule now over the powers of the soul. This is *dominalis iustitia*.[10]

Of course, no reader will wish that the poet had actually staged Virgil attended by four maidens representing the acquired virtues. We prefer the poem as we have it. Indeed such a cortège for Virgil is unthinkable. And yet we are obliged to realize, nonetheless, that the acquired cardinal virtues must be conceived as present with Virgil and as an essential part of the goal to which he leads, even as the infused virtues are an indispensable part of that higher justice which is given when Beatrice comes. We have only to recall the statement by Thomas Aquinas already noted: "Even as the natural light of reason is something besides the acquired virtues, which are ordered to this natural light, so also the light of grace which is a participation of the Divine Nature is something besides the infused virtues, which are derived from and ordered to this light."

When we think of Virgil as leading to a goal at the summit of the mountain, we are bound to conceive this always as having a special qualification put upon it: if it is a goal, it is a first or preliminary goal and not a terminus. Not even as a goal "of this life" is it terminal. Virgil leads to Beatrice, and the man whom he brings as far as he may along the way passes from his guidance to hers. Such had been Virgil's promise at the outset. And now even his last words announcing that he has come as far as he can, that he discerns no further, signal the fact that Beatrice is expected: "Until the beautiful eyes, now happy, come, which by their tears caused me to come to you. . . ."

And the beautiful eyes do come — only Virgil is not there to behold them. How then, in terms of justice, are we to conceive the goal to which Virgil leads in its relation to the goal attained when Beatrice comes? Is Virgil's justice a first attainment somehow preparing for Beatrice's advent? This would seem to imply that the attainment of such a justice as ancient wisdom had been able to discern is a first step or preparation toward a justice lying beyond the limits of ancient wisdom. In terms of the natural light given to ancient wisdom, this would mean that an attainment of justice under the natural light is somehow a first moment or phase in the movement toward that justice of grace, beyond the natural light.

We do well to put such questions as carefully and clearly as possible, since in this context of thought we must always recall the famous last chapter of Dante's treatise *On Monarchy*. There Dante writes of two goals appointed to man in the "journey of our life" and refers to Eden as the figure of the first, happiness in this life ("beatitudo hujus vitae"). On the other hand, that other goal which is the happiness of the life to come ("beatitudo vitae aeternae") is figured by the celestial paradise. The chapter is all the more interesting in that the goals are themselves defined in terms of "operation," and of the virtues, the means by which we reach them. The first goal, figured by the terrestrial paradise, consists in due operation according to the virtues proper to man, these being the moral (and intellectual) virtues, all *acquired* virtues; and to such a goal we attain by philosophy ("per philosophica documenta"). The other goal, signified by the celestial paradise, consists in due operation according to the theological virtues, faith, hope and charity; and this goal we reach through revealed truth and Scripture ("per documenta spiritualia").[11]

One is tempted, of course, to seize at once upon such a scheme of two goals and such means of arriving at them (the more precious because formulated by Dante himself), and to affirm forthwith that this is the very conception which the poet has represented in this *Comedy*, in the two goals to which Virgil and Beatrice guide. For in the poem is not Eden the first goal, and does Virgil not guide to Eden by the natural light of the philosophers? And the virtues referred to as "virtues proper to man," what else would these be if not the acquired virtues which, as we have seen, must be thought to attend Virgil as he guides. Thus attainment of the first goal would mean attainment of due operation according to the acquired virtues, and such operation is surely Plato's kind of justice. Moreover, is not the celestial paradise the end to which Beatrice leads, as the light of grace and revelation, and are not the very colors of her procession and her dress those colors of the three theological virtues, faith, hope, and charity? So that here too, in respect to the second goal, treatise and poem would seem to agree.

Indeed all would seem to fit remarkably well except for one point, and a most important one it is: by the central thesis of *De Monarchia* it is nowhere required that the attainment of the first goal be a first step toward the attainment of the second goal, though all readers of the treatise know how Dante does introduce this requirement in the closing words.[12] One simply does not pass from the one goal to the other, or at least nowhere (except in those last words) is it recognized that this might be the case. And one knows why, of course: Dante's thesis in that work requires that the two goals be, in fact, *two*. Otherwise, if the first were strictly ordered to the second, this would imply an absolute subjection of one to the other, and it would then follow that the Emperor ought to be strictly subject to the Pope.

Now all of this has been observed many times before, and is evident enough to anyone reading the two works with much attention. Certainly, in the action of the poem, Virgil does lead to Beatrice. This may not be doubted. But what is too often overlooked, in testing the scheme of the treatise against the outline of event in the poem, is this: in the poem it is Beatrice herself who is the first goal, and Beatrice is in Eden. Beatrice is the end toward which the journey with Virgil always moves. Beatrice is also a beginning as well as an end, for she too must guide as Virgil does, and she leads to the celestial paradise. Her colors are the colors of those three virtues by which we "ascend to celestial Athens." But we note that Beatrice is attended (most significantly) by the infused cardinal or moral virtues, unknown to "the philosophers," for which reason no mention of them was made in the *De Monarchia*. But where now are the *acquired* virtues which the treatise would have attributed to Virgil? In the poem they are given no personification whatever.

These and other considerations, arising out of the comparison of treatise and poem on this particular issue, can serve to sharpen our view of what Dante has in fact staged as the first goal of his journey to God, at the summit of the mountain and in Eden. The goal is justice. But the goal is a justice which in the poem is acknowledged to include all that Beatrice and her seven handmaids represent, a justice which Christian doctrine knows to be attainable only through the grace and charity of Christ. The goal at the summit, in short, is justice as St. Paul had conceived it; it is the end and completion of a process known as the "justification of the ungodly."

Beatrice is such a goal in Eden and in this life. To attain to her and her handmaids, the seven infused virtues, is to come to such a condition of justice.

As we review thus once more the familiar details of the whole scene at the summit of the mountain, taking thought of Virgil and of the goal to which he declares himself to lead — which is justice on the Philosopher's definition — we come into the clear realization that one most prominent feature of the whole scene or stage-set at the summit is the river Lethe, that stream which seems to draw a dividing line between Virgil and Beatrice. It is readily felt to be some kind of boundary line, even before we understand how this must be so. Dante himself may not cross over this boundary before he has confessed himself to Beatrice, who remains all the while on that further bank where she had come. Matelda too is on the far side of the stream, and Dante may not cross over to possess her. But it is when thought is taken of the figure of Virgil on this scene that the stream as boundary stands out most clearly. Virgil had dismissed Dante with words that declare him to have reached a kind of inner justice. Dante may now be his own guide. Even so, Virgil does not quit the scene at this point, as he might have been expected to do, since he can now "discern no further" and therefore can have no function; Virgil remains and follows Dante into the "divine forest" at the summit and on, to the margin of the stream. And there Virgil remains along with Statius to hear Matelda's words and smile at them. But it is clear that Virgil could well have declared of this very stream that "beyond this I do not go," even as he did of the justice to which he had led but a moment before.

Justice: indeed, if we will but conceive this whole scene in such terms, we may see that the poet has staged, here at the summit, the attainment of two kinds of justice, or justice as seen in two perspectives. One, the justice to which Virgil leads, the other the justice which comes with Beatrice's coming. And between the one and the other justice is the boundary and dividing line of a stream. As for the first, the justice of Virgil, we are now in a position to understand it for what it is. Virgil's justice is justice according to the philosophers, justice as Plato and Aristotle had conceived it by the natural light of reason. This is the only conception of justice that may be had by such a light as theirs. "Più oltre non discerno." But when the wayfarer can cross the stream which Virgil may not cross, and can enter into the company of Beatrice and her handmaids, this is then nothing less than that highest subjection of personal justice given through Christ's grace and through charity alone, and known only by the light of grace. Between the two justices is the line of a river. Whereupon we have only to turn back to that definition of justice by Thomas Aquinas which we were examining to see what the line of this river in Eden means; for we may view it as a line drawn within and through that very formulation:

> Justice is so called inasmuch as it implies a certain rectitude of order in the interior disposition of man, in so far as what is highest in man is subject to God || and the inferior powers of the soul are subject to the superior, i.e., to the reason; and this disposition the Philosopher calls justice *metaphorically speaking.*

The line of the river, in Dante's scene at the summit, falls exactly where we may see a line drawn through the definition. And with this we understand better what Dante has done. Thomas Aquinas chose to take no notice at this point of the fact that the Philosopher had not and could not have conceived of the highest subjection of justice, named first in his definition. Such a subjection, in which what is highest in man is ordered to God, lies quite beyond the Philosopher's range of vision. Thomas draws no line here, though at many another time he did. Dante did draw the line in his poem. In staging the event of justice attained, Dante drew that line in the shape of a stream, a limit for Virgil. Virgil may go only so far as Aristotle's conception actually went, to that justice which is the second and lower subjection only, or, in the ascending order of the journey, to the first justice to be reached.

One might finally bring yet one more term into this matter as a touchstone. This is a verb devised by Dante, giving a name to the journey to God as it begins to move through the area where Beatrice guides and in the upward way with her: *trasumanar*.[13] To come to Beatrice and to move with her is to move beyond the human. And, looking through this striking verb, we may see what the stream in Eden is the boundary of, and what it means to cross that stream. It means to pass beyond the human, to pass over into the trans-human. Indeed, the verb *trasumanar* can suggest a coordinate term which Dante did not use, but clearly implied: *umanar*. And if we permit ourselves such a verb for the moment, may we not see that it properly applies to the area of journey where Virgil guides and to the goal to which he guides? To move with Virgil means to move "within the proportion of man's nature," as Thomas Aquinas liked to express it. To journey with Virgil is to journey by that natural light which may not extend beyond such confines.

But what we should be concerned to remark by way of such ideas is this: both goals, the human and the transhuman, are goals at the summit of the mountain, on either side of a dividing stream. Virgil is on one side, Beatrice on the other.

Since this is represented as an attainment, first with Virgil, then with Beatrice, the two "justices" become two successive moments in a forward movement. Virgil leads to Beatrice. The question then comes to be: Is the human justice of Virgil "ordered to" the transhuman justice attained with Beatrice? What we require, in order to answer the question, or indeed to test it as a legitimate question, is some pattern of established theological doctrine in just these terms, that scheme in the background which could have

guided the poet's hand in shaping the event at the summit as a
return to Eden.

*   *   *

Plantaverit autem Dominus Deus paradisum voluptatis a prin-
cipio; in quo posuit hominem quem formavit. . . . Tulit ergo
Dominus Deus hominem, et posuit eum in paradiso voluptatis, ut
operaretur et custodiret illum. Do the familiar verses of Genesis
not tell us that God first formed Adam outside the Garden, and
then placed him therein? The suggestion of this is plain enough.
It would seem that there were these two moments with Adam. But
if this is fact, it must also be "for the sake of signifying," even as
Augustine had insisted in the case of events and things in the
Paradise. What then can the significance be of these two moments
in Adam's creation?

Hugh of St. Victor, for one, was confident that he saw what
was signified by this; it must be that God did this for the sake of
teaching Adam the important distinction between what is natural
and what is of grace: "God chose to form him outside the Paradise that he might understand that he was placed in the Paradise
not by nature but by grace." [14] For Hugh, therefore, the first
moment of Adam's formation outside the Garden was a moment
in naturalibus puris, and he puts certain questions regarding that
first condition:

> If the question is asked whether the first man in that first state of
> his creation had any virtues, we think without any doubt at all that
> good affections and orders according to justice were implanted in
> his nature from his first origin; through these he was attracted by
> natural desire to seek out goodness and justice, and in these good
> affections, indeed, were natural virtues with which, from the begin-
> ning, the nature of man was fashioned and furnished. Now, regard-
> ing those virtues which are accomplished by good will moved from
> divine love, we do not wish to define anything rashly about this,
> in so far as pertains to that first state, especially since regarding the
> work of His charity we have no certain argument, either from
> authority or from reason. [15]

In spite of Hugh's hesitations respecting the second moment
or condition of grace in Adam, no less an authority than St.

Augustine could be adduced to support the opinion here expressed. And, following Hugh, there were other theologians who held with him that Adam had been created first in a condition of pure nature. Alexander of Hales, for instance, makes use of both Augustine and the above passage in Hugh to support this view, citing words of the former respecting the creation of the angels as well as of man:

> We confess therefore in the sincerity of faith what we hold to be the right belief: that God the Lord of all things Who made all things very good . . . did order the life of angels and men in such wise as to show first what they were capable of by their free will and then what the gift of His grace and the justice of His judgment could do.[16]

Other texts can readily be found in Augustine that affirm, or at least strongly suggest, two such moments in Adam's formation, and these texts were eagerly sought out by those theologians who felt that such an interpretation of Genesis was the correct one, but that it might be challenged. Alexander of Hales cites from the *De Spiritu et Anima* the interpretation which Augustine had made of yet another verse of Genesis: "Faciamus hominem ad imaginem et similitudinem nostram" (I.26). God's thought here, according to Alexander, would be of two distinct moments in Adam's formation: "imago est in naturalibus, similitudo in gratuitis." And for this he calls in the authority not only of Augustine but of Peter Lombard.[17]

There is good evidence that many readers had so understood the verses in Genesis, both as to fact and as to what was signified. Adam would thus have been formed first in nature, *secundum naturam*; then, in a second moment, denoted by his being placed in Eden, Adam would have been elevated to the condition of grace. As for the two moments being accepted as literal fact, we know that Dante recalled this point when he wrote his *De Vulgari Eloquentia*, putting there the question of Adam's language and what the first word spoken by the first man must have been.[18] Dante did not take sides there as to whether Adam was fashioned in the Garden or, first, outside the Garden, but his very hesitation shows clearly enough that he views the point as a matter of debate in his time. Now it is of some interest to note, as we are presently concerned to do, that when in his poem Dante came to represent a "return to Eden," he did take a position on this question in the very outline of literal event as he conceived it at the top of the mountain. This he did not do, of course, in any figure of an Adam. That first man is not seen here where he was first created; instead, a Dante returns to the Garden, is re-formed in a journey in which he comes finally to the place where Adam was first formed.

Once more we have come back to that broad simile of the "return" which can be seen to have guided the poet along the way of the journey he staged. And it will prove worth our while to remain yet a moment with that simile: long enough to observe that Dante has in fact represented the "re-forming" of a man as a return which passes again through the two moments of man's original formation. To see this we have to be aware of that doctrine which held that Adam was created first *outside* the Garden, and consider the full import of such a view.

In this it becomes important to go back to what has already been noted respecting the stream of Lethe as a prominent feature of the scene at the summit. One has the distinct sense that that stream is there as a boundary or limit. Might it not be actually a boundary to Eden proper, or mark off, so to speak, an outer Eden from an inner Eden? A clear answer to this would hold much meaning for us. It would suggest that we ought to understand that Eden proper is not entered until the stream is crossed. Eden proper would thus be where Matelda dwells, even as it was where Adam lived after he was placed therein. And Eden, in this bounded sense, would also be where Beatrice comes. Already one begins to get clear glimpses of the increment in meaning which such a feature would suggest.

The question whether Adam was created *secundum naturam* in a first moment, and then elevated to a condition of grace above nature in a second moment, was a familiar one to the thirteenth century and was, by Dante's time, one long debated. Since Genesis seemed to point to two such moments in the case of Adam's formation, it is of no surprise that a considerable line of theologians had held to that view. Peter Lombard, in so ruling, had claimed to have St. Augustine's support, and many another theologian who followed Peter and wrote commentaries on his *Sentences* ranged himself on that side of the question: Alexander of Hales, as noted, Albertus Magnus, Bonaventura, and others. Indeed, those who took the side of Peter Lombard in this question can easily be counted in the majority, by Dante's time. Hence it seems worth our while to consider some sample opinions on this point. First we may hear the Lombard who formulates in quite precise terms the question, "Why man, created outside the Paradise, was placed in Paradise":

> God took man thus formed, as Scripture teaches, and placed him in the paradise of delights which He had planted from the beginning. In these words Moses clearly suggests that man, created outside the Paradise, was then later placed in the Paradise. It is said that this was done either because man was not to continue to dwell in it, or in order that this be assigned not to nature, but to grace.[19]

A question so clearly stated in the *Sentences* was bound to receive its abundant commentary from subsequent theologians, each obliged to take a position on this point. Thus we have noted that Alexander of Hales agreed with Peter Lombard. Alexander's treatment of the matter in his own *Summa* shows clearly that this was already a question hotly debated, "Whether the first man was created in grace":

> On this many have held differing opinions. Some hold that the first man was created in sanctifying grace [*in gratuitis gratum facientibus*]. And the reason which they give is, on God's part, His perfect liberality; and on man's part, man's sufficient suitability. Others hold that man was created merely in a natural condition, not in sanctifying grace. The latter opinion is to be held, because it is in agreement with reason, is approved by the authorities, and declares the Divine excellence. . . .
>
> It is in praise of Divine majesty that man was first created according to nature, and subsequently informed by grace, that he might recognize grace to be a gift of God and might distinguish grace from those things which are of nature [*a naturalibus*]; and, by so distinguishing, not attribute it to his nature but to God the Creator, and for this render due thanks to God, and thus Divine help be not denied but glory be declared to the Helper.[20]

Alexander goes on to hold that the very Wisdom of God is declared by such a creation *gradatim*, through successive stages and in a process extended in time. This was the characteristic way of meeting the opposition of those who held for the one moment only, *in grace*. "Even the beauty [*decor*] of wisdom is manifest in the fact that man was brought to perfection by stages and according to a process in time: for it is the part of wisdom to distinguish separate things according to the fitness of times." [21]

In his own *Summa*, Albertus Magnus made it quite clear that he sided with Peter Lombard and Alexander of Hales on this question. Adam was not created at once in sanctifying grace but in natural grace first, and then informed by that grace which is meritorious.[22]

St. Bonaventura's complete agreement with Peter Lombard in his own Commentary on the *Sentences* may also be noted, both on the fact itself of the two distinct moments in Adam's formation and on the intended significance:

> It was moreover fitting that man be put in such a place [the Paradise] that it might be easy for him to attain to his homeland, and that God should show His benevolence to man, for whom He had prepared this most pleasant place for habitation; and that thus the delightfulness of the exterior habitation might correspond to the interior delights, which the soul has which is the temple of God, and which the soul of the first man had. But it was fitting that man be produced outside such a place, in order that he recognize better the beneficence of God in seeing himself as one brought from elsewhere; and that it might also be evident from this that man was not made to live there forever, but as a pilgrim there for a time. And because God foreknew the fall of man, He wished to place him in the Paradise, that through his ejection from the place of delights he might know by sense experience how many spiritual goods he lost through sin; and that he should know no less how much difference there is between one who obeys God in humility and one who proudly contemns Him.[23]

It becomes evident, in following out the line of debate, that theology had come to this question with a most passionate interest; and it is likewise clear why this was so. The question touched on nothing less than that most important problem (the biggest which the thirteenth century had been obliged to face) of the sharp distinction to be drawn between two orders, the order of nature and the order of grace. The revival of Aristotle's philosophy had indeed made that line the frontier of a whole range of urgent questions.

One theologian, we know, showed special concern for the distinguishing line to be drawn between two such orders. At first encounter it can surprise us that St. Thomas took his position with the opposition on this question, holding finally that Adam must have been created in grace, and not first *in naturalibus puris*, as the Master of the Sentences and those others noted above had held. To be sure, Thomas was not alone in this. An opposition had already formed its line and advanced its arguments. Nor was Thomas himself at first certain what his position would be. Indeed, in his earliest work to touch on the matter, his own Commentary on the *Sentences* of Peter Lombard, Thomas distinguishes three positions on the question: 1) There are those who hold that man did not have grace or the infused virtues in his first state at all. But such a view does not appear to agree with the authorities who hold that Adam had charity, which may not be had without grace. 2) There are others who distinguish two states in the state of innocence, saying that man at the beginning of his creation was created solely *in naturalibus*, but that before he sinned he was given grace. But this opinion does not appear to agree with what saints and doctors have said about this, who speak of the state of innocence as one state; and therefore this opinion is of no great authority. 3) There are yet others who say that man was created in grace at the instant of his creation; and this opinion appears to agree well enough with the opinion of Augustine, who holds that things were created simultaneously in matter and form.[24]

We note Thomas's hesitation in choosing between the last two positions. One would expect him to side with the third, and perhaps he actually means to do so, since this later became the position of the *Summa Theologiae*. However, at this earlier moment of the *Commentary*, Thomas writes thus:

> As to which of these opinions is truer, this cannot be proved, as in the case of all those things which depend only upon God's will. Yet this is the more probable, that since man was created with his

natural powers intact, he turned to God in the first instant of his creation and got grace; and therefore this opinion is to be maintained.[25]

One sees how ambiguous this particular text of Thomas is. He simply has not made up his mind on the question. The best that we may make of it is that at this time he is willing to allow either the second or the third opinion above.

Already, in his definition of original justice, we have seen why the position of St. Thomas must finally be the one he took. Thomas held that man was created for an end, above and beyond nature, for God himself. Therefore man was given the means of attaining to such an end above nature. That means, we know, was the total order of original justice, a threefold gift having as its third and highest component an ordering to the end, given through sanctifying grace and charity. To hold that Adam was first created without such an orientation to God, his proper end, was to hold to the creation of man as something without due purpose. Why would God create man for Himself and yet in a first moment fashion him as if he were not made for such an end? One could see no possible reason for a first creation *in solis naturalibus*. It would mean a creation without the three subjections of original justice.

> Some say that man was not created in grace; but that it was bestowed on him subsequently before sin: and many authorities of the Saints declare that man possessed grace in the state of innocence. But the very rectitude of the primitive state wherewith man was endowed by God, seems to require that, as others say, he was created in grace, according to Eccles. vii. 20: "God made man right." For this rectitude consisted in his reason being subject to God, the lower powers to reason, and the body to the soul: and the first subjection was the cause of both the second and the third; since while reason was subject to God, the lower powers remained subject to reason, as Augustine says. Now it is clear that such a subjection of the body to the soul and of the lower powers to reason, was not from nature; otherwise it would have remained after sin. . . . Hence it is clear that . . . the primitive subjection by virtue of which reason was subject to God, was not a merely natural gift, but a supernatural endowment of grace.[26]

Of course, St. Thomas is quite ready to concede to the opposition that God could have chosen to form quite another man than Adam in a condition of pure nature and that God might have left such another man in that condition, without the further intention of bestowing grace upon him; but Thomas is also quite ready to contemplate the consequences of this. Such a man would have been left with only the natural light of reason and the possibility of an existence according to the principles inherent in nature alone. Therefore such a man, not created for a higher end, would have felt the struggle of the flesh against the spirit, which Thomas conceives to be natural, even without sin. (Indeed, without the order to the higher end, one might not even conceive of sin.) Such a man would have died naturally, since it is natural for the body to fall into dissolution, even as we see everywhere in nature.[27]

But God did not create man for an end lying within nature's confines merely. He created him for that end above nature which He is Himself. We must therefore think that God created Adam, in the first instant, for just such an end, giving him the means of attaining to it, bestowing upon him original justice which must include the highest subjection of sanctifying grace.

That Adam was created for the end above nature which is God Himself was never denied by the opposing view on this issue. There is never question as to that. Subjection through grace was given to Adam, of course; on this all agree. It is only a question whether in a first moment (and perhaps *outside* the Garden) God had formed Adam *in solis naturalibus*. It is a question whether there were two moments, in Adam's formation, two points in time — or one moment only.

The fascination which such a question held for theology is evident. It rests on the question of a line between nature and grace in point of time, in a succession of two moments. And to this question we may bring the notion of justice, since that is the term used for Adam's condition in Eden. Justice is the essence of the issue. And once more we may take the precise measure of this in terms of the three subjections of original justice. Those who held that Adam was formed first in a condition of pure nature without grace would readily allow that this first condition was a kind of justice. It was indeed that same lower and middle subjection of the three which we can now recognize so clearly. So Albertus Magnus, and one may note his stress on the fact that this is an order within nature:

> Man was created in a grace freely given [*in gratia gratis data*] according to natural virtues. Now, *grace* is spoken of in three ways, as the Gloss says on James i. 17: "Omne datum optimum et omne donum perfectum desursum est, descendens a Patre luminum, etc." For the Gloss says on this that the "data optima" are those which are given with nature and which raise the natural powers to acts which are perfect according to nature, such as a good mind, an ordered will, a luminous intellect, clear sense, perfect and discreet reason, a natural capacity for virtue. . . . And thus, in this kind of grace was man created. And this is seen to be proved by the authority of Augustine. . . .
>
> Secondly, that which is superadded and which raised the powers to acts of merit is called *grace*, and in this grace Adam was not created, as Augustine says.[28]

The question of there being two distinct moments in Adam's formation becomes thus a question of two kinds of justice or, on the scale of the three subjections, a question of two levels of justice. Albertus, and those who range themselves on the side of Peter Lombard, hold that Adam was created first in the lower order of justice, conceived as being without the orientation which the higher subjection of grace would give to it; as being, first, a justice without grace. But it is not thought that God had ever intended to leave man in such a state of justice, *in naturalibus solis*. Such a first moment would have been a preparation, a first condition, for the subsequent reception of grace. And it is this relation of the first moment in nature to the second moment of subsequent grace that concerns us especially.

In fact, this same view commanded such general assent that even St. Thomas was willing to allow it as a plausible hypothesis; and it is clear why this is so: if a first moment in Adam's formation is "ordered to" the higher moment (which is of the *end*), if it is a disposition for this, then Thomas can more readily accept it. There is here no longer a question of man being created *in solis naturalibus* and left in that condition. It is but a matter of two phases in the process of establishing man in that total order of justice which exceeds nature. Thus we find that Thomas, though still holding to the position that the total justice given to Adam included grace and was given in a single moment, can grant in the reply to an "objection" that the other view has some reason in it:

> Such a reason follows the opinion of those who hold that sanctifying grace is not a part of original justice — which opinion I still hold to be wrong, because since original justice first consisted in the subjection of the mind of man to God, which cannot hold if not through grace, original justice could not be without grace. . . . Yet even supposing this opinion, such a reason is not conclusive: for even if original justice did not include grace, still *it was a certain disposition prerequisite to grace.* [My italics.] [29]

Such a notion of a first moment or phase in the formation of man, followed by another completing moment, had good support, by analogy at least, in the view which we know Dante to have held respecting the formation of every human creature since Adam. The fact that Adam must be set apart from all others in this is what makes it a matter of analogy. For Adam was fashioned directly by God, body and spirit, was created "mature," fully formed as an adult; whereas Adam's children and all his posterity come into existence in a mother's womb, developing first as a foetus through a natural formation. Such in fact is the account of the genesis of the human creature which Statius (who can "see further" than Virgil) gives when he has joined the two wayfarers in their climb toward the summit of the mountain. And Statius, we may note, excuses himself here for venturing to explain such a truth in the presence of Virgil, clearly implying that it is not given to Virgil to discern the whole truth by himself. That whole truth goes beyond natural limits.

Beginning with the moment of conception in the womb, Statius' exposition follows out the first stages of the growing foetus as two stages. In a first phase the foetus has life merely, like a plant. Then it grows into a higher stage of formation and is like an animal, having a sensitive nature as well as its first vegetative one. But, then, says Statius, comes the point at which many a wise man has gone wrong: how does the "animal" creature become a human

creature? It is the point at which Statius knows more than Virgil
can discern:

> "Apri alla verità che viene il petto:
>   e sappi che, sì tosto come al feto
>   l'articular del cerebro è perfetto,
> lo motor primo a lui si volge lieto
>   sovra tant'arte di natura, e spira
>   spirito novo, di vertù repleto."
>
> Purgatorio XXV, 67–72.

"Open your breast to the truth that follows, and know that
as soon as the articulation of the brain is perfected in the foetus,
the First Mover turns to it, rejoicing over such handiwork of
nature, and breathes into it a new spirit full of power."

The relevance of such a view to the question of Adam's formation is evident. In the formation of every human creature, two
moments or phases are made distinct by an emphatic line: first,
there is the phase of nature, a moment of formation *in naturalibus*
(and just so far Virgil could have carried the argument), followed
by the moment "above nature" when God, happy (and almost
proud!) of nature's handiwork within her own order, completes
the genesis and full formation of the creature to be fashioned, by
breathing in, infusing, the rational soul.[30] It is a moment "above
nature," the moment of grace. Might Adam's formation not have
followed such a pattern, even though, in Adam's case, God and
not nature is the *faber* at the first stage?

There was also the more difficult question concerning the condition of Adam's posterity, had there been no sin: the question,
namely, of the way in which original justice was to have been
transmitted. It was a thorny problem indeed, and we have already
taken note of some of its aspects. The exact *manner* of the transmission of original justice is the point of most difficulty. Original
sin has replaced original justice as the condition into which all are
born of Adam. It is a sin of the nature, even as the justice was a
rectitude of the nature. But how then was original justice to have
been transmitted, especially if original justice must depend, at its
highest level, on the presence of sanctifying grace and charity?
There precisely is the crux of the problem. Surely if sanctifying
grace and charity must be among the parts of original justice, such

justice could not have been transmitted within the order of nature. Grace and charity are from God, not from nature.

The answer seems to be (though one could wish for more clarity in the actual statements by theologians) [31] that original justice would have been given to each individual human creature at the moment when the rational soul itself is bestowed by God. It too, like the rational soul and together with it, would have been breathed in, infused. And in the sense that the rational soul itself is given to each and every human creature as the due completion of a being formed first in nature, so would it have been with original justice, that gift to the creature which would have bestowed upon him a due order and orientation to his last end. Original justice was thus to have been a gift to the nature, even as the rational soul is such a gift — and such a birthright. Of course, we must not forget that the question of Adam's formation is unique, Adam being the only human being in whose formation nature had no part, unless this be true also of Eve — though she was formed from a part of Adam's body.

There is an even closer analogue to the notion of Adam's formation in a condition first of nature and then of grace, this being the corresponding view of two such moments in the creation of the angels — a doctrine so generally held, indeed, that those who endorsed the position of Peter Lombard with respect to Adam's creation in two moments were quick to appeal to it for support.

It is evident that any theologian holding the view that there were two moments in the creation of the angels would tend to take the corresponding view respecting Adam. It would also seem to follow that those who oppose such a view of Adam would tend to reject the notion that the angels were formed first *in naturalibus solis*, even though the angelic nature is higher than man's and the case may be different. It offers therefore no surprise that Thomas Aquinas does precisely this. Even as with man, so with these higher creatures: their formation is a matter of a single instant. The angels were created forthwith in a condition of grace:

> Although there are some conflicting opinions on this point, some holding that the angels were created only in a natural state, while

others maintained that they were created in grace; yet it seems more probable, and more in keeping with the sayings of holy men, that they were created in sanctifying grace.[32]

And to this Thomas adds in a reply to an objection of the same article: "Grace stands not as the end of operation, because it is not of works, but as the principle of right operation. Therefore it was fitting for grace to be given straightway with nature." [33]

One notes the initial recognition made by Thomas. There were indeed conflicting opinions on this, but mainly one only, the opinion that with the angels there were the two moments, as with Adam, and not one only. In fact, in his earlier Commentary on the *Sentences*, Thomas had recognized that the latter opinion was more commonly held:

> There are two opinions about this, i.e., whether the angels were created in grace. Now some say that the angels were not created in grace, but only in a condition of nature [*in naturalibus tantum*]; and this is the more common opinion. But others say that the angels were created in grace. However, as to which of these opinions be the truer one, this cannot be apprehended effectively by reason, because the beginning of creatures depends upon the simple will of the Creator, which it is impossible for reason to investigate.[34]

The whole purpose of such excursions as these into patterns of doctrine is to bring into clear view the background shapes of such doctrine as might well have supported a poet in his staging of the journey as "return to Eden." The specific doctrine of most interest to us is one which affirms that Adam was created by God first in pure nature, then in grace; and the analogies noted are merely evidence that such a view is a common one on several counts. Therefore, if a certain verse in Genesis seems to state that God first formed man outside the Garden and then placed him within it, it is not surprising that such a first authority should have been cited as the best of evidence in this regard. And we may come back to the scene in the poem where a stream is conceived as a boundary and dividing line between justice with Virgil and justice with Beatrice, justice in the natural proportion and justice above nature, the first being a preparation, or *dispositio*, for the second, since when the first justice is reached the advent of the second is expected. Virgil leads to Beatrice.

What we are finally privileged to see is clear: Dante has continued to work with the metaphor "return to Eden" even in this
respect. At the summit and end of the climb up the mountain,
when Eden is reached, we may see history somehow repeating
itself; as it was with Adam in his formation, so now with this man,
so now with "man," in his re-formation. Only now do we glimpse
an aspect of the metaphor we might otherwise have missed. There
had been a moment in Adam's formation when Adam was not yet
in Eden, when Adam was formed outside of Eden in a first condition *secundum naturam*. What corresponds to this, in a "return"
to Eden, is the moment when Virgil proclaims that Dante the
wayfarer is now reformed in justice, a justice discernible by the
natural light. This then is the moment *secundum naturam* in the
re-formation. Dante advances to a stream which cuts across his
path and blocks his way. He may go no further for the moment,
nor may Virgil ever go further than this. Beatrice is expected and
when she comes Virgil has disappeared. The light of grace flashes
through the forest, from beyond the stream. And when, after contrition and confession, Dante may cross through the water to the
far shore, to attain to Beatrice and the infused virtues, we know
that he crosses to a condition of grace and justice beyond Virgil
and beyond nature. And we come to understand better why that
further bank of the stream where Beatrice comes is called a
"blessed" shore.

The stream of Lethe in Eden is as a boundary, marking the confines of the Paradise proper. Return to Eden is thus not complete
until the wayfarer has crossed over. Only when he stands on the
far shore, where Beatrice and Matelda are, does he stand in that
place where God had placed man *after* He had first formed him
outside the Garden, according to nature. The pattern of the original formation of man is thus seen to repeat itself in the re-formation of a man named Dante, who attains first to a condition of
justice with Virgil, within the proportion of his nature and under
the natural light, and then, in a second moment attains to Eden
proper, crossing the river to a kind of justice with Beatrice that
is truly beyond all human measure.

Notes

1. The relative order and degree among the subjections of original justice which prompts such a figure as that of a "ladder" is witnessed in passages such as the following in Aquinas (*Summa c. G.* III, 141): "Est autem summum bonum hominis felicitas, quae est ultimus finis eius: quantoque aliquid est huic fini propinquius, tanto praeminet inter hominis bonum. Huic autem propinquissimum est virtus (I Ethic. ix, 3) et si quid est aliud quod ad bonam operationem hominem proficiat, qua pervenitur ad beatitudinem. Consequitur autem et debita dispositio rationis, et virium ei subiectarum. Post hoc autem et corporis incolumitas, quae necessaria est ad expeditam operationem. Demum autem ea quae exterius sunt, quibus quasi adminiculantibus utimur ad virtutem. — Erit igitur maxima poena hominem a beatitudine excludi. Post hanc autem virtute privari, et perfectione quacumque naturalium virtutum animae ad bene agendum. Dehinc autem, naturalium potentiarum animae deordinatio. Post hoc autem, corporis nocumentum. Demum autem, exteriorum bonorum sublatio."

2. Jerome notes as follows, in *Epistola LXVI* (*PL* 22.640): "Dicamus aliquid et de Philosophis. Quatuor virtutes describunt Stoici, ita sibi invicem nexas, et mutuo cohaerentes, ut qui unam non habuerit, omnibus careat: prudentiam, justitiam, fortitudinem, temperantiam."

3. *De Bono* (in *Opera Omnia*, ed. Monasteri Westfalorum Aschendorff, XXVIII, 292): "Ex hoc patet quod rectitudo animae quae est iustitia generalis, consistit in debito ordine virium omnium ad actum." The term is everywhere to be found, e. g., Aquinas, *De Ver*, xviii, a. 1, ad 2: "Dicendum quod iustificatio non dicitur a iustitia legali, quae est omnis virtus; sed a iustitia quae dicit generalem rectitudinem in anima, a qua potius quam a gratia iustificatio denominatur: quia huic iustitiae directe et immediate omne peccatum opponitur, cum omnes potentias animae attingat; gratia vero est in essentia animae."

4. *Ethics* V, 11.

5. *Summa Theol.* I–II, q. 113, a. 1, resp.

6. Aquinas, *In III Sent.* d. xiii, q. 1, a. 4, sol. 3: "In omnibus quae agunt propter finem oportet esse inclinationem ad finem, et quamdam inchoationem finis: alias nunquam operarentur propter finem. Finis autem ad quem divina largitas hominem ordinavit vel praedestinavit, scilicet fruitio sui ipsius, est omnino supra facultatem naturae creatae elevatus. . . . Unde per naturalia tantum homo non habet sufficienter inclinationem ad illum finem; et ideo oportet quod superaddatur homini aliquid per quod habeat inclinationem in finem illum, sicut per naturalia habet inclinationem in finem sibi connaturalem: et ista superaddita dicuntur virtutes theologicae ex tribus. Primo quantum ad objectum: quia cum finis ad quem ordinati sumus, sit ipse Deus,

inclinatio quae praeexigitur consistit in operatione quae est circa ipsum Deum. Secundo quantum ad causam: quia sicut ille finis est a Deo nobis ordinatus non per naturam nostram, ita inclinationem in finem operatur in nobis solus Deus: et sic dicuntur virtutes theologicae, quasi a solo Deo in nobis creatae. Tertio quantum ad cognitionem naturae, inclinatio in finem non potest per naturalem rationem cognosci, sed per revelationem divinam: et ideo dicuntur theologicae, quia divino sermone sunt nobis manifestatae: unde Philosophi nihil de eis cognoverunt."

Or, see St. Bonaventura, *In II Sent.* d. xxx, q. 2, a. 1 (ed. Quaracchi, II, 719): "Hanc igitur legem et inordinationem ad Deum si quis velit attendere, nullo modo dubitabit hominem esse peccatorem a sua nativitate, immo ita certum est, ut dubitari non possit de originali, sicut etiam nec de actuali. — Hoc tamen ignoraverunt philosophi et etiam aliqui haeretici, quia nescierunt attendere, in quo attenditur rectitudo animae et iustitia, et pro quanto anima dici debet ad Deum ordinata."

7. Bouillard (*Conversion et grâce*, p. 87) remarks this characteristic tendency in Aquinas: "Par une extrapolation inconsciente, saint Thomas passe sans cesse de la nature selon le philosophe à la nature selon le théologien. Pour lui, la nature humaine est tantôt le principe immanent des opérations de l'homme, tantôt la créature faite à l'image de Dieu. Il passe indifféremment d'une notion à l'autre, sans remarquer que ce passage implique une conversion totale. Sa thèse sur la préparation à la grâce par des actes naturels souffre de cette ambiguité. Elle n'est pas fausse, mais équivoque."

8. *Purgatorio* VI, 42.

9. *Summa Theol.* I–II, q. 110, a. 3, resp.: "Sic igitur lumen naturale rationis est aliquid praeter virtutes acquisitas, quae dicuntur in ordine ad ipsum lumen naturale; ita etiam ipsum lumen gratiae, quod est participatio divinae naturae, est aliquid praeter virtutes infusas, quae a lumine illo derivantur, et ad illud lumen ordinantur."

10. Augustine, *City of God* XIV, 19: "Hence it is that even the philosophers who have approximated to the truth . . . assert that this third part of the mind is posted as it were in a kind of citadel, to give rule to these other parts, so that, while it rules and they serve, man's righteousness is preserved without a breach."

11. *De Monarchia* III, 16, 7 ff.

12. *De Mon.* III, 16, 17: "Que quidem veritas ultime questionis non sic stricte recipienda est, ut Romanus Princeps in aliquo Romano Pontifici non subiaceat, cum mortalis ista felicitas quodam modo ad inmortalem felicitatem ordinetur. Illa igitur reverentia Cesar utatur ad Petrum qua primogenitus filius debet uti ad patrem: ut luce paterne gratie illustratus virtuosius orbem terre irradiet, cui ab Illo solo prefectus est, qui est omnium spiritualium et temporalium gubernator."

13. *Paradiso* I, 70.

14. *Adnotationes in Gen. VII*, PL 175.39: "Extra paradisum voluit eum facere Deus, ut intelligeret se ex gratia, non ex natura, in paradiso locatum."

15. I have cited the trans. by DeFerrari of the *De Sacramentis*, Medieval Academy of America, Pub. No. 58 (Cambridge, Mass., 1951), pp. 106–107. Latin text in PL 176.274.

16. *Summa Theol.* I–II, Inq. IV, tr. iii, q. 3, tit. 1, a. 1, resp. (ed. Quaracchi, II, 730): (after citing Hugh and Augustine) "Saluberrime confitemur quod rectissime credimus Deum dominum rerum omnium, qui creavit omnia bona valde. . . . sic ordinasse angelorum et hominum vitam ut in ea prius ostenderet quid posset eorum liberum arbitrium, deinde quid posset suae gratiae beneficium iustitiaeque iudicium."

17. *Ibid.*, II, 728: "Item, Gen. i. 26: 'Faciamus hominem ad imaginem et similitudinem nostram.' Sed sicut exponit Augustinus, et habetur II Sent. dist. 16, imago est in naturalibus, similitudo in gratuitis." The *De Spiritu et Anima* of Augustine is found in *PL* 40.

18. *De Vulg. El.* I, v, 3: "Et hinc penitus elicere possumus locum illum ubi effutita est prima locutio; quoniam, si extra paradisum afflatus est homo, extra, si vero intra, intra fuisse locum prime locutionis convicimus."

19. *Liber II Sententiarum* d. xvii, ch. 4 (ed. Quaracchi, I, 385): "Hominem autem ita formatum tulit Deus, ut Scriptura docet, et posuit in paradiso voluptatis, quem plantaverat a principio. — His verbis aperte Moyses insinuat, quod homo extra paradisum creatus, postmodum in paradiso sit positus. Quod ideo factum dicitur, quia non erat in eo permansurus, vel ut non naturae, sed gratiae hoc assignaretur."

20. *Summa Theol.* I–II, Inq. IV, tr. iii, q. 3, tit. 1, cap. 1, resp.

21. *Ibid.*

22. *Summa Theol.* II, tr. xiv, q. 90, sol. (ed. Borgnet, XXXIII, 174): "Secundo, dicitur *gratia* quod superadditur talibus adjutoriis potentiarum, et elevat potentias ad actum meriti. Et in hac non fuit creatus Adam, ut dicit Augustinus. Dederat enim ei unde posset stare, sed non unde proficeret ad meritum. Et de hoc consueverunt assignari tres causae, quod scilicet in hoc resultat omnipotentia creatoris, sapientia et bonitas: omnipotentia in creatione naturae, sapientia in ordine naturae ad gratiam, et gratiae ad gloriam, bonitas in perfectione secundum gratiam gratiam facientem, ut sic laudaretur ab homine creator potens, sapiens, et bonus."

23. *In II Sent.* d. xvii, dub. 2, resp. (ed. Quaracchi, II, 427): "In hoc autem loco decuit hominem poni, ut esset ei facilitas perveniendi ad patriam, et ut Deus homini ostenderet benevolentiam, cui locum amoenissimum ad inhabitandum praeparaverat, et sic amoenitas exterioris habitaculi corresponderet deliciis interioribus, quales habet anima, quae est templum Dei, et habebat anima primi hominis. — Extra autem hunc locum debuit homo produci, ut melius cognosceret Dei beneficium, dum se videret quasi aliunde adductum; et ut etiam per hoc ostenderet, quod homo non erat ibi factus ad aeternaliter habitandum, sed temporaliter peregrinandum. Et quia Deus eius eiectionem de loco voluptatis cognosceret sensibiliter, quanta bona spiritualia amisisset per culpam; cognosceret etiam nihilominus, quanta esset differentia inter eum qui Domino humiliter obedit, et eum qui ipsum superbe contemnit."

24. *In II Sent.* d. xxix, q. 1, a. 2, sol.

25. *Ibid.*

26. *Summa Theol.* I, q. 95, a. 1, resp.

27. *In II Sent.* d. xxxi, q. 1, a. 2, ad 3: "Poterat Deus a principio quando hominem condidit, etiam alium hominem ex limo terrae formare, quem in conditione naturae suae relinqueret, ut scilicet mortalis et passibilis esset et

pugnam concupiscentiae ad rationem sentiens; in quo nihil humanae naturae derogaretur, quia hoc ex principiis naturae consequitur." On this point, see Bouillard, *Conversion et grâce*, p. 78.

28. *Summa Theol.* II, tr. xiv, q. 90, mem. 1, resp.: "In gratia gratis data secundum virtutes naturales factus est homo. Gratia enim dicitur tribus modis, sicut innuit Glossa super illud Jacobi, I, 17: Omne datum optimum, et omne donum perfectum desursum est, descendens a Patre luminum, apud quem, etc.' Ibi enim dicit Glossa, quod data optima sunt, quae dantur cum natura, et elevant potentias naturales ad actus perfectos secundum naturam, sicut bonum ingenium, ordinata voluntas, luminosus intellectus, clarus sensus, perfecta et discreta ratio, habilitas naturae ad virtutes, secundum quod vir est extremum potentiae in bono, ut dicit Aristoteles in II *Ethicorum*. Et hoc modo in tali gratia creatus est homo. . . . Secundo dicitur *gratia* quod superadditur talibus adjutoriis potentiarum, et elevat potentias ad actum meriti. Et in hoc non fuit creatus Adam, ut dicit Augustinus."

29. *De Malo* q. 5, a. 1, ad 13: "Ratio illa procedit secundum opinionem ponentium quod gratia gratum faciens non includatur in ratione originalis iustitiae; quod tamen credo falsum quia cum originalis iustitia primordialiter consistat in subiectione humanae mentis ad Deum, quae firma esse non potest nisi per gratiam, iustitia originalis sine gratia esse non potuit. . . . Sed tamen praedicta opinione supposita, adhuc ratio non concludit, quia, licet originalis iustitia .gratiam non includeret, tamen erat quaedam dispositio quae praeexigebatur ad gratiam."

30. Cf. also, *Convivio* IV, xxi, 11: "Per via teologica si può dire che, poi che la somma deitate, cioè Dio, vede apparecchiata la sua creatura a ricevere del suo beneficio, tanto largamente in quella ne mette quanto apparecchiata è a riceverne." and St. Bonaventura, *In II Sent.* d. xxxii, q. 2, a. 3, concl.: "Quoniam igitur Deus sic instituit humanam naturam, ut Adam praepararet corpora, et ipse illis corporibus animas infunderet."

31. On the several debatable points in the whole question see the works of Kors and Van Roo cited above. I have accepted the views of the latter as the more persuasive in the case of Aquinas. The position of St. Thomas appears evident enough, in the *Summa Theol.* (I, q. 100, a. 1, ad 2): "Quidam dicunt quod pueri non fuissent nati cum iustitia gratuita, quae est merendi principium, sed cum iustitia originali. Sed cum radix originalis iustitiae, in cuius rectitudine factus est homo, consistat in subiectione supernaturali rationis ad Deum, quae est per gratiam gratum facientem . . . , necesse est dicere quod si pueri nati fuissent in originali iustitia, quod etiam nati fuissent cum gratia; sicut et de primo homine supra diximus, quod fuit cum gratia conditus. Non tamen fuisset propter hoc gratia naturalis, quia non fuisset transfusa per virtutem seminis, sed fuisset collata homini statim cum habuisset animam rationalem. Sicut etiam statim cum corpus est dispositum, infunditur a Deo anima rationalis, quae tamen non est ex traduce."

32. *Summa Theol.* I, q. 62, a. 3, resp.

33. *Ibid.*, I, q. 62, a. 3, ad 3.

34. *In II Sent.* d. iv, q. 1, a. 3, sol.

Reference List of Theological Writings
Cited in the Notes*

Abelard, Peter:
  Expositio in Hexaemeron (PL 178)
Albert the Great (Albertus Magnus), St.:
  De Bono (*Opera Omnia*, ed. A. Borgnet, Paris, 1890–1899, vol. VII)
  In Quatuor Libros Sententiarum Commentarius (*ed. cit.*, vols. XXV–XXX)
  Summa Theologiae (*ed. cit.*, vols. XXXI–XXXIII)
Alexander of Hales:
  Summa Theologica (Quaracchi, 1924–1930)
Ambrose, St.:
  De Paradiso (PL 14)
Anselm, St.:
  De Conceptu Virginali et de Originali Peccato (PL 158)
  De Veritate (PL 158)
Augustine, St.:
  Confessionum Libri XIII (PL 32)
  Contra Duas Epistolas Pelagianorum (PL 44)
  Contra Julianum Haeresis Pelagianae Defensorem (PL 44)
  De Civitate Dei (PL 41)
  De Genesi ad Litteram (PL 34)
  De Genesi contra Manichaeos (PL 34)
  De Natura et Gratia ad Temasium et Jacobum contra Pelagium (PL 44)
  De Nuptiis et Concupiscentia (PL 44)
  De Peccatorum Meritis et Remissione (PL 44)
  De Spiritu et Anima (PL 40)
  De Vera Religione (PL 34)
  Quaestionum in Heptateuchum Libri Septem (PL 34)

* PL stands for the *Patrologia Latina* of J. P. Migne (222 vols.; Paris, 1844–1864), PG for Migne's *Patrologia Graeca* (166 vols.; Paris, 1857–1866). Sources are included in this list for the reader's convenience; information on other editions used for specific works is to be found in the notes.

Bede:
  In Pentateuchum Commentarii (PL 91)
Bernard of Clairvaux, St.:
  Sermones de Tempore: In Adventu Domini (PL 183)
Bonaventura, St.:
  In Quartum Librum Sententiarum (*Opera Omnia*, Quaracchi, 1882–1902,
    vol. IV)
  Itinerarium Mentis in Deum (*ed. cit.*, vol. V)
Constantine the Great:
  Oratio ad Sanctorum Coetum (PL 8)
Durandus:
  Rationale Divinorum Officiorum (Naples, 1859)
Gregory the Great, St.:
  Homiliae XL in Ezechielem (PL 76)
  Moralium Libri, sive In Expositionem Beati Job Moralia (PL 75)
Honorius of Autun:
  Elucidarium (PL 172)
Hugh of St. Victor:
  Adnotationes in Genesim (PL 175)
  De Sacramentis (PL 176)
  Quaestiones in Epistolas Pauli (PL 175)
Innocent III:
  De Contemptu Mundi, sive De Miseria Conditionis Humanae (PL 217)
Jerome, St.:
  Epistolae (PL 22)
  Liber Hebraicarum Questionum in Genesim (PL 23)
John Damascene, St.:
  De Fide Orthodoxa (PG 94)
Lactantius:
  Institutiones Divinae (PL 6)
Lombard, Peter:
  Sententiarum Libri Quatuor (PL 191, 192)
Origen:
  Commentarii in Genesim (PG 12)
Richard of St. Victor:
  *De Praeparatione Animi ad Contemplationem, Liber Dictus Benjamin
    Minor* (PL 196)
Rabanus Maurus:
  Commentariorum in Genesim Libri Quatuor (PL 107)
Thomas Aquinas, St.:
  Compendium Theologiae ad Fratrem Reginaldum (*Opera Omnia*, Parma,
    1852–1873, vol. XVI)
  De Humanitate Jesu Christi (*ed. cit.*, vol. XVII)
  De Principiis Naturae ad Fratrem Silvestrum (*ed. cit.*, vol. XVI)
  In Epistolam ad Romanos (*ed. cit.*, vol. VIII)
  In Isaiam Prophetam (*ed. cit.*, vol. XIV)
  In X Libros Ethicorum Aristotelis ad Nichomachum (*ed. cit.*, vol. XXI)
  In XII Libros Metaphysicorum Aristotelis (*ed. cit.*, *vol.* XX)
  In VIII Libros Physicorum Aristotelis (*ed. cit.*, vol. XVIII)

In Librum Boetii de Trinitate (*ed. cit.*, vol. XVII)
In Psalmos Davidis (*ed. cit.*, vol. XIV)
In Quatuor Libros Sententiarum P. Lombardi Commentum (*ed. cit.*, vols. VI, VII)
In S. Pauli Epistolas (*ed. cit.*, vol. XIII)
Quaestiones Disputatae: De Caritate (*ed. cit.*, vol. VIII)
Quaestiones Disputatae: De Malo (*ed. cit.*, vol. VIII)
Quaestiones Disputatae: De Veritate (*ed. cit.*, vol. IX)
Quaestiones Disputatae: De Virtutibus Cardinalibus (*ed. cit.*, vol. VIII)
Quaestiones Disputatae: De Virtutibus in Communi (*ed. cit.*, vol. VIII)
Summa contra Gentiles (*ed. cit.*, vol. V)
Summa Theologiae (*ed. cit.*, vols. I–IV)
Walafrid Strabo:
Glossa Ordinaria (PL 113)

The Johns Hop

Baltimo